Transform the way you use your freezer! In *It's Always Freezer Season*, two-time James Beard Award–winning Southern chef Ashley Christensen and cookbook author Kaitlyn Goalen reveal how the freezer can easily become the single most important tool in your kitchen.

By turning your freezer into a fully provisioned pantry stocked with an array of homemade staples, you'll save time and energy. Even on a tight schedule you can now put together delicious, complex dishes such as Cornbread Panzanella with Watermelon, Cucumber, and Za'atar Vinaigrette; Potato Pierogi; Pan-Roasted Chicken Breast with Preserved Lemon–Garlic Butter; Braised Short Ribs with Cauliflower Fonduta; and Provençal Onion Tart (Pissaladière) with Tomato-Olive Relish. Christensen and Goalen also share fully prepared make-ahead dishes for every meal of the day to keep in your freezer, like Pistachio Croissant French Toast with Orange Blossom Soft Cream, Chicken and Kale Tortilla Soup, Pimento Mac and Cheese Custard, and Deviled Crab Rigatoni, plus snacks, sweets, and drinks ready to be enjoyed at a moment's notice. With innovative recipes, helpful technical information, and tips on stocking your new "pantry," this book will allow you to make more delicious meals with a lot less effort.

IT'S *Always* FREEZER SEASON

IT'S *Always* FREEZER SEASON

How to freeze like a chef with 100 MAKE-AHEAD RECIPES

ASHLEY CHRISTENSEN
and **KAITLYN GOALEN**

Photographs by
Lauren Vied Allen

TEN SPEED PRESS
California | New York

TO OUR MOMS, LISA AND
LYNN, WHO TAUGHT US TO
LOVE COOKING AT HOME.

Contents

1   Introduction: Why the freezer?

5   How to use this book.

6   RECIPES ORGANIZED BY COURSE.

PART ONE

HOW TO USE YOUR *Freezer*   9

1 • What to freeze and what not to freeze.   11

2 • How long can I freeze it?   21

     FROZEN FOOD LIFESPAN.   24

3 • How to freeze.   27

4 • How to unfreeze.   39

PART TWO

THE *Freezer* PANTRY   47

5 • Grains.   49

6 • Proteins.   81

7 • Dairy.   111

8 • Vegetables.   133

PART THREE *Freezer*-FRIENDLY DISHES 165

9 ● **Breakfast and brunch dishes.** 167

10 ● **Snacks and bites.** 181

11 ● **Soups and saucy things.** 189

12 ● **Casseroles and bakes.** 209

13 ● **Sweets.** 223

14 ● **Beverages.** 237

253 **Resources.**

255 **Acknowledgments.**

257 **About the authors.**

258 **Index.**

Introduction: Why the freezer?

Both of us love to cook. When we wake up in the morning and choose to cook at home, it is soothing and meditative and fun—an activity that brings us happiness. On those days, it's a luxury to spend a few hours on a single recipe—maybe the music is playing; maybe the windows are open or friends are helping; maybe it's a cold day and the warmth of the stove is making the house cozy. It's a joy.

But even the most beloved activities can be sucked of their pleasure when you are compelled to participate, rather than making the choice. Cooking as a necessity is labor. Whether we do so professionally or simply to feed ourselves or our families, most of us are required to cook daily. Even the most food-loving cooks we know get burned out on the labor of making dinner now and then.

On those nights, you might have options: you may go out to a restaurant; you may pick something up or have it delivered; or you can cook something, even when you don't want to. The latter option becomes *much* more appealing when you have a freezer of dishes that you've cooked on a day when you felt the joy and happiness, rather than the labor, of cooking. A freezer full of the recipes that you'll find in this book is like a savings account of emotional and physical sustenance: draw on it when your day-to-day stores are low.

In this age of obsession with the freshest, most seasonal food and the most cutting-edge flavors and techniques of top restaurants, the freezer may seem like a rather dowdy topic for a cookbook, especially for one cowritten by a professional chef. Freezers feature prominently in the make-ahead recipes of meal-prep blogs, but they rarely get top billing in cookbooks.

Hopefully, by the time you've cooked your way through even a few of the recipes in this book, you'll come to the same realization we have:

> The freezer, more than any other appliance in the kitchen, will help you cook delicious, flavorful meals in less time.

It is at the intersection of quality and taste, approachability and convenience.

The time-saving aspect needs to be contextualized: We're not shaving hours off the clock by cutting corners. There are recipes in this book that require a time commitment because making great food takes time and work. (We should know; we do it for a living.) Instead, we're focused on the idea that you should squeeze as much out of each cooking session as you can. For example, if you're going to spend a few hours making a stock, don't just make enough for one

1

recipe of soup. For almost the same amount of effort, you could make double the stock, freeze half, and thus save yourself time on the next occasion you crave a bowl of something hot and delicious.

Using your freezer more strategically and thoughtfully delivers other benefits, too: it can help you avoid food waste and save money, preserve seasonal ingredients to enjoy throughout the year, and entertain on the fly or provide a meal for a friend or family member who needs the assistance.

We get asked a lot about our "secret weapon" in the kitchen. Home cooks are understandably curious to know what the tools and tricks are for cooking more delicious food. Well, when we're at home, our secret weapon is definitely the freezer. Our freezer is the MVP of our kitchen and the single most important "kitchen tool" we have, as it allows us to cook our favorite things in a way that best satisfies our home-cooking philosophy. Through smart and strategic use of our freezer, we are able to cook deliciously, avoid food waste, and save time by maximizing the time we spend in the kitchen.

With this book, we've laid out our game plan for you to do the same. We love these recipes, and we hope you do, too. But even more so, we hope this approach can inspire in you new possibilities and renewed joy for cooking.

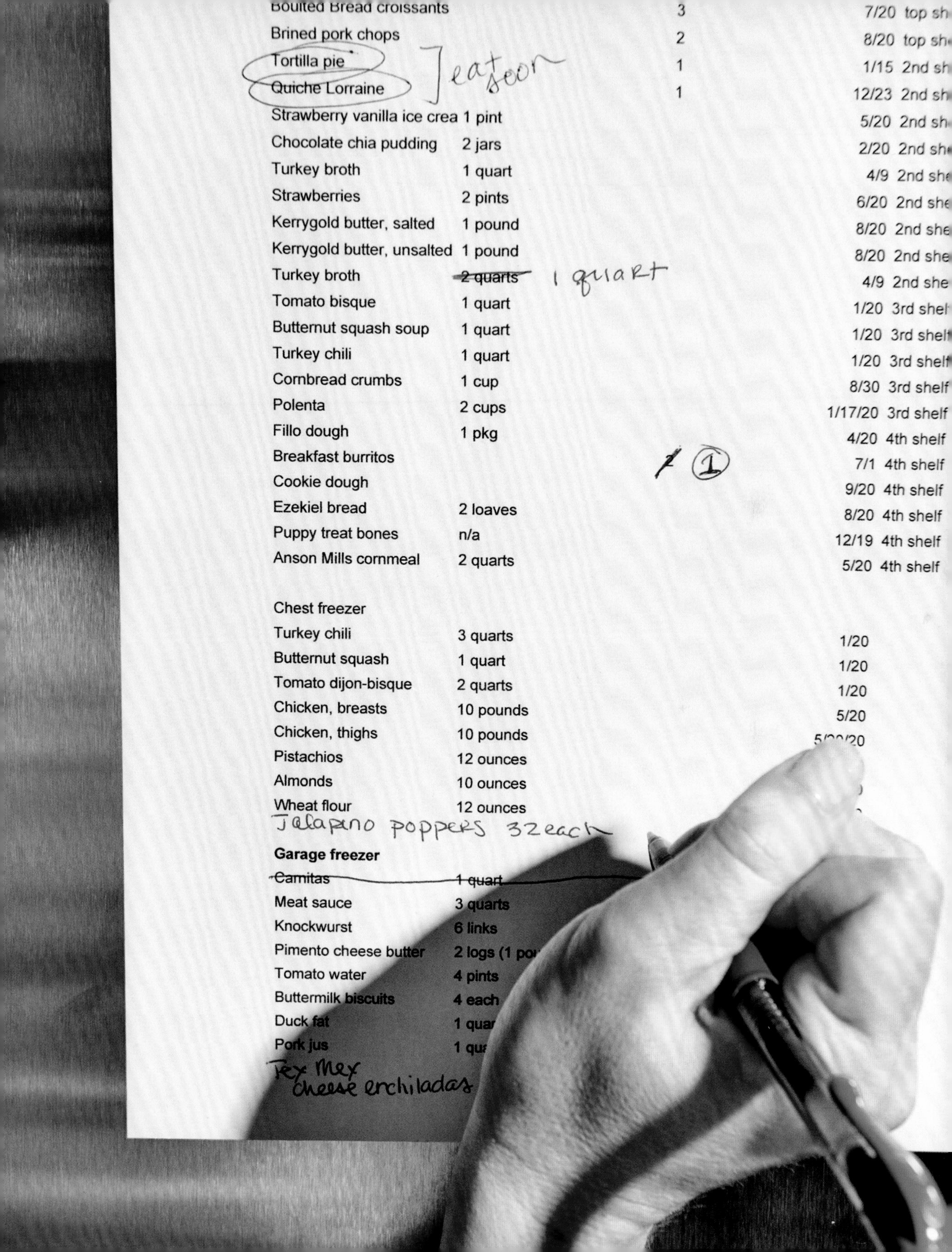

Item	Quantity	Date	Location
Boulted Bread croissants	3	7/20	top sh...
Brined pork chops	2	8/20	top she...
~~Tortilla pie~~	1	1/15	2nd sh...
~~Quiche Lorraine~~	1	12/23	2nd sh...
Strawberry vanilla ice crea	1 pint	5/20	2nd sh...
Chocolate chia pudding	2 jars	2/20	2nd she...
Turkey broth	1 quart	4/9	2nd she...
Strawberries	2 pints	6/20	2nd she...
Kerrygold butter, salted	1 pound	8/20	2nd she...
Kerrygold butter, unsalted	1 pound	8/20	2nd she...
Turkey broth	~~2 quarts~~	4/9	2nd she...
Tomato bisque	1 quart	1/20	3rd shel...
Butternut squash soup	1 quart	1/20	3rd shelf
Turkey chili	1 quart	1/20	3rd shelf
Cornbread crumbs	1 cup	8/30	3rd shelf
Polenta	2 cups	1/17/20	3rd shelf
Fillo dough	1 pkg	4/20	4th shelf
Breakfast burritos		7/1	4th shelf
Cookie dough		9/20	4th shelf
Ezekiel bread	2 loaves	8/20	4th shelf
Puppy treat bones	n/a	12/19	4th shelf
Anson Mills cornmeal	2 quarts	5/20	4th shelf

Handwritten annotations: "eat soon" (bracketing Tortilla pie and Quiche Lorraine); "1 quart" (next to Turkey broth 2 quarts); "1" circled.

Chest freezer

Item	Quantity	Date
Turkey chili	3 quarts	1/20
Butternut squash	1 quart	1/20
Tomato dijon-bisque	2 quarts	1/20
Chicken, breasts	10 pounds	5/20
Chicken, thighs	10 pounds	5/20/20
Pistachios	12 ounces	
Almonds	10 ounces	
Wheat flour	12 ounces	

Handwritten: Jalapeno poppers 32 each

Garage freezer

~~Carnitas~~	~~1 quart~~
Meat sauce	3 quarts
Knockwurst	6 links
Pimento cheese butter	2 logs (1 po...
Tomato water	4 pints
Buttermilk biscuits	4 each
Duck fat	1 quar...
Pork jus	1 qua...

Handwritten: Tex Mex cheese enchiladas

How to use this book.

This cookbook is divided into three main parts. The first section is all about the process of freezing. For such a widely used appliance, there is a lot of confusion and misunderstanding about how to utilize the freezer properly. We've broken things down into practical categories and provide guideposts on everything from packaging and labeling to thawing and reheating. You'll also find some helpful information about freezer "expiration" best practices.

The second section covers what we call the "freezer pantry." The idea for this actually started when we were writing our last cookbook, *Poole's*. During the recipe testing, we found our freezer filling up with many of the elements of more complicated recipes—rabbit confit, parcooked risotto, roasted garlic butter, béchamel—and gradually the freezer became our treasure chest. With these assets ready to be pulled and thawed on any random Tuesday night, a restaurant-worthy meal at home was always within thirty minutes.

So the recipes in this second section are all based around this idea of stocking your freezer as if it were a pantry, with items that may not be a complete recipe on their own but will act as an enhancement (and time-saver) to something else you're trying to cook. We have not only recipes for these items but also recipes for ways to use them: frozen cornbread becomes a Southern-inspired *panzanella* salad (page 53), and braised short ribs transform into short rib stroganoff (page 103).

The third section features complete recipes that are freezer friendly. You could make and eat them now if you wanted, bypassing the freezer altogether. Even better, make a double batch, one to eat now and one to freeze for later. Or you could just get ahead on stocking your freezer and make one to freeze. The recipes in this section are divided into categories like snacks, soups and stews, and casseroles and bakes.

Since the organization of this book is focused on when and how to freeze the recipes, rather than when and how you might serve them, we've created this key to help you navigate your options based on occasion.

RECIPES ORGANIZED BY COURSE.

Morning

Buttermilk Biscuits • 56

Cheesy Sausage and
Sage Waffles • 170

Chocolate Chia Pudding • 178

Egg, Potato, and Cheddar
Breakfast Burritos • 168

Multitasker Smoothie • 238

Orange Biscuits • 57

Pistachio Croissant French
Toast with Orange Blossom
Soft Cream • 173

Quiche Lorraine • 78

Sausage and Cheese Biscuits • 57

Sausage Gravy with
Buttermilk Biscuits • 122

Strawberries for Morning • 251

Tortilla Breakfast Pie • 175

Zucchini–Poppy Seed Bread • 224

Apps

Baked Feta with Roasted Peppers,
Capers, and Salsa Verde • 143

Buffalo Chicken Dip • 100

Chicken Rillettes • 95

Curried Cheddar and
Olive Bites • 184

Ham and Swiss Cheese Rolls • 186

Pimento Cheese Hand Pies • 77

Poole's Three-Cheese
Gougères • 63

Pork Meatballs • 185

Provençal Onion Tart (Pissaladière)
with Tomato-Olive Relish • 150

Roasted Jalapeño Poppers with
Sausage and Tomatoes • 183

Roasted Oysters with Pimento
Cheese Butter • 115

Savory Fritters • 64

Seafood Stuffies • 54

Salads

Cabbage Salad with Crispy Pork
Shoulder, Apples, and Maple-Cider
Vinaigrette • 86

Chicken Niçoise Salad • 96

Cornbread Panzanella with
Watermelon, Cucumber, and
Za'atar Vinaigrette • 53

Kale and Broccoli Slaw with
Pesto-Avocado Dressing • 144

Roasted Beets with Chickpeas,
Herbed Yogurt, and Caramelized
Onion Vinaigrette • 153

Soups and Stews

Basic Butternut Squash Soup • 191

Beef and Coconut Stew with
Root Vegetables • 106

Chicken and Dumplings • 60

Chicken and Kale Tortilla Soup • 203

Chilled Tomato and
Cucumber Soup • 197

Italian Wedding Soup • 129

Miso-Ginger Butternut
Squash Soup • 192

New Manhattan Chowder • 200

Tomato and Greens
Minestrone • 130

Tomato-Dijon Bisque • 199

Turkey Chili with White Beans • 195

Mains

Braised Short Ribs with Cauliflower Fonduta • 105

Broccoli Cheddar Chicken Bake • 101

Carnitas Tacos • 85

Chicken Piccata Farfalle with Sweet Potato • 99

Deviled Crab Rigatoni • 221

Four-Cheese and Greens Lasagna • 126

Harissa Lamb, Eggplant, and Potato Gratin • 155

Hot Dog Casserole • 158

Line Cook's Grilled Cheese • 149

Pan-Roasted Chicken Breast with Preserved Lemon–Garlic Butter • 119

Pan-Roasted Salmon with Chimichurri • 147

Penne alla Vodka • 206

Pimento Mac and Cheese Custard • 217

Pork Reuben on Rye with Swiss, Kraut, and Russian Dressing • 89

Potato Pierogi • 161

Potato Pork Cakes with Marinated Peppers, Summer Squash, and Avocado • 90

The Quickest Risotto Parmigiano • 69

The Quickest Risotto (Add Mushrooms) • 69

The Quickest Risotto (Go Tomato) • 69

Seared Scallops with Butternut Squash, Apples, and Parsley • 192

Short Rib Stroganoff with Egg Noodles • 103

Stuffed Peppers with Short Ribs and Rice • 109

Tea-Brined Pork Chops with Braised Greens and Tomatoes • 137

Tex-Mex Cheese Enchiladas • 211

Sides

Braised Greens and Paneer • 136

Charred Corn, Squash, and Onion Gratin • 215

Cornbread • 50

Green Bean Casserole • 125

Lynn's Thanksgiving Dressing • 55

Twice-Baked Mashed Potatoes • 159

Desserts

Almond Rice Pudding with Rhubarb-Apricot Jam • 71

Apple Pie • 73

Banana Cream Profiteroles • 67

Blueberry-Ginger Cobbler • 59

Churros • 64

Frozen Cheesecake Cookie Sandwiches • 230

Malted Coffee Toffee Cookies • 226

Miso-Caramel Shortbread • 232

Pâte à Choux Doughnuts • 64

Salty Dog Icebox Pie • 228

Spiced Pumpkin Pudding Cakes • 235

Tahini–Brown Butter Chocolate Chip Cookies • 225

Drinks

Boulevardier Slushie • 240

Chai Concentrate • 246

Jalapeño-Ginger Syrup • 248

Kait's Negroni • 242

Margarita Slush • 239

Strawberries for Evening • 251

The Vesper • 242

Vieux Carre • 242

Watermelon Collins • 245

Watermelon Juice • 245

HOW TO USE YOUR *Freezer*

PART ONE

The freezer keeps it simple. To operate it, you plug it in and walk away. You can mess with the temperature setting a little bit, but beyond that, the appliance itself doesn't have a whole lot to manipulate.

The fine-tuning of using a freezer is what happens before and after you place your food in it. In writing this book, we discovered quite a few best practices that will help you get more out of your freezer. In fact, the takeaways of this section are what made us realize that the freezer is arguably the most important appliance in our kitchen. Our hope is that you can use this book as a guide to help you reach the same conclusion.

We built this how-to manual by listening to the questions of family and friends. As we were writing this book, people asked us questions like, "Can I freeze xyz ingredient?" or "Is this casserole that's been in my freezer for six months still safe to eat?" And in testing and freezing the recipes in this book, we were forced to come up with a system to keep our freezer organized, which helped us create guidelines for you.

In this section, you'll find information on which foods to freeze—an important foundation. Freezing alters the makeup of food, and not always in a good way, so it's helpful to know which foods you just shouldn't bother with. You'll also find details about packaging, storing, and organizing food in your freezer—all key to successfully reaping the benefits of your hard work in the kitchen! Plus, we've included some general wisdom on the lifespan of foods in the freezer to help guide your decision-making during a purge (the answer to the question "Should I toss the leftover turkey from two years ago?" is yes).

But perhaps most essentially, you'll find information on how to prepare food for freezing, and how to unfreeze it—whether by thawing or by heating or cooking from frozen. This is the real "technique" piece of cooking for your freezer; it's also at the crux of how to keep food safe to eat, which is another concern that many people have regarding frozen food.

In short, don't skip this part! The recipes will still be there waiting for you when you finish.

Happy freezing!

1

What to freeze and what not to freeze.

Freezing is one of the most common (and easy) methods of food preservation. Long before food brands catered to the freezer with prefrozen foods, the main purpose of the freezer was to extend the lifespan of fresh food. And once you really start thinking of your freezer as primarily a tool for preservation, the doors of possibility open up pretty quickly. Also, unlike some other forms of food preservation, freezing food is incredibly convenient.

But how exactly does a freezer preserve food? What is it about cold temperatures that keeps food from spoiling? At 0°F, the microbacteria that cause food to decay cannot survive or thrive. If food is stored in a frozen state consistently, it'll be "safe" from expiration indefinitely.

Although the freezer halts the decay process where it is, it does not reverse it. So if you put food that's on the brink of spoilage into the freezer, it'll still spoil pretty quickly once it has thawed. You're not turning back the clock; you're just making time stand still. That's why it's important to use fresh ingredients for all of these recipes and to freeze food immediately upon cooking.

Yet you'll see plenty of "expiration" guidelines in this book. These are regarding quality, not safety. Freezing can change the chemical makeup of food, which can have an effect on its texture, flavor, color, and cook time. Remember high-school chemistry? When you freeze food, the water particles in it change from liquid (water) to solid (ice). Water makes up more than 90 percent of most fruits and vegetables, and 60 to 80 percent of most meat, so freezing these items causes considerable change to their makeup. How these changes affect the ingredient dictates which foods are best for freezing and which foods should be enjoyed fresh.

When you are trying to solve the "to freeze or not to freeze" conundrum, think about two things: texture and water. Texture can change drastically during the freezing and thawing processes. Generally speaking, freezing is the enemy of things that are naturally crispy or crunchy. For example, a crunchy stick of celery will be wilted and soft after freezing.

The reason behind this textural change often has to do with water. The more water an ingredient has, the more drastically the ingredient will change during freezing and thawing. The less water it has, the less change.

RAW PRODUCE

In many fruits and vegetables, the water particles that change into ice during freezing are located inside cell walls. Water expands when it turns into ice and often damages the cell walls in the process. Cell walls provide the structure that gives a piece of lettuce its crunch and shape, so the process of freezing alters the texture of most raw vegetables. Freeze a leaf of lettuce and, upon thawing, that leaf will be wilted and droopy. Freeze a fresh tomato and, upon thawing, it will be watery and mushy.

But there are ways to get around this loss in textural integrity. Simply use the previously frozen produce in recipes where you don't need them in their crisp, raw state: as purees or sautés, baked into casseroles, or blended into sauces.

Raw vegetables and fruits are subject to another culprit of deterioration besides your run-of-the-mill bacteria: enzymes. The presence of enzymes is what turns fruits and vegetables brown and decreases their nutrients.

So if you plan to freeze raw produce, whether it's peaches or fresh field peas, take the extra step to kill the enzymes before you freeze to extend the quality of your produce. The easiest way to do this with vegetables is to blanch them briefly in boiling water, then shock them in an ice-water bath.

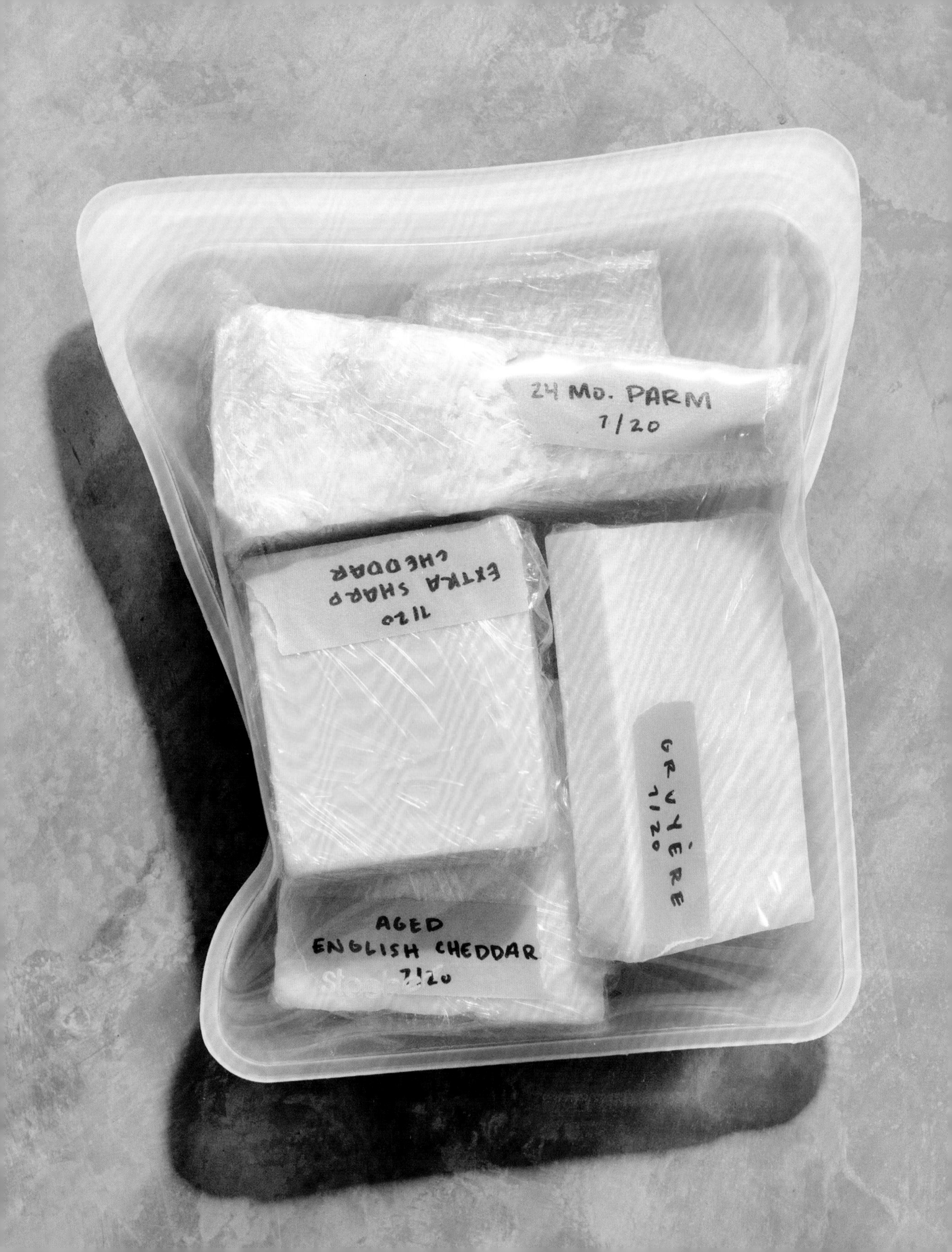
24 MO. PARM
7/20
EXTRA SHARP
CHEDDAR
7/20
GRUYÈRE
7/20
AGED
ENGLISH CHEDDAR
7/20

With fruit, you can employ the same blanching method, but most food scientists recommend the use of ascorbic acid (aka vitamin C) as a way to reduce oxidation and spoilage without subjecting the raw fruit to heat.

COOKED PRODUCE

Cooking, like freezing, breaks down the cell walls in fruits and vegetables, causing them to soften. Thus, the process of freezing isn't going to change the existing texture much more than the cooking process already has.

So great news: Most cooked vegetables make great frozen dishes. You'll find recipes in this book for braised greens and stewed beans and butternut squash soup, plus so many more that are excellent when thawed from frozen. On the fruit side, jams, applesauce, peach puree, and curds all freeze beautifully.

DAIRY

Dairy is finicky in the freezer. It goes back to what happens when certain particles freeze into a solid state. In the case of many types of liquid dairy, the creamy consistency comes from milk-fat globules encased by proteins. When these globules freeze, they form jagged ice crystals that pierce and break the proteins and other particles surrounding them. Because of this, milk, cream, and buttermilk will all lose their viscosity and creamy mouthfeel if frozen and defrosted, and they will likely separate.

You will have better luck freezing dense cheeses, such as Cheddar, Parmigiano, and Gruyère. With cheese, milk-fat globules are typically dispersed more densely and with a stronger emulsification than in liquid dairy, which means the freezing process does less damage to the texture. If you plan to freeze cheese, take care to protect it completely from oxygen, as cheese is particularly susceptible to freezer burn. But if you are melting cheese, there is very little difference between cheese that has been frozen and cheese that hasn't. Creamy soft cheeses, such as cottage cheese and ricotta, are less successful candidates for freezing, as their texture suffers.

Butter, in contrast, may be the dairy product best suited to freezing. Not only does it retain all of its characteristics once it is thawed, but some chefs and food scientists even suggest storing all butter in the freezer instead of the fridge, as its high fat content makes it susceptible to becoming rancid in higher-temperature environments. The fat in butter is distributed differently from the fat in liquid dairy; globules and crystals and water droplets are embedded in a coating of "free fat," which helps butter maintain its texture even after freezing. But there is a downside to freezing butter. It easily absorbs the odors and flavors floating around it, so it can end up tasting like the freezer.

EGGS

There's some competing wisdom on freezing eggs. In the refrigerator, the shelf life of eggs is already fairly long, but you can freeze raw eggs out of the shell (by cracking them into a muffin pan or ice-cube tray, for example). If you try to freeze them in the shell, they'll crack. Freezing produces a noticeable, though not awful, effect on their texture.

SO WHAT ABOUT ICE CREAM?
(And other examples of successful frozen dairy.)

If freezing milk or cream straight from the carton is off-limits, how does that translate to arguably the most famous and popular frozen treat in the world? Ice cream is the product of adding sugar to heavy cream and churning the mixture while it freezes. When this happens, three different elements—ice crystals, cream, and air—organize into a stabilized arrangement. Too much ice or air can alter the ice cream significantly. With larger ice crystals, the texture will be icy and grainy. With too much air churned into the mixture, the volume of the ice cream will increase and the concentration of flavor will lessen. Think of gelato versus Breyers: the former has fewer air cells and is very dense and creamy; the latter has an

almost "fluffy" texture. Meanwhile, the cream holds onto its viscosity thanks to the sugar, which lowers its freezing point and helps maintain the structure of the milk-fat globules and proteins. There's a lot going on in a pint of pistachio!

There are other ways to coax dairy into playing nice in the freezer. These usually involve the presence of a nondairy ingredient to help bind and stabilize the structure. Take béchamel, the thickened cream sauce (page 120). The presence of flour in béchamel allows for successful freezing of a mostly milk–based recipe. Milk or cream that's been cooked into soups or stews also stands up better to freezing.

Cooked egg whites take on a strange, rubbery texture after freezing and thawing, so don't even bother with hard-boiled, soft-boiled, or fried eggs. But egg dishes in which the eggs are beaten (think scrambled eggs in breakfast burritos, or eggs baked into a quiche or casserole) hold up quite well. Here is one pro tip we discovered while working on this book: adding cottage cheese to scrambled or baked eggs helps them maintain their fluffy texture when you reheat them. (It's apparently one of the secret ingredients in the Starbucks sous vide egg bites, too.)

MEAT

You can probably answer this one: yes, meat is okay to freeze. In fact, you've probably already tried it. Meat is one of the most common foods people freeze. Part of this is because meat is expensive. If you've dropped fifty dollars on steaks and don't get around to grilling them within a day or two, you'll want to buy more time on your investment, and the freezer is an easy route.

Meat takes well to being frozen without major sacrifice in quality of flavor or texture. You can freeze it raw, and you can freeze it cooked. You can freeze pretty much any kind of meat, from chicken to beef to pork to last year's Thanksgiving turkey.

SEAFOOD

The seafood industry shares our love for the freezer. Because seafood is especially perishable, most commercially caught or farmed fish is frozen (sometimes on the boat at sea!) before it's shipped to grocery stores. And if you happen to come into a windfall of freshly caught fish, your freezer will help you extend the amount of time you have to enjoy it. The most important thing to note with seafood is to use the pull and thaw method (see page 43) to thaw it. Fish and shellfish both have rather delicate flesh, and rapid thawing or cooking from frozen can dramatically decrease the quality.

GRAINS AND NUTS

Here's a question: What's the advantage to storing shelf-stable foods in the freezer? Although it's perfectly fine to leave your box of pasta and your bag of rice on a pantry shelf, you might want to think about moving tree nuts, flour, and grits to the freezer. Keeping them cold will protect against rancidity, which is more likely to happen with fattier ingredients, such as nuts and nut flours. The fragility of grains is also greater if it isn't highly processed. For example, the all-purpose flour you buy at the supermarket is exceedingly shelf stable because it's been dosed with stabilizers, while the bag of heirloom grits from Anson Mills is much less so. Keep grits in the freezer to ensure a longer shelf life.

You can also successfully freeze quite a few composed grain dishes, from bread to pasta to pie dough, and there's no hard-and-fast rule for when to freeze them—in their raw state or their cooked state. You'll see recipes in this book that go back and forth. But one major consideration is yeast. If the item in question relies on yeast to rise (think breads and rolls), it's best to freeze *after* baking. Cold temperatures can kill yeast, so freezing before baking can sink your loaves before they hit the oven. But after bread has gone through the baking process, the yeast has already activated and created the rise required. Freezing at this point won't have any additional effects.

For items that rely on other ingredients, such as baking soda or baking powder, butter, or eggs, to achieve a rise, freezing before baking is usually okay. Biscuit, pie, and cookie doughs are good examples.

Here's one more general good practice: doughs freeze well and batters do not.

STOCKS, SAUCES, AND CONDIMENTS

Since the composition of sauces and condiments varies so greatly, it's a challenge to summarize any general rules. But here are a few:

→ Raw purees are hit or miss. Avocado-based purees don't work very well, but herb purees, such as pesto or chimichurri, do if the herbs are blanched beforehand.

→ Cooked purees usually freeze well. They may separate slightly upon thawing, but you can usually fix this by putting the puree back into a food processor or blender, or using an immersion blender, and pulsing it a few times. This will work with bean purees like hummus, tomato sauce, eggplant puree, and sweet potato puree.

→ Emulsifications, such as mayonnaise and vinaigrettes, do not freeze well. They break when exposed to freezing temperatures and have negative textural impacts. This means that chicken or tuna salad and other mayo-based dishes are also out.

→ Strained stocks freeze very well.

2

How long can I freeze it?

Expiration dates for frozen foods are a little misleading. At 0°F, the process of decomposition is at a halt, so, theoretically, frozen food will not "expire" in the same way that refrigerated or room-temperature food might.

While a long stint in the freezer won't increase the risk of foodborne illness, it does decrease the quality level of the food. So expiration dates for frozen food are almost always a suggestion for maintaining quality, not a suggestion to ensure safety.

When it comes to expiration dates, we have two major rules. Rule number one: Label *everything* with the name of the dish and the date. We use colored masking tape, which sits in a tape dispenser on our kitchen counter with a Sharpie next to it, just so we're never tempted to skip this crucial step.

To the freewheeling cooking personalities who might be reading this book, cataloging the contents of your freezer may seem a little intense, but you'll be thanking us in six months when the dish you've pulled out of the freezer resembles nothing you've cooked in recent memory. Rather than play a guessing game with yourself, aggressive labeling makes it easy to organize and sort through your freezer inventory (which saves time and makes dinner convenient . . . the whole reason for writing this book!).

Just as important as the identification is the date. Having your freezer inventory labeled will help jog your memory of exactly how long that rock-solid meat loaf has been sitting around in your freezer, taking up real estate.

Which brings us to rule number two: if it's been in your freezer for more than a year, it's time to toss it. One year is the magic cutoff point at which even the most sturdy, freezer-friendly items undergo a sharp decline in quality. After a year, freezer burn is inevitable, flavors become muted, and textures change drastically. So if you're rummaging around in your freezer and you come across items that have crossed over that one-year line, make like Marie Kondo and throw it out.

Some ingredients and recipes won't even make it to a year. Check out the chart on page 24 to see a more detailed breakout of freezer-life expectancy. Our recommendations range from as short as 1 month to as long as 12 months, depending on the ingredients, the composition of the dish, and the packaging.

FREEZER ORGANIZATION

All of this variance in expiration dates begs the question, how do you keep up with what's in your freezer? What are the best ways to organize the contents of your freezer to make sure you're using what you have before it goes bad? We have experienced the "freezer as black hole" scenario, in which items get frozen and then languish, untouched and forgotten, until finally being thrown away. If you're not in the habit of using your freezer regularly for preserving food, this might sound pretty familiar. The best way to avoid this is by staying organized.

Making Your Freezer Inventory

We keep a Google spreadsheet with our freezer inventory. Before you laugh or roll your eyes and stop reading, hear us out. This list of what's in our freezer at any given time allows us to keep up with what we have, when we should eat it by, and what we might need to stock up on. We also have it listed in the same order we have the freezer organized, a strategy we picked up from years of Ashley doing inventory counts in our restaurant walk-ins. There's a reason why professional kitchens operate this way, and doing it at home has made it so much easier to keep up with what we have and to plan our cooking around it.

Here are some tips for keeping a useful freezer inventory:

→ **Organize it into general categories.** This will help you find and use what's on hand. We divide the list into two buckets: ingredients (this includes prepared ingredients, such as compound butters or stocks) and ready-to-eat dishes.

→ **Include the date made, the expiration date, and the quantity.** Every item on our list has these details so we can tell at a glance what might be creeping up toward expiration and make a plan to use it.

→ **Put it somewhere visible.** The whole point of keeping an inventory is to remember what you have on hand. If your list is out of sight, it'll probably be out of mind. Consider keeping it printed out and taped inside a cabinet or pantry door, or even on your freezer door.

→ **Keep it updated.** This is probably the most tedious habit to adopt. We try to update our inventory as we go, rather than wait and do a big update periodically. As we put things in the freezer, we add them to the spreadsheet, and as we pull things out, we remove them from the spreadsheet.

Organizing Your Freezer

It seems obvious, but it's worth saying anyway: the more organized you keep your freezer, the more likely you'll be to utilize it to its full potential. How you organize your freezer depends a lot on what kind of freezer you have and the amount of space at your disposal.

Here are some tips that are beneficial for any kind of freezer:

→ **Store by category.** Keep raw ingredients to one section and prepared dishes or ingredients to another. Keep like with like: uncooked meats together, soups and stocks together, casseroles and main dishes together, desserts together.

→ **Make sure labels are easily visible.** You want to be able to know at a glance what you have, rather than having to dig around to figure out what's in the freezer.

→ **Store food in packaging that takes up the least amount of real estate.** For example, freezing soups and stocks and similar items in vacuum-sealed pouches, laid flat, will take up less room than storing them in upright quart-size containers.

→ **Do a quarterly purge.** We try to do a freezer clean out every three months or so, during which we remove and discard anything that is out of date. We do a quick reorganization of what we have at the same time.

FROZEN FOOD LIFESPAN.

Category	Style	Lifespan
MEAT, RAW	Ground meat	4 months
	Steaks and chops (beef and pork)	6 to 8 months
	Chicken parts	9 months
	Whole chicken	1 year
	Bacon	3 months
	Sausage	4 months
MEAT, COOKED	Ground meat	2 months
	Steaks and chops (beef and pork)	4 to 5 months
	Chicken parts	6 months
	Whole chicken	8 months
	Bacon	6 weeks
	Sausage	2 months
SEAFOOD, RAW	Lean finfish (like bass, cod, tuna, tilapia)	6 to 8 months
	Fatty finfish (like anchovies, sardines, bluefish, mackerel)	3 months
	Shrimp	4 to 6 months
SEAFOOD, COOKED	Lean finfish (like bass, cod, tuna, tilapia)	4 months
	Fatty finfish (like anchovies, sardines, bluefish, mackerel)	6 weeks
	Shellfish (shrimp, lobster meat, crabmeat)	3 months
FRUITS, RAW	Berries, stone fruit	9 months
	Apples, pears	9 months
	Bananas	6 months
FRUITS, COOKED	Fruit puree with sugar	6 months
	Tomato puree	3 months
	Roasted banana puree	4 months
VEGETABLES, RAW	Corn, field peas, green beans, broccoli	1 year
VEGETABLES, COOKED	Greens	4 months
	Sweet potato	8 months
	Eggplant and squash	8 months
	Beans and field peas	6 months
	Onions	6 months

Category	Style	Lifespan
DAIRY	Butter	4 months
	Ice cream	3 to 4 months
	Eggs, cooked	3 months
	Hard cheeses	6 months
GRAINS, COOKED	Bread (loaves, bagels, rolls, English muffins)	4 to 6 months
	Muffins, scones, biscuits, cakes	2 months
	Rice	4 to 6 months
SOUP	Broth	6 months
	Vegetable-based soup	9 months
	Meat-based soup	4 months
	Dairy-based soup	3 months
CASSEROLES	Pasta bakes	4 to 6 months
	Bread puddings, stratas, quiche	3 months
SAUCES	Cream or dairy-based sauce	4 to 6 months
	Vegetable-based sauce	6 months
DOUGH	Cookie dough	9 months
	Piecrust	9 months

3

How to freeze.

It seems self-explanatory, right? The answer to this is as simple as "put the item you wish to freeze into a freezer and wait." But freezing prepared food has some additional steps to ensure you get the safest, most useful, most delicious, and most convenient results.

TIME AND TEMPERATURE

The first step to freezing food properly is to pay attention to how long it takes to get to its frozen state, which is usually between 0° and 10°F. Why is this important?

We talked about how food can't really "go bad" (in a food-safety sense) once it's frozen at 0°F. But it *can* go bad during the process of being cooled to frozen (in the same way, it can go bad during the process of thawing, which we talk about on page 41). The way in which food is frozen can also affect its quality pretty drastically. Improper freezing will lead to things like freezer burn and compromised texture.

In order to avoid foodborne illness and decomposition and to minimize the negative impact on quality, you want to cool your food down to a frozen state as quickly as possible. The first way to achieve this is to prepare your freezer.

Your freezer temperature should be set at 0°F or below. At higher temperatures, food decomposition can continue to occur. If your freezer is struggling to stay at 0°F or below, you may need to defrost it, clean the filters and the fan, have it serviced, or a combination of all three.

There are also ways to prepare your food that will help it to freeze more quickly. One of the biggest factors is the temperature of the food when you put it into the freezer.

Let's start with the biggest no-no: *do not* put hot food into the freezer. It's tempting, after you've spent time and energy on cooking something, to just throw it into a container and stick it into the freezer without waiting for it to cool. But doing so is going to create all kinds of problems, from promoting the growth of bacteria in the dish itself to raising the temperature inside your freezer and thus everything inside it.

Before we dig into the process of freezing, let's talk about the process of cooling hot food. There's a temperature range, known in restaurant kitchens as the "danger zone," in which the bacteria that can lead to foodborne illness are most likely to produce. This is one of the things that health inspectors pay a lot of attention to when doing restaurant inspections; it's unsafe for certain foods to be in this temperature zone for more than a few hours. The danger zone is usually defined as between 40° and 145°F. The most dangerous segment within this range is from about 80° to 115°F.

Hot food should be cooled completely, ideally to 40°F, before transferring it to the freezer. We tend to do this in two parts: We let the food cool to room temperature (65° to 68°F) on the counter or stove, as long as it'll cool to that temp within two hours. If it'll take longer than that, then we take steps to cool it faster (more on this below). Then we portion the dish as we intend to freeze it and cool it in the refrigerator until it's at 40°F. Finally, we place it in the freezer to freeze to 0°F.

Why bother with this multistep process? By doing so, you're basically getting food as cold as you can before putting it into the freezer, which means it'll take less time to reach 0°F than if it started at a higher temp.

There are several things you can do to help the temperature of your food drop quickly. Putting it into the refrigerator is not one of them. Just like slipping hot food into a freezer, putting hot food into the refrigerator can raise the ambient temperature of all the food in the fridge. Not good.

Food cools down faster when it is packaged in smaller quantities or spread out with lots of exposed surface area. If you've ever made a big pot of chili or stock, you know that it can take forever to cool down. Consider portioning big batches of food into smaller containers to speed the cooling process. You can also chill big batches using the ice-bath method, by setting the pot in a sink partially filled with ice water. Similarly, spreading foods like cooked risotto (page 69) or pâte à choux dough (page 62) on a rimmed baking sheet or other shallow pan will help bring down the temperature more quickly than if you try to cool them in the pot in which they were cooked.

Here is a handful of dos and don'ts to help you navigate cooling your food down to freezing quickly:

Do

> → Cool food immediately after cooking and before freezing.
>
> → Portion food in smaller containers to help it cool faster.
>
> → Use an ice-water bath to help cool a large batch of food faster.

Don't

> → Allow at-risk food to stay in the "danger zone" of 40° to 145°F for longer than 4 to 6 hours.
>
> → Put warm or hot food in the refrigerator or freezer.

PORTIONING

When you're getting ready to freeze something, think about how you want to use it later. Is it the type of item that you'll need to thaw out in large quantities? Or is it a batch of individual items that you'd like to be able to pull separately rather than all together? How many people are you typically cooking for at a time? What is the end goal of the ingredient or dish you're freezing?

Part of using the freezer to preserve food is to pull only what you need. There are a couple of reasons for this. First, you lessen the risk of wasting food if you're only thawing and reheating the portions you'll eat on any given occasion.

Second, it's not ideal to freeze and thaw something more than once. It goes back to the "danger zone" standard for food safety: the more you move ingredients through that range of temperatures, the greater the chance bacteria will develop. Additionally, going through multiple stages of thaw and freeze will break down the cellular structure of the ingredients to the point the quality is negatively affected.

So putting some thought into portioning on the front end will make it easier to utilize all of your delicious stores later on. Here are some guidelines for how to portion different types of things.

Prepared Ingredients

We are big on freezing prepared "ingredients" (often referred to in cookbooks as "subrecipes") that we can use later to make a complete dish. This is what we dub our "freezer pantry," and it's the focus of the entire second section of this book. When freezing recipes like this, you want to divide them into portions that will be easy to incorporate when you're ready to cook.

For example, you may prepare a batch of chicken stock that yields two quarts. Rather than freezing it all in one container, divide the stock into two quart-size portions. One quart is a common measurement in soup and stew recipes. Similarly, for things like compound butter or chimichurri, think about how you'll use them. Usually we add compound butter by the tablespoon to recipes like pan sauces, so portioning the butter into tablespoons you can easily pull one at a time makes more sense than portioning a cup or two in a single container.

Individual Portions

Quite a few recipes in this book, from crispy pork and potato cakes (page 90) to biscuits (page 56) to jalapeño poppers (page 183), make individual portions. This is where the freezing technique we call "formative freezing" comes into play. To freeze a recipe in individual portions, the portions need to be spread out on a flat surface like a baking sheet, with enough space around each portion to prevent touching. This is hardly a feasible way to store individual portions, as you'd run out of freezer space pretty quickly. So instead we do a formative freeze, first spreading the portions out flat on a baking sheet for freezing and then transferring them to a storage vessel. Once frozen, the portions will hold their shape and won't stick to one another or get crushed or flattened in the storage vessel (like a plastic bag or container). A formative freeze usually takes about 4 hours to set the portions fully.

What kinds of things should you portion individually for a formative freeze?

→ Biscuit dough (portioned into rounds, frozen on a baking sheet, then transferred to a plastic bag to store)

→ Cookie dough (portioned into balls, frozen on a baking sheet, then transferred to a plastic bag to store)

→ Meatballs (laid flat on a baking sheet for freezing, then transferred to a plastic bag to store)

→ Muffins (frozen in the muffin pan, then transferred to a plastic bag to store)

→ Jalapeño poppers (laid flat on a baking sheet for freezing, then transferred to a plastic bag to store)

You can also use a formative freeze for individual portions of already baked casseroles, such as lasagna and egg strata, or pies and tarts. Cool the dish to 40°F (this will make it much easier to portion), then cut it into single-serving squares or slices. Arrange the portions on a baking sheet and do a formative freeze. Individually wrap the frozen portions in plastic wrap and store in a plastic bag or container. You can do this with the following:

→ Squares of lasagna

→ Slices of quiche

→ Slices of fruit pie (custard pies don't freeze well after baking)

Family-Style Portions

Even when portioning recipes for a larger yield, keep in mind that the larger the portion, the longer it'll take to thaw and reheat. We often break out larger yield recipes into portions of four to six servings.

PACKAGING

Good packaging is critical to successful freezing. One of the major threats to food quality during the freezing is exposure to air, which causes freezer burn. Proper packaging is the last line of defense in protecting food quality in the freezer and is equally important to a smooth transition to thawing and reheating.

Since air exposure is the enemy of frozen food, vacuum-sealed packaging is the standard bearer. When using a vacuum-sealing appliance to package food in plastic pouches you remove the air by vacuum before the pouches

are sealed. The pro? It's airtight, so it's arguably the best of all packaging options. The con? It has size limitations. Most countertop vacuum-sealing appliances have a maximum width of twelve inches, which means you probably won't be vacuum sealing whole casseroles, pies, or large loaves of bread. Additionally, if you don't have a vacuum sealer, there's the con of investing in a new piece of equipment.

Also, while we've already gone over why it's important to cool food before freezing, it's especially true of food packaged using a vacuum sealer. Warm food creates steam that will turn into air pockets in the pouch. These air pockets not only create a perfect petri dish for bacteria to form but can also produce leaks and penetrations in your seal.

If you're not vacuum sealing, you're probably using a combination of glass, plastic, or silicone vessels and plastic or aluminum wrapping.

Before you decide on how to package your food, keep in mind that you may be storing the dish in question for months. Don't accidentally take all of your best pans and containers out of kitchen rotation by using them for freezer storage. Either commit to purchasing a handful of vessels for freezer-only use or rely on disposable packaging.

Plastic or Glass?

There is a lot of conversation around the safety of using plastic. Although almost all plastic food-storage containers are now made without BPA (the compound that was at the center of the public-health debate), some people still have lingering concerns over the safety of plastic in the long term. If you don't feel comfortable storing your food in plastic containers, it's easy enough to work around them. We use a mix of plastic and glass containers, and there are advantages and disadvantages to both.

Glass is great because it is odor and stain resistant; it's oven, dishwasher, and microwave safe; and it does a great job of protecting food. Plastic wins points for being lightweight, cheap, and kid friendly, in addition to success-fully protecting food. (Most plastic containers are also dishwasher and microwave safe, but don't stick them in your oven.)

Zip-Top Plastic Bags

Honestly, these bags are one of the more important tools in our freezer arsenal. The downside, of course, is that they are single-use when you're putting them in the freezer. But it's hard to beat their utility, performance, and convenience. You'll see us call for them a lot in the recipes in this book, but do make sure that you are using the freezer-specific bags. They are more durable than regular zip-top bags and stand up better to the cold, which means better protection for your food.

Shape and Size

Whether you go plastic, glass, or a different material, such as silicone or stainless steel, you want to choose containers that are the right size for your portions. The food should fill the vessel completely. If the vessel is too large, you'll have excess air exposure, which can lead to freezer burn. If it's too small, you'll have difficulty with spillage when thawing and reheating. Shallow dishes are preferred over deeper dishes because they will quicken both freezing and thawing.

Choosing the container is only half the equation. Just as important is choosing the lid or cover. You want to package your food to be as airtight as possible for the best results. Lids with silicone gaskets or clips are particularly good at keeping air out. If you are packaging your food in a dish that doesn't have a lid, using plastic wrap with aluminum foil is a good option.

Wrapping for the Freezer

We prefer to wrap food in plastic wrap, rather than aluminum foil, for freezing. In our opinion, it creates a better seal. We approach it with a "cater-wrapping" mentality. Early in her career, Ashley had a small catering side hustle called Notorious Pear. She'd spend hours cooking and then load up everything in the back of her Isuzu Trooper to take to whatever private party had hired her. She became very skilled at wrapping dishes in a way that ensured they wouldn't spill in transit. It turns out that wrapping items for the freezer requires a similar approach. The key is to do a complete 360-degree wrap of the dish—underneath and over the top. This guarantees the plastic is adhering to itself, not to the dish, because as the dish gets cold, condensation can begin to form, and your plastic seal can come loose.

Think of wrapping for the freezer kind of like wrapping a present. You want to pull enough plastic wrap so that if you set the dish on top of the layer of plastic, you'll have enough on each side to wrap around and overlap in the middle. Then pull more wrap, lay it flat, and do the same thing, but with the dish turned ninety degrees. This should create full coverage and a completely airtight seal.

Prepackaged Food

So what about already packaged food that you're buying at a store or market and putting directly into the freezer? Do you need to do anything to repackage it? The answer is, it depends. If the item was already frozen when you purchased it (think ice cream or frozen vegetables), you don't need to do anything else. The manufacturers have already packaged it with the freezer in mind. However, fresh ingredients may need to be transferred into new packaging. Raw meat is the most common and important example. Whether you buy it in the prepackaged plastic-wrapped shell or wrapped in paper from the meat counter, it's essential to transfer raw meat into a more freezer-appropriate package for freezing and storing. Vacuum-sealed plastic pouches are ideal, but we also use zip-top plastic bags.

LABELING

We've already talked about this a little bit as it relates to expiration dates and organization. But let us reemphasize the point: you should be labeling everything you're putting into your freezer. This can be as simple as writing the name and date in Sharpie directly on the container, or it can be more involved. Here's a list of our labeling suggestions:

Required Information

→ Name of item

→ Date it was made

Optional Information

→ Suggested expiration date (see the chart on 24 for guidance)

→ Reheating instructions

→ Initials of who made it

→ Yield or number of portions

Practically, you want to make sure to label your food in a way that will still be legible after weeks or months in the freezer. We use masking tape for most things. It typically works well on glass or plastic containers as long as it's applied when the container is at room temperature. On zip-top plastic bags and plastic pouches for vacuum sealing, masking tape tends to come off, so use a Sharpie to write directly on the bag.

CHEESY SAUSAGE
+ SAGE WAFFLES
7/20 EXP. 8/20

AC

4

How to unfreeze.

When getting ready to cook with food that's starting from a frozen state, there's a prologue that needs to take place before the first step of any recipe: How will you thaw that food? There are a number of ways to do it and a number of ways *not* to do it, and it all depends on the ingredient or dish in question and the end result.

COOKING FROM FROZEN

The first and arguably easiest way to go about this is to bypass the thawing step altogether and start the cooking process from a frozen state. This works best for ready-to-eat dishes that you're reheating with the intention of eating immediately. It also works for some dishes that are not yet cooked but are otherwise completely composed and require no additional steps before cooking.

Oven

Oven-baked dishes, like a pan of Tex-Mex enchiladas (page 211) or apple pie (page 73), are a great example of foods that are ideal to cook directly from frozen. Dishes like these can be put into the oven straight from the freezer and cooked until hot and ready to eat. The only downside is that these types of dishes typically require quite a long baking time: in our experience, a fully frozen 9 by 13-inch baking dish will take from 2½ to 3 hours to bake. Keep that in mind when planning your cooking time.

Sous Vide

If you've used vacuum-sealed packaging, one great way to reheat or cook from frozen is the sous vide method. It requires an immersion circulator, a professional kitchen tool that used to feel out of reach to most home cooks but has made major inroads to accessibility in the last five years. This appliance, which looks like a wide wand and is clipped to the side of a container, will typically run you less than two hundred dollars. The circulator allows you to keep a hot-water bath at a constant temperature. You can add vacuum-sealed bags of frozen food to the water bath to cook or reheat. We've used the sous vide method to bring frozen soups, stews, and even mashed potatoes to a hot temperature. It's a lifesaver on Thanksgiving when you're running out of stove-top or oven space.

Instant Pot

One of the most exciting discoveries of this cookbook was the utility of the Instant Pot for cooking and reheating frozen food. It's particularly great for reheating stock or soup. You may have to run the container under warm water to make it easy to transfer the contents to the Instant Pot, but from there, it's pretty easy: slide the Instant Pot lid to lock, set the timer to high pressure for 6 minutes, and then, when the time is up, release the pressure with the quick release method.

Microwave

An oldie but a goodie, the microwave and frozen food have a long-established, very close relationship. Most prepackaged frozen food encourages microwave reheating, and college students everywhere have survived by using this appliance. But with all of that said, the microwave has a negative connotation among some cooks. In certain culinary circles, cooking with a microwave is looked down on.

On this pretentious attitude, we call BS. Microwaves have as much of a place in the home kitchen as any other appliance. Whether you prefer to use it frequently or at all is up to you, but let's all separate that decision from any kind of moral or cultural high ground. Convenience and quality do not have to be mutually exclusive.

In the past, criticism of microwaves generally focused on the quality of the food: the high-power heating process was hard to control and could lead to some unfortunate quality issues. But the microwaves of today are significantly more calibrated, often with multiple power levels and settings to help you control your cooking. As we've rekindled our love of the microwave with this book, we've also come up with a few rules:

1. Avoid the highest power setting. Even though it's the default setting on most microwaves, it's not necessary and creates the least-consistent results.

2. Rethink your expectations of cook time in the microwave. Microwaves are used for their speed; what takes twenty minutes in the oven takes three minutes in a microwave. But using a microwave at a lower power setting over a longer period of time can be a real game changer.

When thawing something from frozen, we typically start on a power setting below 5 (out of 10, with 10 being the max), and microwave in 3-minute increments. Depending on the size and vessel, it can take from 8 to 12 minutes to thaw and heat.

THAWING

Thawing is different from reheating. When we talk about thawing, we mean the process of raising the temperature of a frozen ingredient to the point at which it is no longer frozen but ideally is not yet in the danger zone of 40° to 145°F. (As a reminder, the danger zone is a temperature range in which bacteria that can lead to foodborne illness are most likely to produce.) We want to thaw, not reheat, ingredients we plan to continue to cook with, rather than immediately reheat and eat. For example, quite a few of the freezer pantry items in Part Two require thawing, not reheating, to be used in a recipe.

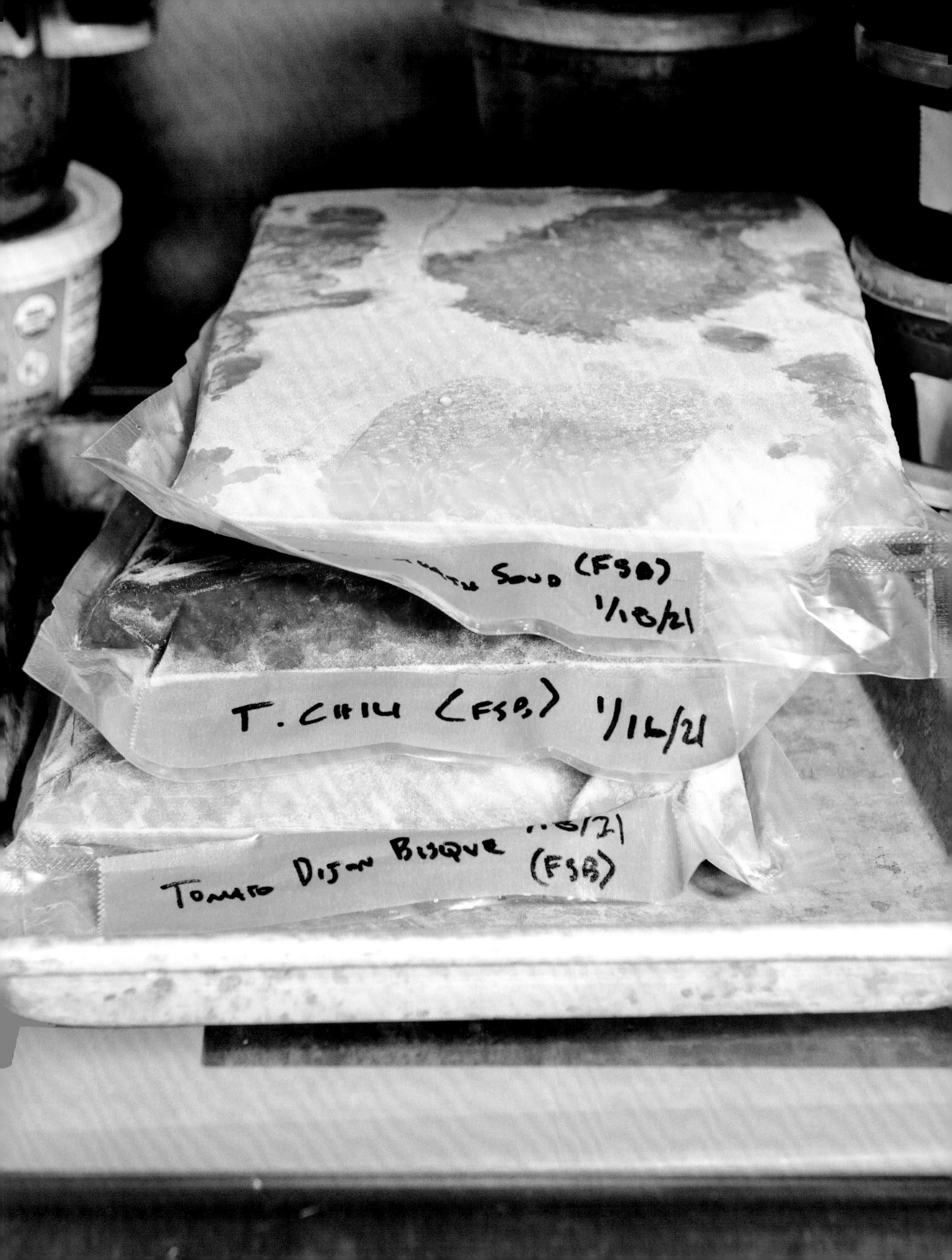

Soup (FSB)
T. CHILI (FSB)
TOMATO DIJON BISQUE
(FSB)

Pull and Thaw (Refrigerator Thawing)

The most controlled and accurate way to thaw something is to move the dish or ingredient from your freezer to your refrigerator, and wait. We call this the pull and thaw method. This ensures that the rise in temperature never exceeds the temperature of the refrigerator, keeping the item below the threshold of the danger zone at all times. But it is also the longest thawing process. In our experience, *it takes a minimum of 24 hours for a previously frozen recipe or dish to thaw in the refrigerator.* You'll often see instructions in recipes elsewhere stating that you can thaw something "overnight," but 8 to 12 hours has rarely been enough time to thaw frozen food completely in our house.

It's easy to get around the time commitment, as long as you're planning ahead. Try to get in the habit of pulling what you need and moving it to the refrigerator about 2 days before you're ready to cook. Your foresight will result in the best quality and safety of your dish.

Countertop Thawing

We don't recommend leaving frozen food out at room temperature to thaw. Most frozen food will require several hours to thaw at room temperature, which means prolonged exposure in the danger zone as the temperature of the item rises. The only exceptions to this would be less perishable items that you might keep on a counter anyway, such as breads, bread crumbs, muffins, cookies, or pie dough. But even then, if it's going to take more than 2 hours for the item to thaw, it's best to move it to the refrigerator.

Cold Water Thawing

Let's face it: Sometimes, we forget to pull our frozen ingredients with enough notice to thaw them in the refrigerator. Sometimes we need to thaw something quickly. In these instances, the next best approach is the cold running water bath. To do this, put your packaged ingredient into a larger bowl or other vessel, or even a plugged sink, and run a slow steady trickle of cold water over it until it thaws. While it's way faster than thawing in the refrigerator, this process isn't exactly quick—expect 20 to 30 minutes for most items. This method is preferred by the health department (at least here in North Carolina), but it's not ideal from a water conservation perspective. You can also try the water bath method: submerge the packaged item in cold water, and change out the water every 30 minutes until it is thawed.

Resist the urge to use hot water to speed up either version of the process; doing so can heat up the exterior of the food to a temperature in the danger zone, where bacteria can start to multiply.

Speed Thawing

If even 20 to 30 minutes is out of the question, there are other ways to move your frozen food into a thawed state with greater haste.

We typically rely on the low power settings of the microwave, or a short round in the Instant Pot (try 2 to 3 minutes instead of 6). But proceed with caution. Anytime you're applying heat to frozen food in order to thaw it, you're risking the chance the temperature of the ingredient will rise into the danger zone. What does that mean? Is it a guarantee that you'll get sick? No, definitely not. But it means that you should start an internal clock in your head: to minimize the risk, prepare and eat the food in question within 4 to 6 hours.

THE Freezer PANTRY

DRY-AGED RIBEYE 7/20

COCKTAIL ICE 3/20

ANSON MILLS 6/20 CORNMEAL

PART TWO

It's time to talk strategy.

The recipes and ideas in this chapter were actually the seed from which this book was born. While we were writing the *Poole's* cookbook, we ended up with so many prepared ingredients—things like half pints of porcini butter, bags of herbed béchamel, and containers of chicken confit. Into the freezer they went.

Then over the course of the several months after we finished testing, we'd pull from these supplies to come up with a dinner plan. The ability to incorporate these flavorful additions was a game changer. It gave our meals at home depth and deliciousness but allowed us to still keep the time spent in the kitchen relatively short.

Once we'd run through the staples from the cookbook, we found ourselves carving out time to replenish our supplies—restocking our freezer pantry with chicken stock and pesto, biscuit dough and piecrusts. At some point, it just became a part of our overall cooking strategy at home.

Here's what we suggest: When the urge to cook strikes, think about what you can make for dinner that night, yes, but also about what you can make for later. Stock your freezer pantry when you feel like being in the kitchen and you'll be grateful the next time you *don't* feel like being in the kitchen.

The recipes in this chapter operate like little nesting dolls. There's a single "pantry" recipe that you can make and freeze, followed by a handful of recipes on how to use that staple (some of which you can also freeze). The idea is that, with your freezer well stocked, your options for delicious meals multiply.

5

Grains.

50 CORNBREAD

CORNBREAD CRUMBS • 51

Cornbread Panzanella with Watermelon, Cucumber, and Za'atar Vinaigrette • 53

Seafood Stuffies • 54

Lynn's Thanksgiving Dressing • 55

56 BUTTERMILK BISCUITS

BISCUIT DUMPLINGS OR "GNOCCHI" • ORANGE BISCUITS • SAUSAGE AND CHEESE BISCUITS • 57

Blueberry-Ginger Cobbler • 59

Chicken and Dumplings • 60

62 PÂTE À CHOUX

Poole's Three-Cheese Gougères • 63

PÂTE À CHOUX DOUGHNUTS • 64

Banana Cream Profiteroles • 67

68 RISOTTO

The Quickest Risotto Parmigiano • 69

Almond Rice Pudding with Rhubarb-Apricot Jam • 71

72 PIECRUST

Apple Pie • 73

Pimento Cheese Hand Pies • 77

Quiche Lorraine • 78

CORNBREAD

**MAKES ONE 12-INCH
SKILLET LOAF**

Kait grew up with cornbread from a JIFFY box mix as an occasional side with chili. It wasn't until she moved to the South—and got to know cornbread through Ashley—that she came to think about cornbread as an ingredient and a staple.

Ashley's recipe for cornbread has no sugar and is an exercise in simplicity (part of the charm for her): just good cornmeal, eggs, buttermilk, butter, salt, and baking powder. The result is a denser, naturally gluten-free loaf that holds up beautifully in the freezer, toasts nicely in the presence of butter and heat, and soaks up the flavors of broths and vinaigrettes.

Why is it worth keeping cornbread as part of your pantry? You can freeze it in whole loaves, in individual wedges, or crumbled into crumbs. Pull the whole loaf to accompany your next large pot of soup. For breakfast, griddle individual slices in butter and eat with yogurt and jam the way you would toast. Use the crumbs to add texture to dishes (they'd work great sprinkled on top of a vegetable gratin, for example) or to form the base of a holiday dressing. Cornbread holds up well, reheats well, and pivots well—a freezer MVP if we ever saw one.

●

6 large eggs, beaten

2½ cups whole (full-fat) buttermilk

¾ cup unsalted butter, melted and cooled, plus 1 tablespoon cold butter for the skillet

2½ cups coarse-grind cornmeal

1½ cups corn flour or fine-grind cornmeal

1 tablespoon plus 2 teaspoons baking powder

1 tablespoon plus 1 teaspoon kosher salt

Preheat the oven to 400°F. Place a 12-inch cast-iron skillet in the oven to heat.

In a medium bowl, whisk together the eggs, buttermilk, and melted butter. In a second large bowl, whisk together the cornmeal, corn flour, baking powder, and salt. Add the wet ingredients to the dry ingredients and fold together with a rubber spatula, mixing well.

Pull the hot skillet from the oven. Add the 1 tablespoon cold butter to the pan and swirl to melt, coating the bottom and sides. Pour the batter into the hot buttered skillet. Return the skillet to the oven and bake the cornbread for 25 to 30 minutes, until set. Flip the cornbread out onto a wire rack.

Serve warm.

TO FREEZE: Let the cornbread cool completely. Wrap the loaf in two layers of plastic wrap. Label and date and freeze for up to 6 months. Alternatively, cut the loaf into wedges, wrap each wedge individually in two layers of plastic wrap. Place the wedges in a zip-top plastic bag or lidded container and freeze for up to 6 months.

TO THAW: Use the pull and thaw method (see page 43) or let the loaf or wedges sit on a counter (see page 43) until at room temperature.

TO REHEAT: For best results, reheat from thawed, not from frozen. Wrap individual slices in a damp paper towel and place on a microwave-safe plate. Place in the microwave, set the microwave on a medium setting (5 out of 10 on ours), and microwave in 2-minute increments. Alternatively, to griddle your cornbread, place a skillet over medium-high-heat and add 1 tablespoon unsalted butter. When it has melted completely, add the cornbread, cut side down, and sear until golden brown. Flip the cornbread and sear on the other side.

● **CHEFFIN' IT UP**

One loaf of cornbread will make 16 cups crumbs. You can also make crumbs out of frozen and thawed cornbread following the same instructions, but these crumbs should not be frozen a second time.

Cornbread Crumbs

Allow the loaf to cool completely, then cut into wedges and, working in batches, pulse in a food processor until reduced to crumbs. (We usually pulse to a coarse texture, because we can always pulse them more for finer texture later.) Divide the crumbs into your preferred portion sizes (we suggest 4 cups), and transfer to zip-top plastic bags. Then label and date, and store in the refrigerator for up to 1 week or in the freezer for up to 1 month.

TO THAW: Use the pull and thaw method (see page 43) or let the crumbs sit on a counter (see page 43) until at room temperature. They will thaw pretty quickly on the counter, typically within 1 hour.

CORNBREAD PANZANELLA

with Watermelon, Cucumber, and Za'atar Vinaigrette

SERVES 4

The unwritten ingredient in *panzanella* is time. This salad thrives at room temperature because the slowly released juices of the fruits or vegetables—traditionally tomato, but in this case watermelon—are pivotal to the overall experience.

The watermelon is matched with the extra element of bright, acidic sumac in the za'atar vinaigrette (which you could use in place of an Italian vinaigrette in other recipes with great results)—all of it soaked up by toasted cornbread cubes, their edges sharpened with butter. It's like an Israeli salad romping through the American South.

●

Preheat the oven to 450°F.

Make the vinaigrette: In a medium bowl, combine the olive oil, canola oil, vinegar, mustard, za'atar, oregano, and salt and whisk well. The vinaigrette won't emulsify; it is a broken vinaigrette by design. You should have about 1½ cups. It will keep in a lidded container in the refrigerator for up to 2 weeks.

Cut the cornbread into 1½-inch cubes and put them into a large bowl. Pour the butter over the cubes and toss to coat evenly. Arrange the cubes in a single layer on a rimmed baking sheet and bake for 5 to 6 minutes, until golden brown and toasted on the first side. Flip the cubes over and bake for 4 to 5 minutes longer, until toasted on the second side. Set the cornbread aside to cool to warm.

Assemble the salad: In a large bowl, combine the cucumber, watermelon, and onion. Drizzle with ¼ cup of the vinaigrette and season with salt and pepper. Mix gently, taking care not to break up the watermelon too much. Add the cornbread cubes and fold together a few times to mix well.

Pour the salad out onto a platter and sprinkle with the feta, mint, basil, and dill. Drizzle with an additional 2 to 4 tablespoons of the vinaigrette and serve.

Vinaigrette

⅔ cup extra virgin olive oil

⅓ cup canola oil

¼ cup red wine vinegar

1 tablespoon Dijon mustard

½ cup za'atar

3 tablespoons dried oregano

1 tablespoon kosher salt

4 wedges (½ loaf) Cornbread (page 50), at room temperature

4 tablespoons unsalted butter, melted

1 English cucumber, quartered lengthwise and cut into ½-inch pieces

2 cups cubed watermelon

¼ red onion, thinly sliced

Kosher salt and freshly ground black pepper

4 ounces feta cheese, crumbled

2 tablespoons fresh mint leaves

2 tablespoons fresh basil leaves

1 tablespoon chopped fresh dill

SEAFOOD STUFFIES

SERVES 8

Native to the New England coast, these are best described as little clam cakes that you bake right in the shell. They are typically made with large quahog clams, which we don't have in North Carolina, so this recipe channels what we love about stuffies but uses the ingredients we have around. We call for littlenecks or top necks instead of quahogs and for cornbread crumbs to bind. In place of the clam shells, you can bake the stuffies in ramekins, individual gratin dishes, or store-bought oven-safe shells.

●

24 top neck clams,
48 littleneck clams,
or about 8 ounces
drained canned clams

1 egg

½ cup mayonnaise

2 tablespoons
Dijon mustard

½ cup chopped fresh
curly parsley

¼ teaspoon sweet paprika

1 teaspoon kosher salt

¾ teaspoon freshly
ground black pepper

8 ounces large shrimp,
peeled, deveined, and
chopped

8 ounces lump crabmeat,
picked over for shell
fragments

6 ounces Cornbread
Crumbs (page 51),
about 2 cups, at room
temperature

Finely grated zest
of 1 lemon

½ cup finely grated
Parmesan cheese

If using fresh clams, place the clams in a bowl and cover with cold water. Let soak for 30 minutes; drain the clams and cover with fresh cold water. Let soak for another 30 minutes. Drain once more and set aside.

In a large, high-sided sauté pan or Dutch oven over medium heat, arrange the clams in a single layer, working in batches if you need to, and add water until it reaches halfway up the depth of the shells. Bring to a boil, cover, and cook the clams, checking them and stirring them frequently, until they begin to open. As they open, transfer them to a plate and reserve; discard any clams that fail to open after 10 minutes.

Once the clams cool, pull the meat from the shells and set aside. Using the edge of a spoon, scrape the shells clean of any membrane, and reserve. Coarsely chop the clam meat, and reserve.

In a bowl, mix together the egg, mayonnaise, mustard, parsley, paprika, salt, and pepper. Add the shrimp and clams and then flake the crabmeat into the bowl. Add the cornbread crumbs and, using a rubber spatula, gently fold the ingredients together.

Break the reserved shells into halves and fill the halves with 2½ table-spoons of the seafood mixture (you'll have extra shells, so choose the pretty ones). Round the filling up for a nice full shell.

TO FREEZE: Arrange the stuffed shells on a rimmed baking sheet and freeze for at least 4 hours or up to overnight for a formative freeze (see page 31). Transfer to a gallon-size zip-top plastic bag, label and date, and freeze for up to 2 months.

TO BAKE: Preheat the oven to 400°F. Place the stuffies on a rimmed baking sheet and bake for 15 minutes if cooking immediately after preparing, or for 20 minutes if baking from frozen, until the mixture sizzles and turns golden brown. Top each of the stuffies with some of the lemon zest and ½ teaspoon Parmesan and bake for 5 minutes more. Let sit for 5 minutes before serving.

LYNN'S THANKSGIVING DRESSING

SERVES 10 TO 12

There's never a Thanksgiving at our house at which this dish isn't present. It's a take on the classic cornbread dressing, a fixture in the South that came to us by way of Ashley's mom, Lynn, by way of her grandmother. Because it calls for cornbread crumbs, you end up with a dressing that is more uniform and custardy, rather than the craggy, bread pudding–like texture that sometimes comes with cubed bread. But the straightforward nature of the texture and flavors of this dressing place a heavier burden on the stock: the higher the quality, the better the dish. There's nothing to hide boxed stock in this recipe, so it's worth pulling out your homemade stuff.

2 cups minced celery
(about 4 large stalks)

1½ tablespoons grated
red onion

1 cup chopped fresh
curly parsley

5 fresh sage leaves,
minced

2 tablespoons kosher salt

1 teaspoon freshly ground
black pepper

7 cups Cornbread Crumbs
(page 51), at room
temperature

8 large eggs

2 tablespoons unsalted
butter, melted

4 cups Freezer Chicken
Stock (page 204), thawed

Preheat the oven to 350°F. Grease a 9 by 13-inch baking dish with nonstick cooking spray or butter.

In a large bowl, combine the celery, onion, parsley, sage, salt, pepper, and cornbread crumbs. In a medium measuring cup, whisk together the eggs and butter. Pour the egg-butter mixture over the vegetable-crumbs mixture and mix well.

Add the stock to the bowl 1 cup at a time, stirring the mixture as you go. Transfer the mixture to the prepared baking dish and let sit for 20 minutes at room temperature to allow the cornbread crumbs to fully absorb the liquid. Bake for 1 hour, until the dressing is golden brown on top and set in the center.

Serve hot.

CHEFFIN' IT UP

Ashley would say that adding anything to this recipe is blasphemy. But Kait wouldn't mind if you added 8 ounces crumbled fennel sausage to it with the vegetables and crumbs.

BUTTERMILK BISCUITS

**MAKES ABOUT
24 BISCUITS**

Biscuits are one of those rare things that actually *improve* when frozen (pie dough and cookie dough also fall into this category). It's likely about the butter. For this recipe, we use the grated frozen butter method. This technique suspends little butter flakes throughout the dough, which rise and create flaky pastry during cooking. Freezing the dough before baking ensures the fat and milk solids stay put (essential for creating a flaky result).

Biscuits bake quickly and can lean sweet or savory with ease. Use them to top a blueberry cobbler (page 59), or treat your biscuit dough like gnocchi, slicing it into small pillows or dumplings (opposite page).

2½ pounds self-rising flour (9 cups), plus more if needed

1 tablespoon kosher salt

1 pound unsalted butter, frozen

4 cups whole (full-fat) buttermilk

Unsalted butter or jam, for serving (optional)

In a large bowl, stir together the flour and salt. Using the large holes of a box grater, grate the frozen butter into the flour mixture, stirring and coating the butter with flour as you grate. Once all of the butter is in, use a pastry blender to distribute the butter evenly in the flour. It should have a pebbly texture.

Next, pour in the buttermilk and, using your hands, incorporate it with the flour mixture until a shaggy dough ball forms. Turn the dough out onto a well-floured work surface and, still using your hands, carefully pat it into a loaf shape, incorporating more flour as needed until the dough is not sticky and is easy to manipulate. Gently pat the dough out into an even layer about ¾ inch thick.

Using a 2½-inch round biscuit cutter, and firmly pressing straight down (without twisting the cutter), punch out as many biscuits as possible. Gather up the dough scraps and gently form into a ball. Press the dough out into a ¾-inch-thick layer and repeat to punch out more biscuits until you have about 24 total.

TO FREEZE: Arrange the cut biscuit dough on a rimmed baking sheet and freeze for at least 4 hours or up to overnight for a formative freeze (see page 31). Transfer to a gallon-size zip-top plastic bag, label and date, and freeze for up to 4 months.

TO BAKE: Preheat the oven to 400°F. Place the biscuits, with their edges touching, on a rimmed baking sheet and top each with a small pat of butter. Bake for 10 to 13 minutes from room temperature or 14 to 16 minutes from frozen, until puffed and golden brown on top.

Serve warm, with more butter or jam for spreading if you like.

● **CHEFFIN' IT UP**

This biscuit recipe is malleable. Use it as a template to experiment with biscuit flavors and applications, both sweet and savory.

Biscuit Dumplings or "Gnocchi"

Instead of punching out the biscuit dough into rounds, cut it into strips about ¾ inch wide. Then cut each strip crosswise into 1-inch-long pieces (they'll look like little dough pillows). Freeze as directed for the biscuits.

Orange Biscuits

In a medium bowl, combine ½ cup granulated sugar and the finely grated zest of 2 oranges. Use your fingers to rub the zest into the sugar until the sugar is damp like wet sand. Mix the sugar with the flour and salt at the beginning of the recipe and proceed as written. While the biscuits are in the oven, make a glaze: In a medium saucepan over medium heat, whisk together 3 cups confectioners' sugar, ½ cup fresh orange juice, ½ teaspoon kosher salt, and the finely grated zest of 2 oranges. Bring the mixture to a simmer and let cook for about 6 minutes, until the mixture is smooth and the sugar has dissolved. Remove from the heat and let cool for 10 minutes. Whisk in 8 ounces softened cream cheese until the glaze is smooth. Let the biscuits cool for 10 minutes after removing them from the oven. Then drizzle some of the glaze over each biscuit before serving.

Sausage and Cheese Biscuits

In a medium skillet over medium-high heat, brown 8 ounces loose breakfast sausage, breaking it up with the back of a wooden spoon, for 5 to 7 minutes, until no pink remains. Transfer to a paper towel–lined plate and let cool. In a food processor, pulse the sausage until it's finely minced (you can also do this by hand with a knife). Put the sausage into a medium bowl, add 1 cup shredded sharp Cheddar cheese, and mix well. Fold the sausage-cheese mixture into the biscuit dough before you turn it out onto a work surface to shape it. Proceed with the recipe as written.

BLUEBERRY-GINGER COBBLER

SERVES 8

When you have frozen biscuits in your freezer, you have a cobbler topping at the ready. We get a bountiful blueberry season in early summer in North Carolina, but you could make this recipe with any summer fruit of your choosing. It'd be a knockout with a mix of berries or with peach or plum slices.

The ginger, in both fresh and crystallized form, adds a dynamic spiciness that really sets off the tartness of the berries.

½ cup turbinado sugar

2 tablespoons
all-purpose flour

½ teaspoon ground
cinnamon

½ teaspoon freshly
grated nutmeg

½ teaspoon kosher salt

¼ cup finely chopped
crystallized ginger

1 teaspoon peeled and
finely grated fresh ginger

4 cups fresh blueberries,
stemmed, then rinsed
and patted dry

6 Buttermilk Biscuit
rounds (page 56), frozen

Vanilla ice cream or
crème fraîche, for serving

Preheat the oven to 400°F. Butter a 2-quart baking dish.

In a medium bowl, whisk together the sugar, flour, cinnamon, nutmeg, and salt. Add the crystallized ginger, fresh ginger, and blueberries and toss to coat.

Pour the blueberry mixture into the prepared baking dish. Bake for 30 minutes, until the berries begin to break down and turn slightly jammy.

Remove the baking dish from the oven and arrange the biscuit rounds on top, carefully nestling them into the blueberry mixture. Return the dish to the oven and bake for another 20 minutes, until the biscuits are puffed and golden brown and the blueberries are bubbling.

Serve warm or at room temperature with ice cream.

CHICKEN AND DUMPLINGS

SERVES 4

Making this dish during the summertime, when corn is in season, will bring out the best flavor. In other seasons, you could use frozen corn or swap out the corn for other vegetables: hearty greens in the fall, sweet potato in the winter, peas in the spring. *Gochujang*, a spicy fermented chile paste, is a staple of Korean cooking. Here it adds a touch of heat and funk, but you can leave it out if you prefer.

●

1 tablespoon neutral vegetable oil

1½ pounds bone-in, skin-on split chicken breasts (about 2 whole breasts)

2 tablespoons unsalted butter

1 small yellow onion, chopped

1 carrot, chopped

1 celery stalk, chopped

½ cup dry white wine

8 ounces waxy potatoes, cut into 1-inch pieces

1 cup fresh corn kernels

2 garlic cloves, minced

1 teaspoon gochujang (optional)

¼ cup all-purpose flour

3 cups Freezer Chicken Stock (page 204), thawed

Kosher salt and freshly ground black pepper

20 biscuit dumplings (page 57)

Preheat the oven to 400°F.

Heat a large cast-iron skillet over high heat. When the pan is hot, add the oil. When the oil is shimmering, add the chicken breasts, skin side down, then lower the heat to medium-high and let cook undisturbed for about 5 minutes, until the skin turns golden brown. Flip the breasts and cook for an additional 4 minutes.

Transfer the skillet to the oven and cook for 4 to 5 minutes, until an instant-read thermometer inserted into the thickest part of a breast (not touching bone) registers 150°F. Transfer the chicken breasts to a cutting board to rest.

Return the skillet with all of the cooking juices to the stove top over medium heat and add the butter. When the butter melts, add the onion, carrot, and celery and cook, stirring occasionally, for 5 to 7 minutes, until the carrot and celery have softened and the onion is beginning to turn translucent. Pour in the wine, bring to a simmer, and deglaze the pan, scraping up any browned bits. Let cook for about 10 minutes, until the wine reduces completely.

Add the potatoes, corn, garlic, and gochujang and stir to mix well and to coat everything with the gochujang. Sprinkle the flour over the mixture and cook, stirring, until it begins to smell toasty. Add the stock, increase the heat to high, and bring to a boil. Turn down the heat to a simmer and let cook, stirring occasionally, for 10 minutes. The liquid will thicken to the consistency of a gravy. Season to taste with salt and pepper.

With the liquid simmering, add the dumplings and cook for about 8 minutes from room temperature or 15 minutes from frozen, stirring occasionally, until puffed and cooked through.

While the dumplings are cooking, pull the chicken from the bone and remove and discard the skin. Shred the chicken meat.

Add the chicken to the skillet and stir until combined and heated through. Taste and adjust the seasoning, then spoon into bowls and serve hot.

PÂTE À CHOUX

MAKES 1¾ POUNDS

Pâte à choux is a light, versatile pastry dough that gets heavy play in our restaurants. We use it as the base for our sweet churros and doughnuts, as well as for our savory fritters studded with ingredients like lump crabmeat or turnip greens and cheese. Ashley likes the dough because it's technically already "cooked"—you scald milk and butter and add flour and eggs. That allows you to control the second cook—whether in the fryer or the oven—and never worry about if it's fully cooked through or not.

Its precooked status is also what makes pâte à choux freezer friendly, even though it seems pretty batter-like. We suggest freezing the dough in zip-top plastic bags because, upon thawing, you can treat them like a preloaded pastry bag: simply cut off the corner and pipe the dough into whatever shape you're after.

1 cup whole milk

½ cup unsalted butter

Sea salt

¾ cup plus 2 tablespoons all-purpose flour

5 large eggs, at room temperature

In a medium saucepan over medium heat, bring the milk, butter, and ¾ teaspoon salt to a boil. Add the flour all at once and stir vigorously with a wooden spoon until the ingredients come together into a ball. Continue stirring over medium heat for 3 to 5 minutes, until the dough develops a smooth texture and pulls away from the sides of the pan. Remove from the heat.

Transfer the mixture to a stand mixer fitted with the paddle attachment. With the mixer on low speed, add the eggs one at a time, beating after each addition until incorporated and scraping down the bowl before adding the next egg. The finished dough will be sticky and shiny.

TO FREEZE: Let the dough cool completely. Spoon into a zip-top plastic bag, label and date, and freeze for up to 6 weeks.

TO THAW: Use the pull and thaw method (see page 43) or the cold water method (see page 43).

POOLE'S THREE-CHEESE GOUGÈRES

**MAKES ABOUT
25 GOUGÈRES**

At our first restaurant, Poole's, the mac au gratin has a reputation. It's a pretty basic recipe, but one of the things that gives it an edge is a blend of three cheeses: two parts sharp Cheddar to one part each grana padano and Jarlsberg. But this cheese mix is hardly proprietary to macaroni. We use it regularly for other recipes, including here, where it lends a dynamic layer to *gougères*, the classic baked puffy bites.

If the dough hasn't been previously frozen, you can bake these *gougères* off and freeze them.

●

½ cup grated sharp
Cheddar cheese

¼ cup grated grana
padano cheese

¼ cup shredded
Jarlsberg cheese

1¾ pounds Pâte à Choux
(opposite page), freshly
made or thawed and
at room temperature

Preheat the oven to 400°F. Line two rimmed baking sheets with parchment paper.

In a large bowl, stir together the cheeses. Set aside one-third of the cheese mix for sprinkling over the tops of the gougères. Add the pâte à choux to the cheese mix remaining in the bowl and mix well.

Transfer the pâte à choux to a pastry bag fitted with a ½-inch round tip and pipe tablespoon-size mounds onto the prepared pans, spacing them 2 inches apart. Sprinkle the reserved cheese mix on top of the mounds, dividing it evenly.

Bake for about 22 minutes, until puffed and golden brown. Serve hot.

TO FREEZE: If the dough was not previously frozen, let the gougères cool completely. Arrange them on a rimmed baking sheet and freeze for at least 4 hours or up to overnight for a formative freeze (see page 31). Transfer to a zip-top plastic bag, label and date, and freeze for up to 6 weeks.

TO REHEAT: Arrange the gougères on a rimmed baking sheet and place in a preheated 350°F oven for 8 to 10 minutes, until hot throughout.

PÂTE À CHOUX DOUGHNUTS

It's not always fun to deep-fry at home, but on the occasions when you're feeling up to it, remember pâte à choux (page 62). This dough is a canvas for your fritter-based dreams, growing a custardy interior and crispy exterior when exposed to hot oil. Here's a quick rundown on how to make different types of doughnuts.

CHURROS: Make cinnamon sugar by mixing together 2 cups sugar and 1 teaspoon ground cinnamon in a shallow dish and set aside. Spoon 1¾ pounds Pâte à Choux, thawed, into a pastry bag fitted with a large star tip. Working in batches to avoid crowding, pipe the dough in 6-inch-long logs into hot (350°F) canola or soy oil, cutting them free with a knife or offset spatula. Fry, turning occasionally, for 5 to 6 minutes, until deep golden brown on the outside. Transfer to a large, paper towel–lined plate to drain, then add to the cinnamon sugar and turn to coat evenly. Serve warm. Makes 15 to 20 churros.

DOUGHNUTS: Spoon 1¾ pounds Pâte à Choux, thawed, into a pastry bag fitted with a ¾-inch round tip. Cut parchment paper into 3½-inch squares. You will need a square for each doughnut. The dough is sticky and hard to handle, and the parchment makes it easier to drop the piped doughnut into the oil. Have canola or soy oil heated to 350°F. Pipe a 4-inch circle onto each square, leaving a hole 2 inches in diameter in the center. Working in batches to avoid crowding, pick up each parchment square and carefully lower it, paper side up, into the hot oil, using tongs to peel away the parchment as the doughnut releases from it. Fry, turning once, for 5 to 6 minutes total, until golden brown all over. Transfer to a wire rack and let cool. Dip the top of each doughnut into the icing of your choice and let set before serving. Makes 15 to 20 doughnuts.

SAVORY FRITTERS: Add 8 to 12 ounces of your ingredient of choice, such as shredded cheese, minced greens, or flaked crabmeat or minced shrimp meat, drained of excess moisture, to 1¾ pounds Pâte à Choux, thawed. Once the dough is mixed thoroughly, working in batches, scoop rounded tablespoons of the dough into hot (350°F) canola or soy oil. Fry, turning as needed, for about 5 minutes, until golden brown on all sides. Transfer to a large, paper towel–lined plate to drain. Serve warm. Makes about 30 fritters.

BANANA CREAM PROFITEROLES

MAKES
25 PROFITEROLES

1 ripe to overripe large banana in its peel

⅔ cup whole milk

2 large egg yolks

⅔ cup heavy cream

2 teaspoons cornstarch

1 tablespoon water

1 teaspoon pure vanilla extract

½ cup granulated sugar

Pinch of sea salt

1¾ pounds Pâte à Choux (page 62), thawed

Confectioners' sugar, for dusting

One of the most classic uses for pâte à choux is profiteroles, the dainty French handle for cream puffs. You can get really creative with the filling, from classic pastry cream to chocolate. For this version, we adapted our banana pudding recipe. The end result is banana cream pie in one bite.

Preheat the oven to 425°F. Line a rimmed baking sheet with parchment paper.

Put the banana on the prepared pan and bake for about 25 minutes, until it is black. Let the banana cool to room temperature.

Peel the banana and transfer the flesh and any juices that collected on the pan to a food processor and process until smooth. Add the milk and process until well mixed. Set a fine-mesh strainer over a medium heavy saucepan and press the banana mixture through the strainer.

In a medium bowl, whisk together the egg yolks and cream. In a small bowl, whisk together the cornstarch, water, and vanilla.

Set the pan with the banana-milk mixture over medium heat and add the granulated sugar and salt. Cook, stirring constantly, until the mixture registers 150°F on an instant-read thermometer. Remove the pan from the heat. While whisking the egg yolk mixture constantly, slowly drizzle in about ¼ cup of the hot milk mixture. Repeat two more times. Pour the egg yolk mixture into the saucepan, whisking well, and return the saucepan to medium heat. Cook, whisking constantly, until the mixture registers 150°F. Whisk the cornstarch mixture briefly to recombine, then add to the pan and continue to cook, whisking, until the pudding has thickened and registers 177°F.

Remove from the heat, pour into a medium bowl, and press a piece of plastic wrap directly onto the surface of the pudding. Let cool to room temperature, then move to the fridge to chill well.

Meanwhile, make the profiteroles: Preheat the oven to 425°F. Line two rimmed baking sheets with parchment paper. Spoon the pâte à choux into a pastry bag fitted with a ¾-inch round tip and pipe tablespoon-size mounds onto the prepared pans, spacing them 2 inches apart. Bake, rotating the pans 180 degrees halfway through baking, for about 22 minutes, until puffed and golden brown. Transfer the pan to a wire rack and let the puffs cool to room temperature.

Spoon the chilled banana pudding into a pastry bag fitted with a ¼-inch round tip. To fill the puffs, pierce the bottom of each puff with the tip and squeeze some pudding (2 to 3 teaspoons) into the cavity. Dust the profiteroles with confectioners' sugar and serve immediately.

RISOTTO

MAKES ABOUT 4 CUPS

This risotto does two things at once to unlock your risotto-making manacles—you know, the ones that have kept you attached to your stove for an hour as you ladle small amounts of hot stock into a pan that you've been stirring for what feels like hours.

The first: It skips that whole stock-ladling technique and treats the risotto like pasta. You bring the liquid and rice together to a boil, then lower the heat to a simmer and let the rice cook, stirring frequently. We learned this approach from Sarah Grueneberg, the chef of Monteverde in Chicago, whose advice about anything pasta or risotto related is as good as gold.

The second: You can parcook risotto ahead of time and freeze it, knocking out about twenty minutes of work. It also means you can have a stash of parcooked risotto for other applications, such as rice pudding (page 71). Look to the note for what to do if you are making the risotto to eat now.

When shopping for Arborio rice, look for Acquerello brand. It's our favorite because it has a nutty, unique flavor and a distinctive texture, both of which it owes to being aged before it's packaged. Also, you can switch up the liquid, from stock to tomato water to milk and beyond. Making a seafood risotto? Use fish or shrimp stock. But if you're making risotto ahead and you're not sure how you may use it down the road, use water to keep your options open.

•

2 cups water

2 cups Arborio rice

In a medium saucepan over medium-high heat, combine the water and rice and bring to a boil. Cook, stirring frequently, until the water has mostly evaporated and the mixture thickens, 10 to 12 minutes. Lower the heat to medium and stir constantly until the liquid has evaporated, about 5 minutes.

TO FREEZE: Spread the parcooked risotto out on a rimmed baking sheet and let cool to room temperature. Transfer to the refrigerator and chill well, then transfer to lidded plastic pint containers or quart-size zip-top plastic bags, label and date, and freeze for up to 3 months.

TO THAW: Use frozen (see pages 69 and 71), or use the pull and thaw method (see page 43) or the cold water method (see page 43) to thaw.

NOTE

If you are *not* parcooking to freeze, and you want to make risotto to eat immediately, increase the liquid to 6 cups, and increase the cooking time to 30 minutes. The ratio of 6 cups liquid to 2 cups rice yields the texture and creaminess you're after.

THE QUICKEST RISOTTO PARMIGIANO

SERVES 2

Half-batch frozen Risotto (opposite page), about 2 cups

3 cups water, Parm Stock (page 128), or Freezer Chicken Stock (page 204), thawed

½ teaspoon kosher salt

2 tablespoons unsalted butter

½ cup finely grated Parmigiano-Reggiano cheese, plus more for serving

Juice of ½ lemon

A bowl of cheesy, buttery risotto on a cold day is a simple gift, especially when you can accomplish it in under half an hour. There is an obscene amount of Parmigiano-Reggiano in this recipe, but it's the featured ingredient, not the sidekick.

In a medium saucepan over high heat, combine the risotto, water, and salt and bring to a boil. Lower the heat to medium-high and simmer, stirring frequently, for 8 to 10 minutes, until the liquid has evaporated and the rice is porridge-like.

Remove from the heat and stir in the butter. Then stir in the Parmigiano until evenly incorporated. Stir in the lemon juice. Serve immediately, spooning the risotto into bowls and finishing with more Parmigiano.

CHEFFIN' IT UP

Add Mushrooms

Make a porcini puree: In a small skillet, combine 2 ounces dried porcini and ½ cup boiling water and let sit for 10 minutes. Bring to a simmer over medium heat and cook for about 10 minutes, until almost all of the water has evaporated. Remove from the heat, season with ¼ teaspoon kosher salt, and transfer to a food processor. Puree until smooth. Mix the puree into the risotto.

Go Tomato

Use tomato water in lieu of the stock and top with a relish of diced tomato, extra virgin olive oil, salt, and chopped fresh basil. To make 1 cup tomato water, core 1 pound tomatoes and cut into large chunks. Transfer to a food processor, add ¾ teaspoon kosher salt, and pulse until coarsely chopped. Line a fine-mesh strainer with cheesecloth, allowing it to overhang the sides, and set the strainer over a medium bowl. Transfer the tomatoes to the strainer and let drain; you can gather together the edges of the cheesecloth and squeeze to wring more of the liquid from the tomatoes. Use immediately or cover and refrigerate for up to 2 days.

ALMOND RICE PUDDING

with Rhubarb-Apricot Jam

SERVES 4

This dessert is a marriage of our tastes. Ashley tends to go for pudding and custard-based desserts, while Kait prefers starchy things. This creamy rice pudding, augmented with a touch of almond extract, appeases us both. The rhubarb-apricot jam is worthwhile because it extends the short-lived overlap of two very seasonal ingredients. Fresh apricots are just beginning when rhubarb is on its way out.

●

Jam

1½ pounds rhubarb, trimmed and cut into ½-inch pieces

1½ pounds apricots, halved and pitted

1 cup water

4 cups sugar

Juice of 1 lemon

1 teaspoon kosher salt

Pudding

Half-batch frozen Risotto (page 68), about 2 cups

4 cups water

½ teaspoon kosher salt

4 cups half-and-half

½ cup sugar

½ teaspoon pure almond extract

Make the jam: In a large pot over medium-high heat, combine the rhubarb, apricots, and water and bring to a boil over medium-high heat. Lower the heat to a simmer and cook, stirring occasionally, for about 15 minutes, until the fruit is very soft. Stir in the sugar, lemon juice, and salt and continue to cook, stirring often and skimming off any foam that forms on the surface, for about 8 minutes, until the mixture registers 220°F on a candy thermometer.

Remove from the heat and let cool completely. Transfer the jam to two 1-pint glass jars, cap tightly, and store in the fridge for up to 3 weeks.

Make the pudding: In a medium saucepan, combine the risotto, water, and salt. Bring to a boil over medium-high heat, stirring frequently, until the water is absorbed, about 10 minutes. Add the half-and-half, bring it up to a simmer, then lower the heat to medium. Add the sugar and stir constantly, until it forms a thick and creamy porridge, 18 to 20 minutes.

Remove from the heat, transfer to a medium bowl, and let cool. Cover and refrigerate for at least 2 hours or until ready to serve.

To serve, spoon the pudding into dessert bowls and top each serving with a spoonful of the jam.

PIECRUST

**MAKES ENOUGH
DOUGH FOR TWO
9-INCH PIECRUSTS**

Piecrusts have a reputation of being a pain to make from scratch. But here's our case for doing just that. If you're making one, the amount of time to make a few more is nominal (especially if you're making only the dough). The real estate that a few wrapped-up disks of dough take up is minimal, and homemade piecrusts taste way better than what you'll find in your grocer's freezer aisle.

This recipe makes a dough that is flexible—it can go sweet or savory. You can also freeze the dough in disk form, which is great for hand pies and top crusts, or you can roll it out to preserve in shell form.

●

1 cup cold unsalted butter, cut into ½-inch cubes

1¼ cups plus 1 tablespoon all-purpose flour

4 teaspoons sugar

¼ teaspoon kosher salt

2 tablespoons plus 1 teaspoon ice water

In a large bowl, whisk together the butter, flour, sugar, and salt. Place the bowl in the freezer for 30 minutes. Remove from the freezer and use two butter knives to cut the butter into the flour mixture until pea-size pieces form. Then massage the butter pieces between your fingers, stretching them into thin ribbons.

Add the ice water by the tablespoon to the flour mixture, stirring to mix as you go. Add water only to the point that the dough holds together when pinched between your fingers; you may not need all of it. Divide the dough in half and gather each half into a ball. Press each ball into a thick disk, wrap the disks separately in plastic wrap, and refrigerate for 1 hour before rolling.

TO FREEZE AND THAW IN DISK FORM: Label and date the plastic-wrapped disks and place in a zip-top plastic bag (you can store multiple disks in one bag). Freeze for up to 9 months. When ready to use, pull the dough from the freezer and let it thaw for about 1 hour on the counter before rolling it out.

TO FREEZE IN SHELL FORM: Lightly dust a work surface with flour and roll out a dough disk into an 11-inch round. Drape the dough over a 9-inch disposable pie pan and press onto the bottom and sides. Trim the overhang to ½ inch and roll the overhang under itself to create a thicker crust edge. Crimp as desired. Freeze the unwrapped pie shell for 4 hours or up to overnight for a formative freeze (see page 31), then wrap the shell in two layers of plastic wrap. Label and date and freeze for up to 3 months.

Because the dough is already in a thin layer, you don't need to thaw it before baking. You can blind bake the shell directly from frozen, or you can fill it and bake it without thawing. Just add about 5 minutes to the cook time of the recipe you're using.

APPLE PIE

This recipe is pretty straightforward except for one thing: it's a make-ahead apple pie, and you freeze the whole dang thing *before* baking it. Then it goes into the oven, rock-solid from the freezer, and you look like a wizard for bringing out a homemade apple pie from a clean kitchen—no flour on the counters, no bits of apple peel, nothing. (You don't need to tell anyone what it looked like before.)

Baking fruit pies from a frozen state has some advantages. Time in the freezer evaporates some of the natural moisture in the fruit, so the juiciness is more contained and you get less of a juice explosion. This is especially true of stone fruits, which have the tendency to release excess amounts of juice. For this same reason, you shouldn't store fruit pies in the freezer for longer than about 1 month, lest there's too much evaporation—nobody wants a dry pie.

It'll take every minute of 2 hours to bake this pie from frozen, and that extra time really helps to concentrate flavors. Although you could pull and thaw (see page 43) this ahead of time to shorten the bake, we think the results are better when you bake from frozen.

Don't use previously frozen pie dough for this recipe. You're freezing the pie unbaked, so you don't want to take the dough through freezing and thawing twice.

2 freshly made Piecrust dough disks (opposite page)

½ teaspoon powdered ascorbic acid (see Note)

4 tablespoons water

10 apples, peeled and cut into ½-inch chunks

½ cup apple cider

½ cup granulated sugar

¼ cup firmly packed light brown sugar

¼ cup all-purpose flour

½ teaspoon ground ginger

½ teaspoon ground cinnamon

¼ teaspoon ground cloves

¼ teaspoon freshly grated nutmeg

½ teaspoon kosher salt

Lightly dust a work surface with flour and roll out one dough disk into an 11-inch round. Drape the dough over a 9-inch pie pan and press onto the bottom and sides. Trim the overhang to ½ inch (you will crimp when you've added the top crust), then refrigerate while you make the filling.

In a small bowl, stir together the ascorbic acid and water. Put the apples into a large bowl, sprinkle the acid water over them, and toss to coat. Let the apples stand for 5 minutes to absorb the acid water.

In a small skillet over high heat, bring the apple cider to a boil and boil until reduced by half, about 5 minutes. Remove from the heat and set aside to cool slightly. In a medium bowl, stir together both sugars, the flour, ginger, cinnamon, cloves, nutmeg, and salt.

Pour the reduced cider over the apples and toss to coat. Add the dry ingredients and toss again to coat, making sure the apples are thoroughly coated. Transfer the apples to the pie shell, arranging them evenly. Refrigerate the filled pie shell while you roll out the top crust.

Lightly dust the work surface again with flour and roll out the second dough disk into a round about 11 inches in diameter. Bring the pie out

continued →

APPLE PIE

continued

of the fridge and drape the round over the filled pie shell. Trim the edges of both top and bottom piecrust so that they are even, leaving about ¼ inch of overhang. Fold the overhang under itself to form a ridge around the edge of the pie. Use a fork or your fingers to crimp if you like. Cut a few vents in the top crust.

TO FREEZE: Wrap the whole pie completely in plastic wrap. If you have a pie-shaped container, place the wrapped pie in it for added protection; otherwise, wrap the plastic-wrapped pie in one layer of aluminum foil. Label and date and freeze for up to 1 month.

TO BAKE: Unwrap the frozen pie, then cover the top with foil. Place in a cold oven and set the oven to 425°F. When the oven reaches temperature, bake for 45 minutes, then lower the heat to 350°F and bake for another hour. Remove the foil and bake for 15 to 20 minutes longer, until the crust is golden brown and a knife inserted through a vent into the center of the pie meets no resistance and the tip of the blade is hot to the touch.

Let cool for 10 minutes before cutting and serving.

NOTE

Ascorbic acid is also called vitamin C. Look for it in powdered form in a pharmacy or health food store.

PIMENTO CHEESE HAND PIES

MAKES ABOUT
18 HAND PIES

These little pimento cheese pockets feel somehow approachable and a little fancy at the same time—which basically sums up where we like to live our lives. Ashley makes a seriously delicious pimento cheese, but recommends store-bought here because her pimento uses a house-made cider aioli, which can be finicky and break when exposed to heat. Store-bought pimento cheese, made with shelf-stable mayonnaise, works better for this application.

While you could definitely fill and form the hand pies and refrigerate them up to a day ahead of baking, we don't recommend freezing them (again, that pesky mayo). Hand pies with other fillings, such as fruit, would be fair game for freezing ahead before baking.

●

1 Piecrust dough disk (page 72), thawed

1 large egg

Neutral vegetable oil, for deep-frying

¾ cup store-bought pimento cheese

Lightly dust a large work surface with flour and roll out the pie dough ¼ inch thick. Working quickly, use a 2½-inch round pastry or biscuit cutter to cut out as many rounds as possible (you should get about 18). Transfer the rounds to a large rimmed baking sheet and place in the refrigerator for 10 minutes; discard any dough scraps.

In a small bowl, beat the egg well for an egg wash and set aside. Pour oil to a depth of 3 inches into a large, deep cast-iron skillet and heat to 350°F on a deep-fry thermometer.

Working in batches, remove three or four rounds at a time from the refrigerator. Brush the edge of each dough round lightly with egg wash. Place 1 to 2 teaspoons pimento cheese in the center of each round and fold the round in half to form a half-moon. Seal the edges by pressing down with fingers or a fork, making sure the edges are well sealed. Transfer the finished hand pies to the refrigerator while assembling the remaining ones.

Working in batches, add the hand pies to the hot oil and fry, turning once, for about 2 minutes on each side, until golden brown and cooked through. Transfer to a paper towel–lined plate and let cool slightly before serving.

NOTE

You can also bake the pies on a rimmed baking sheet in a preheated 350°F oven for about 14 minutes, until the crust is golden and cooked through. If you choose to bake the pies, brush the tops with egg wash before slipping them into the oven.

QUICHE LORRAINE

SERVES 8

This quiche, distinguished by mushrooms, Swiss, and bacon, was a fixture of the holidays during Ashley's childhood; it's her mom's riff on the classic quiche Lorraine. It has since become a tradition for our house, too. You can freeze the quiche whole after baking—use a disposable pie pan if going this route, which makes reheating easier and won't lock up your good pie pan in the freezer for months. Or you can freeze individual slices for a quick and luxurious breakfast.

•

One 9-inch pie shell
(see Piecrust, page 72),
freshly made or thawed

3 large eggs

¾ teaspoon sea salt

¾ cup heavy cream

¾ cup whole milk

6 ounces Jarlsberg
cheese, shredded

2 ounces grana padano
or Parmigiano-Reggiano
cheese, finely grated

8 ounces cremini
mushrooms, sliced

½ cup thinly sliced shallots

5 slices bacon, cooked
until crispy and coarsely
chopped

Preheat the oven to 350°F. Line the pie shell with parchment paper and fill with pie weights (dry beans or raw rice works great). Bake for 30 minutes. Remove the weights and parchment and bake for another 15 minutes, until the crust is cooked through and golden brown. Let cool completely on a wire rack.

In a large bowl, whisk the eggs and salt until the eggs are blended. Add the cream and milk and whisk to incorporate fully. Set aside.

In a small bowl, mix together the Jarlsberg and grana padano. Layer one-third of the cheese in the pie shell. Next, layer half of the mushrooms, followed by half of the shallots, and then half of the bacon. Repeat these four layers, beginning with half of the remaining cheese, and ending with the remaining cheese. Pour the egg mixture over the layers.

Cover the edge of the crust with aluminum foil to prevent overbrowning. Bake the quiche, rotating the pan 180 degrees halfway after the first 20 minutes, for 40 to 50 minutes, until the filling is set. Transfer to a wire rack and let cool for about 10 minutes if serving immediately. If freezing, let cool to 70°F, then transfer to the refrigerator to cool to 40°F.

TO FREEZE: If freezing the whole quiche, wrap it in two layers of plastic wrap. Label and date and freeze for up to 3 months. To freeze individual portions, cut the quiche into eight slices and arrange on a rimmed baking sheet. Freeze for at least 4 hours or up to overnight for a formative freeze (see page 31). Wrap each frozen slice in plastic wrap, place all of the slices in a zip-top plastic bag, label and date, and return to the freezer for up to 1 month.

TO REHEAT: If reheating the whole quiche, unwrap, place in a cold oven, and set the oven to 325°F. When the oven reaches temperature, bake for 60 to 70 minutes, until warm throughout or an instant-read thermometer inserted into the center registers 150°F. If reheating individual slices, unwrap, place on a rimmed baking sheet, place in a cold oven, and set the oven to 325°F. When the oven reaches temperature, bake for 10 to 15 minutes, until warm throughout.

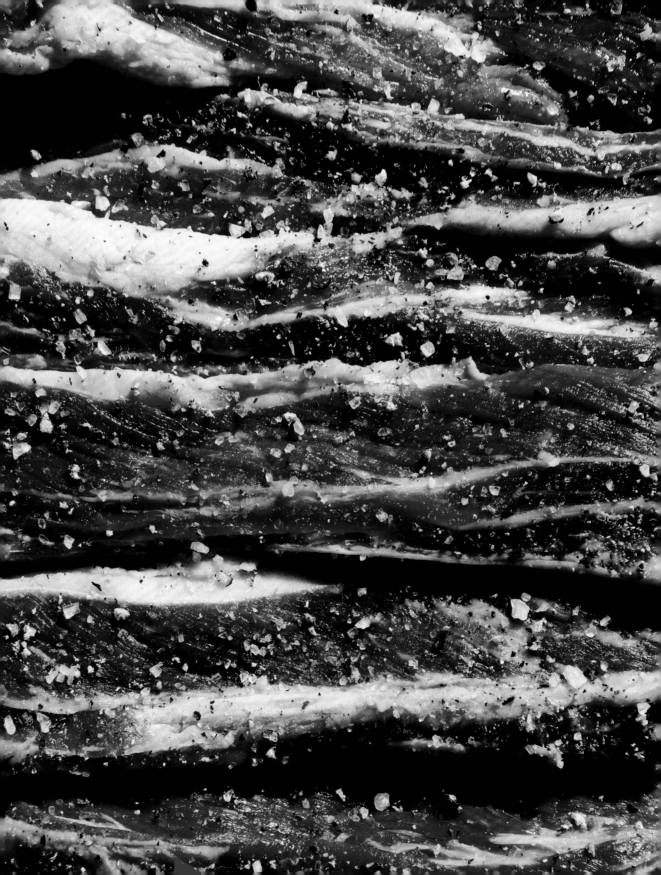

6

Proteins.

82 **PULLED PORK SHOULDER, MIKE'S WAY**

Carnitas Tacos • 85

Cabbage Salad with Crispy Pork Shoulder, Apples, and Maple-Cider Vinaigrette • 86

Pork Reuben on Rye with Swiss, Kraut, and Russian Dressing • 89

Potato Pork Cakes with Marinated Peppers, Summer Squash, and Avocado • 90

94 **CHICKEN CONFIT**

Chicken Rillettes • 95

Chicken Niçoise Salad • 96

Chicken Piccata Farfalle with Sweet Potato • 99

Buffalo Chicken Dip • 100

Broccoli Cheddar Chicken Bake • 101

102 **BRAISED SHORT RIBS**

Short Rib Stroganoff with Egg Noodles • 103

Braised Short Ribs with Cauliflower Fonduta • 105

Beef and Coconut Stew with Root Vegetables • 106

Stuffed Peppers with Short Ribs and Rice • 109

PULLED PORK SHOULDER, MIKE'S WAY

MAKES 5 POUNDS

This method for achieving tender pulled pork is unusual—no salt in the braise, no browning ahead of time for flavor—but trust us, it works. We got the method from our dear friend Mike Blasberg, who uses it as his carnitas recipe (page 85), but the pork itself is so versatile that we chose it to anchor a number of recipes for this book.

One aspect of this recipe is especially important to note: once you've braised the pork, you strain the braising liquid and then reduce it down to a thick, glossy, collagen-rich sauce, which you pour over the pork. This coating is particularly useful when it comes to freezing. Think of it as Chapstick on a ski slope, protecting from wind chill and dehydration.

•

1 boneless pork shoulder, 6 to 7 pounds, cut into 2-inch pieces

1 large orange, cut into eighths

8 garlic cloves, crushed with the side of a knife

1 jalapeño chile, stemmed, halved lengthwise, and seeded

2 medium fresh bay leaves

4 small yellow onions, halved through the equator

5 quarts water

2 tablespoons kosher salt

In a large stockpot or Dutch oven, combine the pork, orange, garlic, jalapeño, bay leaves, onions, and water and bring to a boil over medium-high heat. Skim off any foam from the surface and turn down the heat to a simmer. Cover and simmer for 2 hours, opening and stirring every 30 minutes. After 2 hours, pull one piece of pork out of the pot and check to see if it can be shredded by pressing it against the side of a bowl. If it's not yet ready, re-cover the pot and continue to simmer the pork until it can be shredded, checking every 15 minutes.

When the pork is ready, drain the contents of the pot through a fine-mesh strainer set over a large heatproof bowl or other vessel. Transfer the pork to a metal bowl. Discard the orange pieces, garlic, jalapeño halves, bay leaves, and onion halves. Return the liquid to the pot and place on the stove to reduce over high heat.

While the liquid is reducing, use two forks to shred the pork. Once the liquid has reduced to about 4 cups (it will be thick and bubbly), remove from the heat and stir in the salt. Pour the liquid over the shredded pork and use a rubber spatula to fold the meat and liquid together until the liquid is fully incorporated.

TO FREEZE: Let cool to room temperature. Divide into 1-pound portions and package in your preferred freezer-safe container (we suggest vacuum pouches or zip-top plastic bags). Label and date and freeze for up to 9 months.

TO THAW: Use the pull and thaw method (see page 43) or the cold water method (see page 43).

TO REHEAT: You can reheat the pork from frozen using the sous vide method (if you've used vacuum pouches) or in a microwave. For sous vide, set the water bath temperature to 150°F and drop in a pouch. It will take 1 hour to reach temperature. To use a microwave, use the defrost setting to thaw and reheat the pork slowly. If your microwave doesn't have an auto-defrost setting, set the microwave on a medium-low setting (3 out of 10 on ours) and microwave in 4-minute increments, stirring after each increment. Make sure the container is microwave safe and vented.

CARNITAS TACOS

SERVES 8

Our favorite thing about carnitas is the textural contrast between the crispy seared bits and the tender chewy bits of the pork, achieved here by pressing the shredded pork into a thin layer in a skillet for maximum surface exposure. With that in mind, you can keep the accoutrements for your taco bar relatively simple—no need to gild the lily. But if you're a toppings fanatic and want to add on things like guacamole, radish slices, or additional types of salsa, we certainly won't stop you.

●

2 pounds Pulled Pork Shoulder, Mike's Way (page 82), thawed

16 to 20 corn tortillas

1 white onion, finely diced

1 bunch cilantro, finely chopped

3 limes, cut into wedges

Salsa of choice, for serving

Put half of the pork into a large skillet and press it out into an even layer. Place the skillet over medium-high heat and let the meat sear, undisturbed, for 8 to 10 minutes. The fat from the pork will render and make the seared side crispy. Use a flat spatula to flip the pork in sections and sear the other side by letting it cook, undisturbed, for another 8 to 10 minutes. Transfer the seared pork to a platter and keep warm. Repeat with the other half of the pork.

Meanwhile, warm the tortillas, either in the oven or in a skillet on the stove. Keep warm in a clean kitchen towel while you finish searing the pork.

To serve, spoon the pork onto a platter and set out the tortillas, onion, cilantro, limes, and salsa. Invite guests to fix their own tacos by placing some of the pork on a tortilla and topping it with onion, cilantro, a squeeze of lime juice, and salsa.

CABBAGE SALAD

with Crispy Pork Shoulder, Apples, and Maple-Cider Vinaigrette

SERVES 4

Here's a conundrum: most days, lunch is some form of salad that we bring with us to work, but tender lettuces don't hold up great in transit and at the office. Heartier salads, with a base of shredded cabbage or kale, have become the norm for us because they actually get better when they sit for a bit. The vinaigrette breaks down the toughness of the greens just enough to make them more enjoyable as a raw ingredient.

•

Preheat the oven to 400°F.

Make the vinaigrette: In a small bowl, combine the shallots and vinegar and let soak for 15 minutes. In a medium bowl, whisk together the shallots and vinegar, maple syrup, and both mustards, mixing well. Slowly add the oil in a thin stream while whisking constantly. Whisk in salt to taste. You should have about 2 cups. The vinaigrette will keep in a lidded container in the refrigerator for up to 2 weeks.

Make the salad: Thinly slice the cabbage as you would for slaw. Put it into a large bowl along with the parsley. Cut each apple in half from tip to tail and cut away the core. Place each half, cut side down, on a cutting board and slice into thin half-moons. Add the apples to the bowl with the cabbage and season the dry salad with the salt and pepper, tossing to distribute. Drizzle with ¼ cup of the vinaigrette and toss to coat well. Let sit while you prepare the pork.

Spread the pork shoulder out in an even layer on a rimmed baking sheet and bake for 15 to 18 minutes, until crispy and browned in spots. Meanwhile, spread the pepitas on a separate rimmed baking sheet or in a pie pan and toast in the oven for 3 to 4 minutes, until aromatic and slightly darker in color. Let cool to warm, about 10 minutes.

Add the pork and half of the pepitas to the cabbage mixture and fold in gently, mixing well. Add another ¼ cup of the vinaigrette and fold a few more times. Spoon the salad onto individual plates and garnish with the remaining pepitas. Serve immediately.

Vinaigrette

2 teaspoons minced shallots

⅓ cup cider vinegar

½ cup pure maple syrup

⅓ cup whole-grain mustard

2 tablespoons Dijon mustard

1 cup neutral vegetable oil

Sea salt

1 small to medium head red cabbage, halved lengthwise and cored

½ cup firmly packed fresh flat-leaf parsley leaves

2 apples

½ teaspoon sea salt

½ teaspoon freshly ground black pepper

8 ounces Pulled Pork Shoulder, Mike's Way (page 82), thawed

½ cup pepitas

PORK REUBEN ON RYE

with Swiss, Kraut, and Russian Dressing

MAKES 2 SANDWICHES

Kait used to consistently burn grilled cheese sandwiches. The perfect grilled cheese—golden brown on the outside, gooey melted cheese on the inside—was a culinary white whale. The game changer was the oven. Once she started using the oven to address the interior of her sandwich, she never burned a grilled cheese again.

So for this Reuben, we decided to treat the interior and exterior of the sandwich separately. The interior is built entirely in the oven, which allows for more control over heating and for melting cheese, while the bread is toasted and dressed, free of toppings until the very end. It's a foolproof way to get a hot, gooey, melted interior with toasted (but not overtoasted) bread.

•

Preheat the broiler. Line a rimmed baking sheet with aluminum foil.

Make the dressing: In a medium bowl, whisk together the mayonnaise, ketchup, horseradish, Worcestershire sauce, hot sauce, and onion powder. You should have about ⅔ cup. The dressing will keep in a lidded container in the refrigerator for up to 1 week.

Make the sandwiches: Divide the pork in half and form each half into a thick disk. Place the disks on the prepared pan and, with your hand, flatten them out into sandwich-size cakes. Slide under the broiler and broil for about 4 minutes, until the tops are caramelized and brown. Remove the pan from the broiler and top each cake first with half of the sauerkraut and then with a slice of cheese. Return to the broiler and broil just until the cheese is melted and bubbly.

Spread a generous layer of the Russian dressing on two of the bread slices. Spread the mustard on the other two slices. Use a spatula to lift one of the cakes from the baking sheet and place it on one of the mustard-slathered bread slices. Top with a Russian dressing–slathered slice, dressing side down. Repeat with the remaining cake and bread. Slice each sandwich in half and serve.

Dressing

½ cup mayonnaise

1 tablespoon ketchup

2 teaspoons prepared horseradish

½ teaspoon Worcestershire sauce

4 dashes of hot sauce

½ teaspoon onion powder

Sandwiches

4 ounces Pulled Pork Shoulder, Mike's Way (page 82), thawed

½ cup sauerkraut, well drained

2 slices Swiss cheese

4 slices rye bread, toasted

2 teaspoons whole-grain mustard

POTATO PORK CAKES

with Marinated Peppers, Summer Squash, and Avocado

SERVES 4

This recipe has a few components, but the main ones can be made ahead: you can make and freeze the pork cakes (do this the same day you're making the pulled pork; see Note) and the marinated peppers.

But even if you've done nothing ahead and are debating whether this recipe is worth making, we urge to you to decide that it is. It makes an any-time-of-day meal. You can skip the peppers and the squash, add a fried egg to the pork cake, and call it breakfast. You can serve the dish as written for dinner. Or forget the pork cakes and serve the peppers, squash, and avocado as a great summer side dish. Maneuver through it as you like and you'll come out happy that you opted in.

●

Make the pork cakes: Fill a large pot with water and salt it generously (it should taste salty like the ocean). Add the potatoes and bring to a boil over high heat. Cook for about 25 minutes, until tender when pierced with a knife.

Drain the potatoes well. Let them cool just until they can be handled, then use your hands to crumble them up. You don't want them fully "mashed," but they should be pretty broken up. Put the potatoes into a large bowl, add the pork, and mix well. Season with 1 teaspoon kosher salt and the pepper. Form the mixture into eight equal disk-shaped cakes. (If you make the pork cakes from pulled pork shoulder that has not been previously frozen, they can be frozen either at this point or after they are cooked below. See freezing directions on the next page.)

Make the salad: Cut the summer squash in half lengthwise. Cut the onion half in half from tip to tail. Season the cut sides of both vegetables with salt and pepper.

In a large cast-iron or other heavy skillet over high heat, warm 1 tablespoon of the oil. When the oil is very hot, add the squash and onion, cut side down, and sear until very dark brown, about 5 minutes. Flip the vegetables and cook for 1 minute more, then transfer to a cutting board. Return the skillet to medium-high heat.

Add 1 tablespoon of the oil to the skillet. When it shimmers, place four of the pork cakes in the skillet and sear until deeply browned on one side, about 6 minutes. Flip and sear on the other side an additional 6 to 8 minutes. Remove to a plate and keep warm. Add the remaining 1 tablespoon oil to the skillet and repeat with the remaining four pork cakes.

Pork Cakes

Kosher salt

1 pound Yukon gold potatoes

8 ounces Pulled Pork Shoulder, Mike's Way (page 82), freshly made or thawed

¼ teaspoon freshly ground black pepper

1 pound summer squash (whatever variety you're excited about will work)

½ yellow or Vidalia onion

Sea salt and freshly ground black pepper

3 tablespoons neutral vegetable oil

½ cup Marinated Peppers (recipe follows)

Juice from ½ lemon

2 ripe avocados, halved, pitted, and peeled

continued →

POTATO PORK CAKES

continued

While the cakes finish cooking, cut the charred squash and onion into thin slices and transfer to a large bowl. Drain ½ cup of the marinated peppers and add to the bowl along with 2 tablespoons of their oil and the lemon juice. Stir to mix well, then season to taste with salt and pepper. In a medium bowl, mash the avocados until smooth. Season with ¼ teaspoon salt.

To serve, spoon some of the salad onto each plate and top with a potato-pork cake. Finish with a spoonful of the mashed avocado and serve.

TO FREEZE THE POTATO PORK CAKES: Arrange uncooked cakes or fully cooled cooked cakes on a rimmed baking sheet and place in the freezer for at least 4 hours or up to overnight for a formative freeze (see page 31). Transfer the cakes to a zip-top plastic bag or individually wrap them in plastic wrap and place in a lidded plastic container. Label and date and freeze for up to 3 months.

TO BAKE UNCOOKED CAKES FROM FROZEN: If the cakes are wrapped, unwrap them. Place the cakes on a rimmed baking sheet, place in a cold oven, and set the oven to 400°F. When the oven reaches temperature, bake for 40 minutes, until hot throughout.

TO REHEAT COOKED CAKES FROM FROZEN: Thaw the cakes using the pull and thaw method (see page 43). Preheat the oven to 400°F. Arrange the cakes on a rimmed baking sheet and bake for 20 to 25 minutes, until warm throughout.

3 large red bell peppers
(about 1½ pounds total)

Sea salt

1 cup extra virgin olive oil

1 fresh bay leaf

12 thyme sprigs

3 garlic cloves

Zest of 1 lemon, removed
in wide strips with a
Y peeler

Marinated Peppers

To roast the peppers, one at a time, place them directly over a high gas flame and, using metal tongs to rotate them, char the entire surface of each pepper. To char the top, balance the pepper on its curvy stem end on the grate of the burner. (If you don't have a gas range, roast the peppers under the broiler, rotating them with metal tongs so they char evenly.)

Transfer the roasted peppers to a metal bowl, cover with plastic wrap, and let sit for 15 minutes. Use a dish towel to gently rub off the skins of the peppers. Don't run them under water, as this will wash away some of the flavor. Tear the peppers in half and remove the stems and seeds. Lay the peppers flat and cut in half horizontally. Slice each half vertically into ¼-inch-wide strips so you have batons measuring roughly 2 inches by ¼ inch. Transfer the batons to a medium bowl and season with ½ teaspoon salt, tossing to distribute.

In a small saucepan over medium heat, combine the oil, bay leaf, thyme, garlic, and lemon zest and heat until the oil begins to slowly bubble. Once it begins bubbling, turn down the heat to low and cook for 4 to 5 minutes more, then remove from the heat. Pour the oil and aromatics over the peppers, let cool, cover, and marinate in the refrigerator for at least 6 hours or up to 24 hours before using. Pick out and discard the bay, thyme, garlic, and lemon zest before using or storing.

To store the peppers, transfer them, still submerged in their oil, to a lidded container and refrigerate for up to 2 weeks. You can also freeze them, submerged in their oil, in a lidded plastic or glass container. Label and date and freeze for up to 2 months. To thaw, use the pull and thaw method (see page 43).

CHICKEN CONFIT

**MAKES ABOUT
1½ POUNDS**

Frozen chicken meat is an essential component of any well-stocked freezer pantry. We make extra chicken for the freezer when we're grilling or smoking chicken. But if we're making chicken specifically for the freezer, our favorite method is confit. With this technique, chicken legs are slowly cooked in duck fat, which creates a rich, very tender finished product. The legs can be frozen whole or the meat pulled from the bone.

●

4 cups cold water

6 tablespoons kosher salt

3 tablespoons sugar

4 cups ice-cold water

3½ pounds bone-in, skin-on chicken legs

8 thyme sprigs

3 fresh bay leaves

10 garlic cloves

4 cups duck fat, melted and cooled to room temperature

Neutral vegetable oil, for covering, if needed

In a medium saucepan over medium heat, combine the cold water, salt, and sugar and heat, stirring, until the salt and sugar dissolve. Transfer to a large bowl and stir in the ice-cold water. Submerge the chicken legs in the brine, cover, and refrigerate for 12 hours.

Preheat the oven to 275°F. Drain the chicken legs and arrange them snugly in an even layer in a 9 by 13-inch baking dish. Distribute the thyme, bay leaves, and garlic evenly over the surface. Pour the duck fat over the chicken legs; they should be submerged. Add more duck fat or vegetable oil if needed to cover them completely. Cover the dish with aluminum foil or a lid.

Transfer the dish to the oven and bake for 2 hours, until you can easily pull the meat with a fork. Remove from the oven and let the chicken rest at room temperature for 1 hour. Then refrigerate the dish, still covered, overnight.

The next day, remove the legs from the fat. Let the fat come to room temperature, then push through a strainer, discarding the solids, and reserve.

TO FREEZE WHOLE: Put the chicken legs into vacuum pouches or zip-top plastic bags and add about ½ cup fat per leg to the containers. Seal, label and date, and freeze for up to 9 months.

TO FREEZE PULLED: Use your hands to pull the meat from the bones, discarding the bones and the skin (or reserve the skin to make gribenes). Portion the confit into vacuum pouches, zip-top plastic bags, or lidded plastic or glass containers. Add about ½ cup fat per leg to the containers. Seal, label and date, and freeze for 6 to 7 months.

TO THAW: Use the pull and thaw method (see page 43) or the cold water method (see page 43).

TO REHEAT: If stored in vacuum pouches, reheating from frozen using the sous vide method works very well. Set the sous vide water bath to 150°F and drop in the pouch. It will take 1½ hours to reach temperature. Otherwise, thaw first and then reheat to your preference—in a pan on the stove, in the oven, or in the microwave.

CHICKEN RILLETTES

MAKES 1 PINT

Chicken rillettes are about as far as we're willing to go in making charcuterie at home. Seasoned confit becomes a spreadable snack that pairs beautifully with a gin Martini on a Sunday evening. Even better: You can make this ahead and freeze it. We've even relied on our freezer inventory for last-minute hostess gifts when invited to someone's house for dinner.

●

1½ cups pulled Chicken Confit in its fat (opposite page), freshly made or thawed and at room temperature

1 medium shallot, finely minced

1 teaspoon finely grated lemon zest

1 teaspoon minced fresh flat-leaf parsley

½ teaspoon minced fresh tarragon

¼ teaspoon minced fresh thyme

Kosher salt and freshly ground black pepper

Crackers, Dijon mustard, and pickled onions, for serving

Drain the chicken meat, reserving the meat and fat separately.

In a medium bowl, combine the shallot and lemon zest and let sit for 10 minutes. Add the parsley, tarragon, thyme, and chicken and mix with a wooden spoon until the chicken has an almost feathery texture. Add the reserved fat by the tablespoon, adding just enough to form a spread. Season to taste with salt and pepper.

Pack the rillettes into four 4-ounce glass jars and top each jar with a few more spoonfuls of the fat to form a seal. Cover and store in the refrigerator until ready to serve. If properly sealed with fat, the rillettes will keep in the fridge for up to 2 weeks.

To serve, spread the rillettes on crackers and top with a dab of mustard and some pickled onions.

TO FREEZE: If the chicken wasn't previously frozen, you can freeze the jars of rillettes for up to 4 months.

TO THAW: Use the pull and thaw method (see page 43).

CHICKEN NIÇOISE SALAD

SERVES 4

A few minor tweaks to a very iconic recipe can help breathe new life into it. In this case, the protein that anchors the salad, typically oil-poached tuna, has gone to land in the form of chicken confit. We've also moved the anchovies from a starring role to the ensemble, as part of the herbaceous vinaigrette.

This isn't a salad for tossing; it's a platter salad, one that you build in layers and could eat with your fingers if you wanted (at least that's what you'd do if you ate it at our house). Serve with a very cold glass of rosé.

●

Vinaigrette

2 tablespoons
white wine vinegar

1 medium shallot, finely
minced

1 tablespoon whole-grain
mustard

2 oil-cured anchovy fillets

10 large fresh basil leaves

¼ cup loosely packed
fresh tarragon leaves

1 cup canola oil

½ teaspoon kosher salt

½ teaspoon freshly
ground black pepper

4 large eggs

Kosher salt

8 ounces haricots verts

4 radishes, greens removed

1 cup pitted niçoise or
Castelvetrano olives

8 ounces heirloom
tomatoes

Freshly ground black pepper

1 head Bibb or other butter
lettuce, cored and leaves
separated

1 cup pulled Chicken
Confit (page 94), thawed,
drained, and at room
temperature, or shredded
cooked chicken

Make the vinaigrette: In a food processor, combine the vinegar, shallot, mustard, anchovies, basil, and tarragon and pulse to a paste. With the motor running, slowly add the oil until emulsified and incorporated. Season with the salt and pepper. You should have about 1¼ cups. The vinaigrette will keep in a lidded container in the refrigerator for up to 3 days.

Make the salad: Fill a medium saucepan with water and bring to a boil over high heat. Gently lower the eggs into the water and boil vigorously for 1 minute. Turn down the heat to low, cover, and simmer for 8 minutes. Meanwhile, fill a large bowl with ice water. When the eggs are ready, scoop them out with a slotted spoon and transfer them to the ice water to shock them.

Return the heat to high, bring the water back to a boil, and salt it generously (it should taste salty like the ocean). Add the haricots verts and blanch for 1 to 2 minutes, until bright green but still crunchy. Drain the beans and immediately immerse them in the ice water to shock them.

Cut each radish in half from tip to tail, then cut each half into small wedges. Tear the olives with your fingers. Cut the tomatoes into wedges and season with salt and pepper.

Arrange the lettuce leaves in a bed on a platter. Drizzle ¼ cup of the vinaigrette over the leaves. Layer the radishes, olives, and tomatoes over the lettuce. Drain the green beans, pat dry, and layer them over the lettuce. Break up the chicken with your hands and spread it over the salad. Drizzle the salad with another ¼ cup of the vinaigrette.

Peel the eggs and cut lengthwise into quarters. Season the eggs with salt and pepper and arrange them across the salad. Serve immediately.

CHICKEN PICCATA FARFALLE

with Sweet Potato

SERVES 4

We're not sure who the audience is for this recipe. It has enough sophistication to be squarely pegged for adults, but something about it strikes us as so kid-like and familiar—the effect of butter and bow ties in the same proximity will take you right back to childhood.

If you prefer to leave the sweet potatoes out (one less step on those particularly lazy nights), you'll still get something delicious (again, butter and bow ties). Likewise, if you prefer to chef this up with other additions, it'll make room. Bacon wouldn't be out of place here, nor would a handful of spinach or kale.

●

2 medium sweet potatoes, peeled and cut into ¼-inch cubes (about 3 cups)

¼ cup plus 3 tablespoons extra virgin olive oil

Kosher salt

4 quarts water

8 ounces farfalle

2 garlic cloves, minced

¼ cup minced shallots (about 2 shallots)

2 tablespoons drained capers, plus 1 tablespoon of their juice

Finely grated zest and juice of 2 lemons

½ cup dry white wine

4 tablespoons unsalted butter

Freshly ground black pepper

1½ cups pulled Chicken Confit (page 94), thawed and drained, or shredded cooked chicken

1 cup chopped fresh flat-leaf parsley leaves

Finely grated Parmesan cheese, for serving (optional)

1 lemon, cut into wedges

Preheat the oven to 400°F.

In a medium bowl, combine the sweet potatoes and 2 tablespoons of the oil, season with ½ teaspoon salt, and toss to coat. Spread the sweet potato cubes in a single layer on a rimmed baking sheet and roast, stirring occasionally, for 13 to 15 minutes, until fork-tender and browned in spots. Let cool slightly.

Fill a medium pot with the water and add ¼ cup salt. Bring to a boil over high heat, add the farfalle, and cook for 11 to 12 minutes, until al dente. Drain the pasta, reserving 1½ cups of the pasta water.

In a high-sided sauté pan over medium heat, heat ¼ cup of the oil. Add the garlic and shallots and cook, stirring occasionally, for 4 to 5 minutes, until the shallots have softened. Add the capers and lemon zest and stir to incorporate. Add the reserved sweet potatoes and cook, stirring, for about 2 minutes, until the ingredients are well coated.

Add the caper juice and white wine, bring to a simmer, and let reduce for 2 to 3 minutes. Add the pasta water, lemon juice, and butter and season with pepper. Stir until the butter dissolves into the sauce, about 2 minutes. Add the farfalle and chicken and stir well to coat in the sauce. Stir in the remaining 1 tablespoon oil and the parsley.

Spoon into pasta bowls and top with Parmesan. Serve with the lemon wedges.

BUFFALO CHICKEN DIP

SERVES 8

Our friend Eliza is the ultimate party thrower. She has a beautiful home and loves to fill it with people and celebrate . . . well, whatever needs celebrating. We've had some late nights there (including our wedding), and that's how we learned this very important life lesson: keep a stash of buffalo chicken dip in your freezer. She keeps frozen trays of it, ready to bake, and then pulls them out for the most satisfying and indulgent late-night snack.

There's a recipe for this dip on every hot sauce website, but this is our version. The chicken confit takes it to the next level, though it'll still taste delicious with any pulled chicken meat. Do not use previously frozen chicken if you plan to freeze the dip.

8 ounces cream cheese, at room temperature

4 tablespoons hot sauce (see Note)

1 tablespoon minced red onion

1 tablespoon fresh lemon juice

1 teaspoon kosher salt

1 cup shredded Cheddar cheese

½ cup finely grated Parmigiano-Reggiano cheese

1 cup crumbled blue cheese

8 ounces pulled Chicken Confit (page 94), freshly made or thawed, drained, and at room temperature, or shredded cooked chicken

2 green onions, light and dark green parts, thinly sliced on the diagonal

Fritos or tortilla chips, for serving

In a stand mixer fitted with the paddle attachment (or in a medium bowl with a hand mixer), cream together the cream cheese, hot sauce, red onion, lemon juice, and salt on medium speed until smooth. Fold in the Cheddar, Parmigiano-Reggiano, blue cheese, and chicken confit until evenly distributed.

Transfer the mixture to a 9 by 9-inch baking dish and spread into an even layer.

TO FREEZE: If made from chicken not previously frozen, spread the mixture in the baking dish as directed and wrap the dish in two layers of plastic wrap. Label and date, then freeze for up to 4 months.

TO BAKE FROM FROZEN: Unwrap the baking dish, place in a cold oven, and set the oven to 400°F. When the oven reaches temperature, bake for about 40 minutes, until bubbling and gooey.

TO BAKE WITHOUT FREEZING: Preheat the oven to 400°F. Bake for about 20 minutes, until bubbling and gooey.

Sprinkle the green onions over the top and serve hot directly from the dish, with the Fritos for dipping.

NOTE

For the hot sauce in this dip, we like a combination of 2 tablespoons Tabasco and 2 tablespoons Texas Pete.

BROCCOLI CHEDDAR CHICKEN BAKE

SERVES 10 TO 12

If you're making food to freeze and give to someone else (new parents, a friend recovering from an illness, just because), this is a good recipe to fall back on. It yields two good-size casseroles, and it's approachable for particular eaters (including kids).

•

4 cups water

2 cups quinoa, rinsed

Kosher salt

1 head broccoli, steamed and coarsely chopped, or 14 ounces frozen broccoli

3 cups pulled Chicken Confit (page 94), freshly made or thawed and drained, or shredded cooked chicken

2 tablespoons neutral vegetable oil

1 yellow onion, diced (about 2 cups)

1 garlic clove, minced

2 cups Freezer Chicken Stock (page 204), freshly made or thawed

4 cups Herbed Béchamel (page 120), freshly made or thawed

3 cups shredded sharp white Cheddar cheese

In a medium saucepan, combine the water, quinoa, and ½ teaspoon salt and bring to a boil over high heat. Turn down the heat to a simmer and cook for about 15 minutes, until the water has evaporated and the quinoa is fluffy. Transfer to a large bowl and add the broccoli and chicken.

In a large skillet over medium heat, warm the oil until it shimmers. Add the onion and cook, stirring often, for 5 to 7 minutes, until softened and translucent. Add the garlic and cook, stirring, for 1 minute, until fragrant. Season with 2 teaspoons salt and stir to combine. Add the stock, increase the heat to medium-high, and bring to a simmer. Add the béchamel, lower the heat to medium, and simmer for 2 minutes, stirring constantly to combine. Gradually add the Cheddar in handfuls, stirring constantly, until it is completely incorporated into the sauce.

Pour the sauce over the quinoa, broccoli, and chicken and stir to mix well. Season to taste with salt. Divide the mixture between two 8 by 12-inch baking dishes.

TO FREEZE: If made from ingredients not previously frozen, let the assembled casseroles cool to room temperature, then chill in the fridge for 1 hour. Wrap the dishes in two layers of plastic wrap, label and date, and freeze for up to 3 months.

TO BAKE FROM FROZEN: Unwrap the dishes, place in a cold oven, and set the oven to 375°F. When the oven reaches temperature, cook for 60 to 70 minutes, until hot throughout. Remove from the oven and let sit for 5 minutes before serving. Spoon hefty scoops into bowls and enjoy.

TO BAKE WITHOUT FREEZING: Preheat the oven to 375°F. Bake for 35 to 40 minutes, rotating the dishes 180 degrees halfway through baking, until bubbling. Remove from the oven and let sit for 5 minutes before serving. Spoon hefty scoops into bowls and enjoy.

BRAISED SHORT RIBS

MAKES 3 POUNDS, ENOUGH FOR 6 SERVINGS

Short ribs require time to coax out their best texture and flavor, which is why they're a natural choice for freezing. Do the work up front and reap the rewards of that rich, stewy savoriness quickly and easily down the road. Forget about the ribs as they slow cook in the oven, then meal prep with recipes like short rib–stuffed peppers (page 109) or beef and root vegetable stew (page 106) before enjoying some of your efforts with cauliflower *fonduta* (page 105).

You can freeze the short ribs on the bone, or you can cut the meat from the bone and store it shredded or cubed.

●

One 5-pound slab bone-in beef short ribs

Sea salt and freshly ground black pepper

2 cups red wine

2 cups water

1 head garlic, halved across the equator

8 thyme sprigs

4 rosemary sprigs

Preheat the oven to 450°F.

Dust the short ribs on all sides with salt and pepper so they are well coated. Place the ribs bone side down in a large roasting pan and roast for about 20 minutes, until the meat forms a caramelized crust. Remove from the oven and lower the oven temperature to 275°F.

Let the ribs rest for 10 minutes, then pour the wine and water into the bottom of the pan and add the garlic, thyme, and rosemary. Cover the pan tightly with aluminum foil and return it to the oven. Roast for about 4 hours, until the short ribs are very tender when tested with a fork but not falling apart.

Transfer the pan, still covered, to a heatproof surface. Turn up the corners of the foil so the heat will release gradually and let the ribs rest for 20 minutes. To serve, cut between the bones to separate the ribs and divide among individual plates. Alternatively, cut the entire slab of meat off the bones and then cut against the grain into 1-inch-thick slices and divide among individual plates.

TO FREEZE ON THE BONE: Let the whole short rib slab cool completely, then put it into a zip-top plastic bag. Label and date and freeze for up to 5 months.

TO FREEZE OFF THE BONE: Let the whole short rib slab cool completely. Cut the meat from the bones and cut into 1-inch cubes, or shred the meat with your fingers. Put the meat into vacuum pouches or zip-top plastic bags, label and date, and freeze for up to 5 months.

TO THAW: Use the pull and thaw method (see page 43) or the cold water method (see page 43) to thaw a whole short rib slab or short rib meat off the bone.

TO REHEAT: Do not reheat a whole short rib slab from frozen. If short rib meat is stored in vacuum pouches, you can reheat from frozen using the sous vide method. Set the sous vide water bath to 150°F and drop in the pouch. It will take 1½ hours to reach temperature.

SHORT RIB STROGANOFF

with Egg Noodles

SERVES 4

When Kait was growing up, beef stroganoff was on the dinner rotation at her house, made with either flank, top round, or sometimes even ground beef (which created a pretty incredible creamy Bolognese effect).

For this version, which gets slightly fancier than the one from Kait's childhood, we borrow from a long-standing dish on the menu at Poole's: oyster mushrooms with sherry and cream. Using a mix of mushrooms, like oyster, trumpet, and maitake, and deglazing the pan with sherry elevate this dish without adding more work for you. If you're looking to add more work, though, doing this with fresh pasta would be pretty divine.

•

1 tablespoon unsalted butter

1 tablespoon olive oil

1 pound cubed Braised Short Ribs meat (opposite page), thawed

½ cup thinly sliced shallots

4 cups mixed sliced mushrooms (such as oyster, trumpet, and maitake)

Kosher salt and freshly ground black pepper

¼ cup dry sherry

2 tablespoons all-purpose flour

1½ cups heavy cream

1 teaspoon Worcestershire sauce

1 teaspoon dark soy sauce

1 teaspoon prepared horseradish

12 ounces dried egg noodles

In a medium Dutch oven or heavy skillet over medium-high heat, warm the butter and oil. When the butter has melted, add the short rib meat and brown, stirring occasionally, for 5 to 7 minutes, until the meat is caramelized and hot throughout. Using a slotted utensil, transfer the meat to a plate, leaving the fat in the pan.

Lower the heat to medium, add the shallots, and cook, stirring occasionally, for about 5 minutes, until beginning to soften. Add the mushrooms and cook, stirring occasionally, for about 15 minutes, until the moisture has evaporated and they are caramelizing in spots. Season with salt and pepper. Add the sherry and simmer until the liquid evaporates.

Sprinkle the flour over the mushroom mixture and cook, stirring, until it begins to smell nutty and toast in the pan. Add the cream and stir, cooking, until the liquid begins to simmer and thicken slightly. Let simmer, stirring occasionally, for 5 minutes. Stir in the Worcestershire sauce, soy sauce, and horseradish. Cook gently, stirring for 1 minute more, then stir in the reserved meat. Keep warm while you cook the pasta.

Fill a large pot with water and salt it generously (it should taste salty like the ocean). Bring to a boil over high heat, add the egg noodles, and cook for 7 to 9 minutes, until al dente. Drain thoroughly.

To serve, divide the noodles among individual plates and spoon the short rib meat and its sauce over the top.

BRAISED SHORT RIBS

with Cauliflower Fonduta

You could go the classic meat-and-potatoes route and pair your short ribs with mashed potatoes (page 154). But if you're looking to do something different, this velvety, creamy cauliflower *fonduta* is elegant and rich. *Fonduta* essentially translates to "fondue," but the Italian version is fortified with eggs and cream.

•

Short Ribs

2 cups beef stock

½ cup dry red wine

4 Braised Short Ribs on the bone (page 102), thawed

4 tablespoons cold unsalted butter

Fonduta

Kosher salt

1 head cauliflower, cored and cut into florets

2 tablespoons cream cheese

¼ cup whole milk

¼ cup heavy cream

3 large eggs

8 ounces Fontina cheese, shredded

Make the short ribs: Preheat the oven to 400°F. In a large Dutch oven or other heavy pot, combine the stock, wine, and short ribs. Roast for about 20 minutes, until the short ribs are warm throughout and the liquid has reduced to 1 cup.

Meanwhile, make the fonduta: Fill a medium saucepan with water and salt lightly. Bring to a boil over high heat, add the cauliflower, and cook for about 10 minutes, until fork-tender. Drain the cauliflower and transfer to a food processor. Add the cream cheese and ½ teaspoon salt and process until a smooth puree forms. Keep warm.

Wipe out the saucepan, add the milk and cream, and bring to a simmer over medium heat. Do not let the mixture scorch! In a medium bowl, whisk the eggs until blended. Add about ¼ cup of the simmering milk mixture to the eggs while whisking constantly to mix well. Then slowly pour the egg-milk mixture into the pan with the remaining liquid, turn down the heat to low, and cook, whisking, for 5 to 7 minutes, until the mixture thickens and coats the back of a spoon. Remove from the heat and whisk in the Fontina until melted. Stir in the cauliflower mixture until completely incorporated. Keep warm.

Finish the short ribs: Transfer the short ribs to a plate. Whisk the butter, 1 tablespoon at a time, into the reduced liquid, until all the butter is incorporated.

To serve, spoon the cauliflower fonduta into individual shallow bowls. Lay a short rib in each bowl and top with a few spoonfuls of the braising liquid.

BEEF AND COCONUT STEW

with Root Vegetables

SERVES 6 TO 8

The savoriness of short ribs pairs nicely with equally intense aromatics (ginger and chiles) and an array of spices here. After going through the motions on a snowy or wet or blustery day, a bowl of this stew and sweatpants are a great reward. If you're planning to make this and freeze it, omit the coconut milk or it'll separate upon thawing. Add it to the stew after reheating.

●

1 medium sweet potato, peeled and cut into ½-inch cubes (about 2 cups)

1 medium rutabaga, peeled and cut into ½-inch cubes (about 2 cups)

1 medium turnip, peeled and cut into ½-inch cubes (about 2 cups)

¼ cup extra virgin olive oil

Kosher salt

1 tablespoon chili powder

2 teaspoons freshly ground black pepper

1 teaspoon garam masala

1 teaspoon ground coriander

½ teaspoon ground turmeric

¼ cup neutral vegetable oil

1 medium red onion, thinly sliced (about 2 cups)

1 hot green chile (such as bird's eye or serrano), stemmed and thinly sliced

6 garlic cloves, sliced

2 tablespoons peeled and minced fresh ginger

2 tablespoons tomato paste

4 cups beef stock

2 pounds shredded Braised Short Ribs meat (page 102), freshly made or thawed

Two 13½-ounce cans coconut milk

Cooked basmati rice, for serving

Preheat the oven to 375°F. Line a rimmed baking sheet with aluminum foil.

In a medium bowl, toss together the sweet potato, rutabaga, and turnip with the olive oil and 1 teaspoon salt. Spread the vegetables on the prepared pan and bake, flipping the vegetables with a spatula halfway through baking, for 25 minutes, until tender.

In a small bowl, stir together the chili powder, 1 tablespoon salt, the black pepper, garam masala, coriander, and turmeric.

In a large Dutch oven or other heavy pot over medium heat, warm the vegetable oil until it shimmers. Add the onion and cook, stirring, for about 5 minutes, until it starts to soften. Add the chile, garlic, and ginger and cook, stirring frequently, for about 3 minutes, until fragrant. Add the roasted vegetables and stir to combine. Add the reserved spice mixture and stir to mix well. Cook, stirring occasionally, for 2 to 3 minutes, until the spices are fragrant. Add the tomato paste and cook, stirring constantly, for 2 minutes, until it begins to slightly caramelize.

Add the stock, increase the heat to high, and bring to a boil. Turn down the heat to medium and simmer, stirring occasionally, for 10 minutes, until the liquid is slightly thickened. Fold in the short ribs and cook, stirring, for 3 to 4 minutes. Remove from the heat.

TO FREEZE: If the short rib meat has not been previously frozen, you can freeze the stew at this point. Let cool to room temperature, then refrigerate until well chilled. Portion into pint-size lidded containers, label and date, and freeze for up to 3 months.

TO THAW: Use the pull and thaw method (see page 43) or the Instant Pot method (see page 40). Reheat the stew to serving temperature, then proceed with the recipe as written.

Stir in the coconut milk and cook for another 5 minutes to heat through and blend the flavors. If you are reheating in batches, estimate 1 can coconut milk for each 4½ cups stew.

To serve, spoon the stew over rice.

STUFFED PEPPERS

with Short Ribs and Rice

MAKES 8 PEPPERS

You can freeze tahini! We don't often have the need to, because the sesame paste is exceedingly shelf stable, but it's good information to have. It also means you can use tahini as a binder in recipes that you might freeze, like this one. Tahini is the magic glue holding together a filling of chopped short rib meat, rice, and spices. By stuffing the filling into hollowed-out bell peppers, you get a cute vegetable-as-vessel effect. But you could also make this recipe as a casserole: just chop up the peppers and stir them in.

●

1 cup tahini

2 garlic cloves

1 teaspoon fresh lemon juice

Kosher salt

About ¾ cup ice water

1 pound shredded Braised Short Ribs meat (page 102), freshly made or thawed

3 cups cooked long-grain white rice, at room temperature

¼ teaspoon freshly ground black pepper

⅛ teaspoon ground allspice

⅛ teaspoon freshly grated nutmeg

⅛ teaspoon ground cloves

⅛ teaspoon ground cinnamon

8 medium red bell peppers

¼ cup olive oil

2 cups tomato juice

2 cups vegetable stock or freshly made or thawed Freezer Chicken Stock (page 204)

Plain Greek yogurt, for serving

Preheat the oven to 375°F.

In a food processor, combine the tahini, garlic, lemon juice, and ½ teaspoon salt and process for 1 to 2 minutes, until the mixture lightens in color. With the motor running, gradually add up to ¾ cup ice water, processing until the mixture is super smooth and creamy, like mayonnaise. The mixture will seize at first before emulsifying.

Place the short rib meat in a large bowl. Add the rice, pepper, allspice, nutmeg, cloves, and cinnamon and mix well. Add the tahini mixture and stir to distribute evenly. Season with 2 teaspoons salt.

Cut the top off each pepper and use a spoon to scrape out the seeds and ribs, working carefully to keep the peppers intact. Stuff the peppers with the rice mixture, dividing it evenly.

TO FREEZE: If the ingredients have not been previously frozen, you can freeze the stuffed peppers at this point. Wrap the individual peppers in plastic wrap, place in a zip-top plastic bag, label and date, and freeze for up to 3 months. Thaw before cooking using the pull and thaw method (see page 43) or the cold water method (see page 43). Proceed with the recipe as written to bake.

Nestle the peppers upright in a 9 by 13-inch baking dish and drizzle them evenly with the oil. In a large measuring cup, mix together the tomato juice, stock, and 1 teaspoon salt and pour into the dish at the base of the peppers.

Cover the dish with aluminum foil and carefully transfer to the oven. Bake the peppers for about 1 hour, until the flesh of the peppers is tender when pierced with a knife. Remove the foil and cook for another 30 minutes, basting the peppers with some of the cooking liquid every 10 minutes, until the filling is browned on top.

Scoop the peppers out into shallow bowls, top with a spoonful of yogurt, and serve.

Dairy.

ABOUT COMPOUND BUTTER • 112

113 **PIMENTO CHEESE BUTTER**

Roasted Oysters with Pimento Cheese Butter • 115

116 **PRESERVED LEMON–GARLIC BUTTER**

Pan-Roasted Chicken Breast with
Preserved Lemon–Garlic Butter • 119

120 **HERBED BÉCHAMEL**

Sausage Gravy with Buttermilk Biscuits • 122

Green Bean Casserole • 125

Four-Cheese and Greens Lasagna • 126

128 **PARM STOCK**

Italian Wedding Soup • 129

Tomato and Greens Minestrone • 130

ABOUT COMPOUND BUTTER

Fat is a vehicle for flavor. The chemical compounds that create "flavor" as we experience it open up in oil or butter. A compound butter is butter into which you've mixed one or more flavors, and your options are pretty vast. Typically you want to make compound butter with ingredients that are high in flavor, whether they are aromatics, like garlic, onion, herbs, ginger, or chiles, or umami rich, such as mushrooms, soy, cheese, or fermented fish (anchovies, fish sauce, Worcestershire sauce).

Compound butter, like regular butter, freezes well. Even ingredients that don't typically fare well in a freezer, like raw vegetables, will hold up fine in compound butter. When they're suspended in fat, they are essentially locked in an airtight vacuum, and the effects of the freezer are held at bay. In the fridge, a compound butter lasts a long time, at least a month; in the freezer, it will keep for 6 months, as long as it's well wrapped.

Think about portioning a compound butter before you freeze it. Most often, we reach for compound butter in small amounts, a few tablespoons at a time. So we tend to package compound butter accordingly; by forming it into a log, you can slice off small nubs without thawing the whole batch.

Butter is susceptible to absorbing external smells and flavors, so keeping your butter in a sealed package is crucial. We recommend plastic wrap *and* a zip-top plastic bag for extra protection.

PIMENTO CHEESE BUTTER

MAKES 3 CUPS

One of the sadder discoveries of testing recipes for this book was realizing that pimento cheese didn't make the cut of foods that can be successfully frozen. We couldn't quite stomach the idea of a cookbook without a pimento cheese recipe, so this here is our workaround. Butter *loves* the freezer, and butter protects the cheese from freezer burn, and basically butter answers all our problems (doesn't it always?).

You could, in theory, still treat this pimento-flavored butter like a spread to put on crostini, but it's even more interesting when it is melted over things. Baked potatoes, roasted oysters, and grilled steak are just a few of the pairings that jump to mind.

2 medium red bell peppers

¼ cup cider vinegar

2 cups unsalted butter, at room temperature

2 tablespoons finely grated red onion

1 tablespoon freshly ground black pepper

¾ teaspoon kosher salt

8 ounces 3-year-aged Cheddar cheese, shredded

8 ounces sharp Cheddar cheese, shredded

To roast the peppers, one at a time, place them directly over a high gas flame and, using metal tongs to rotate them, char the entire surface of each pepper. To char the top, balance the pepper on its curvy stem end on the grate of the burner. (If you don't have a gas range, roast the peppers under the broiler, rotating them with metal tongs so they char evenly.)

Transfer the peppers to a metal bowl, cover with plastic wrap, and let sit for 15 minutes. Use a dish towel to gently rub off the skins of the peppers. Don't run them under water, as this will wash away some of the flavor. Tear the peppers in half, remove the stems and seeds, and finely dice the flesh. You should have about ¾ cup.

In a small bowl, combine the diced peppers and the vinegar, cover, and refrigerate overnight. (Or if you can't wait, let sit at room temperature for at least 3 hours.)

Drain the peppers and add to the bowl of a stand mixer fitted with a paddle attachment. Add the butter, onion, pepper, salt, and both cheeses and mix on low speed until everything is evenly mixed.

TO FREEZE: Lay a sheet of plastic wrap on a work surface and scrape the butter onto the center of it. Fold the plastic wrap from the bottom edge over the top of the butter and then use your hands to shape the butter into a cylinder 1½ to 2 inches in diameter within the plastic wrap. Roll up the cylinder the rest of the way in the plastic wrap and put it into a zip-top plastic bag to protect it from odors. Label and date and freeze for up to 3 months.

TO THAW: Use the pull and thaw method (page 43) to thaw the entire cylinder. To thaw a smaller portion, slice what you need from the cylinder and allow to thaw at room temperature (depending on the amount, it should thaw in 20 minutes to 1 hour).

ROASTED OYSTERS

with Pimento Cheese Butter

MAKES 24 OYSTERS

We cook and eat a lot of roasted oysters, and 99.9 percent of the time they're topped with compound butter. We've made them with roasted tomato butter, with chili butter, with curry butter, and now with Pimento Cheese Butter. The butter and the natural liquid from the oysters commingle to create a rich, delicious thimble of the world's best broth; the oyster itself is almost secondary.

With Pimento Cheese Butter, you get the added bonus of a brûléed cheesy crust. Because of that, you may need forks to eat these, though we'll never judge you for slurping straight from the shell.

●

Rock salt, for the pan

24 oysters, shucked, on the half shell

1 cup Pimento Cheese Butter (page 113), thawed and at refrigerator temperature

Position an oven rack in the upper third of the oven and preheat the broiler.

Line a rimmed baking sheet with rock salt. Arrange the oysters on the baking sheet in an even layer (you may have to work in batches), being careful not to tip them. Top each oyster with about 2 teaspoons of the butter.

Transfer the pan to the oven and broil for 5 to 7 minutes, until the butter has melted and is bubbling and the oysters have begun to turn opaque. Serve warm.

PRESERVED LEMON–GARLIC BUTTER

MAKES 2½ CUPS BUTTER

The combination of lemon, garlic, and butter is enough to flavor a whole dish (here's looking at you, chicken piccata). When you take the extra step of preserving the lemons in salt and sugar, the applications of this compound butter are endless. Note that the preserved lemons require 4 days of wait time, so factor that into your planning.

•

Preserved Lemons

8 lemons

1 cup kosher salt

1 cup sugar

½ preserved lemon

15 garlic cloves, minced

1 cup unsalted butter, at room temperature

½ teaspoon kosher salt

Make the preserved lemons: Thoroughly scrub each lemon under running cold water. Cut each lemon lengthwise into quarters, starting from the stem end and stopping within ½ inch of the bottom, so the quarters remain attached. In a medium bowl, stir together the salt and sugar.

Carefully pack each lemon incision with the salt mixture and place the lemons, with the incisions facing up, in a container just large enough to fit them snugly. Cover the lemons with a piece of plastic wrap, laying it directly on them inside the container. Select a plate or lid a bit smaller in diameter than the container and set it on the lemons to weight them down. Keep the container at room temperature for at least 4 days or up to 1 week.

Remove the weight and plastic. The lemons are now ready to use. Cover the container with a tight-fitting lid and store in the refrigerator for up to 1 month. The lemons can also be frozen. Transfer them to a zip-top plastic bag, label and date, and freeze for up to 3 months.

Make the butter: Remove the rind from ½ preserved lemon, being careful to remove all of the pith, then discard the pith and flesh. Finely dice the rind and add to the bowl of a stand mixer fitted with the paddle attachment. Add the garlic, butter, and salt and mix on low speed until everything is evenly mixed.

TO FREEZE: Lay a sheet of plastic wrap on a work surface and scrape the butter onto the center of it. Fold the plastic wrap from the bottom edge over the top of the butter and then use your hands to shape the butter into a cylinder 1½ to 2 inches diameter within the plastic wrap. Roll up the cylinder the rest of the way in the plastic wrap and put it into a zip-top plastic bag to protect it from odors. Label and date and freeze for up to 3 months.

TO THAW: Use the pull and thaw method (page 43) to thaw the entire cylinder. To thaw a smaller portion, slice what you need from the cylinder and allow to thaw at room temperature (depending on the amount, it should thaw in 20 minutes to 1 hour).

PAN-ROASTED CHICKEN BREAST

with Preserved Lemon–Garlic Butter

SERVES 1

Chicken breast is weirdly polarizing. There's the camp of devotees for whom boneless, skinless chicken breast is the main form of protein consumed and who proselytize it as the healthiest, leanest way to eat meat. Then there's the camp of haters, who decry the chicken breast for its lack of flavor and tendency to be overcooked.

We'll stay happily in the middle ground. We love it for its ease, and, yes, we appreciate that it's a healthy option. We work around the criticisms by building flavor through supplementary ingredients and a little bit of attention to technique. We also split the difference in terms of preparation—we keep the skin (that's where the flavor comes in), but otherwise cook it simply, without brine.

Compound butter plays an important role in building flavor here: together with the pan juices, vermouth, and mustard, it creates a rich pan sauce. If you don't have any Preserved Lemon–Garlic Butter in the freezer, you could use regular cold butter.

One 6-ounce boneless, skin-on split chicken breast

2 tablespoons Wondra flour or cornstarch

½ teaspoon kosher salt

½ teaspoon freshly ground black pepper

1 tablespoon canola oil

¼ cup dry vermouth or dry white wine

½ teaspoon Dijon mustard

2 tablespoons Preserved Lemon–Garlic Butter (page 116), thawed and cold

Preheat the oven to 400°F.

Pat the chicken breast dry with a paper towel. In a shallow dish, mix together the flour, salt, and pepper. Dredge the breast in the flour mixture, carefully coating it on all sides.

Heat a medium oven-safe skillet over high heat and add the oil. When the oil is very hot and shimmering, add the chicken breast, skin side down. Turn down the heat to medium and cook undisturbed for about 5 minutes, until the skin is crispy and releases from the pan. Flip the chicken and cook for an additional 5 minutes.

Transfer the skillet to the oven and cook the chicken for 8 to 10 minutes, until an instant-read thermometer inserted into the center of the breast registers 155°F. Move the chicken breast to a plate to rest.

Return the skillet with all of the chicken drippings to the stove top over medium heat. Add the vermouth and mustard and use a spatula or spoon to scrape up any browned bits from the pan bottom. Bring the liquid to a simmer and reduce slightly. Remove from the heat and add the butter, 1 tablespoon at a time, swirling the pan to incorporate the first addition completely before adding the second one.

Cut the chicken against the grain into ½-inch-thick slices and transfer to a plate. Spoon the sauce on top and serve.

HERBED BÉCHAMEL

MAKE 8 CUPS

Béchamel, a cream sauce bound by a roux of flour and butter, holds up well in the freezer, maintaining the same gooey, melty texture that the freezer too often destroys in other dairy. It's pivotal for casseroles, such as lasagna (page 126) or the green bean dish (page 125) that falls on so many Thanksgiving menus. It's the halfway point to sausage gravy (page 122) or cheese sauce. Long story short, béchamel helps bridge the gap when thinking about foods that freeze well. Just like duct tape, you should never be without it.

•

½ cup unsalted butter

8 thyme sprigs

3 shallots, minced

2 garlic cloves, minced

1 cup dry white wine

1 cup all-purpose flour

4 cups whole milk

4 cups heavy cream

1 tablespoon kosher salt

1½ teaspoons freshly ground black pepper

In a medium Dutch oven or other heavy pot over medium heat, melt the butter. Add the thyme, shallots, and garlic and cook, sweating the shallots, for 3 to 5 minutes, until fragrant and softened. Add the wine, bring to a simmer, and reduce for about 10 minutes, until almost completely evaporated. Remove and discard the thyme sprigs. Sprinkle the flour over the vegetables and stir well to coat. Continue to cook, stirring, for 5 to 7 minutes, until the flour smells nutty and has begun to take on a hint of light tan.

While stirring constantly, slowly add the milk and cream. The mixture will seize up and the flour will clump for a moment but will ultimately reincorporate and the mixture will become smooth. Bring to a gentle simmer, continuing to stir to avoid scorching, and cook until the mixture thickens to the consistency of thick gravy. This will take about 6 minutes. Season with the salt and pepper to taste.

TO FREEZE: Spread the béchamel on a rimmed baking sheet and let cool to room temperature. Portion and transfer the béchamel to freezer-safe containers, such as vacuum pouches, quart-size zip-top plastic bags, or pint-size lidded plastic containers. Label and date and freeze for up to 3 months.

TO THAW: Use the pull and thaw method (see page 43) or the cold water method (see page 43).

TO REHEAT: If you used vacuum pouches, reheating from frozen using the sous vide method works well. Set the sous vide water bath to 145°F and drop in the pouch. It will take about 1 hour to reach temperature, depending on the volume. Otherwise, thaw first, then transfer to a saucepan and reheat on the stove over medium heat, stirring frequently, until it begins to gently simmer.

SAUSAGE GRAVY

with Buttermilk Biscuits

**SERVES 4 TO 6
(MAKES 5 CUPS
GRAVY)**

Ashley's mom, Lynn, was an air force brat. Before the age of thirteen, she lived in both Japan and England. A holdover from her military upbringing was a breakfast of beef gravy over dry toast, which she made for Ashley as a kid. If you soften this around the edges and give it a Southern accent, you get biscuits with sausage gravy. It's a meal in and of itself, but you could always add a fried egg on top for extra indulgence.

●

1 pound loose breakfast
sausage

4 cups Herbed Béchamel
(page 120), thawed

8 Buttermilk Biscuits
(page 56), baked
from frozen

In a large skillet over medium heat, cook the sausage, breaking it up with the back of a wooden spoon, for 5 to 6 minutes, until no pink remains. Transfer the sausage to a paper towel–lined plate; leave the browned bits and drippings in the pan.

Return the skillet to medium heat, add the béchamel, and heat, stirring constantly. Stir in the crumbled sausage and simmer for 2 to 3 minutes to allow the flavors to blend.

To serve, split the biscuits and arrange two biscuits, cut side up, on each plate. Ladle a large spoonful of the gravy over each plate of biscuits.

GREEN BEAN CASSEROLE

SERVES 6 TO 8

Holiday menus are always a fine balance for us. The cooks in us want to experiment, try new things, improvise on whatever has been inspiring us lately. But then there's our traditionalist side that craves the classic recipes that we've been making in our families for generations. This is the side that usually comes out victorious.

But our cheffy side still peeks out with tweaks and improvements to the old reliables. Making "cream of mushroom" from scratch is one such tweak; using fresh green beans is another.

While we wouldn't freeze the completely assembled casserole (you'll lose the crisp-tender texture of the green beans), you can definitely freeze the porcini béchamel if the béchamel has not been previously frozen.

●

2 ounces dried porcini mushrooms

½ cup boiling water

Kosher salt

2 pounds green beans, trimmed

1 tablespoon unsalted butter

1 pound fresh button or cremini mushrooms, thinly sliced

1 teaspoon fresh oregano leaves

1 teaspoon fresh thyme leaves

¾ cup thinly sliced red onion

5 cups Herbed Béchamel (page 120), freshly made or thawed and at room temperature

4 cups store-bought crispy onions, such as French's

Preheat the oven to 375°F.

In a small skillet, cover the porcini with the boiling water and let sit for 10 minutes. Then bring to a simmer over medium heat and simmer for about 10 minutes, until almost all of the water has evaporated. Remove from the heat and season with ¼ teaspoon salt. Transfer to a food processor and process until a smooth paste forms. Set aside.

Bring a large pot of salted water to a boil over high heat. Set a large bowl filled with ice water on the counter next to it. Add the green beans to the boiling water and blanch for 1 minute. Drain the beans and immediately add them to the ice water to shock them. Drain well and reserve.

In a large skillet, melt the butter. Add the button mushrooms and cook, stirring occasionally, for 8 to 10 minutes, until they begin to caramelize in spots. Add the oregano, thyme, red onion, and ½ teaspoon salt; stir well, and continue to cook, stirring occasionally, for 4 to 5 minutes, until the onion softens. Stir in the green beans, mixing well, and remove from the heat.

In a large bowl, mix together the béchamel and porcini puree until thoroughly combined. (You can freeze the porcini béchamel if the béchamel wasn't previously frozen; use the storage instructions for the béchamel.) Fold in the green bean–mushroom mixture. Transfer to a 3-quart gratin or baking dish.

Bake for 20 minutes, until warm throughout. Increase the oven temperature to 425°F, arrange the crispy onions in an even layer over the top, and bake for 15 minutes more, until the crispy onions are a deep golden brown. Remove the casserole from the oven and let sit for 5 minutes before serving.

FOUR-CHEESE AND GREENS LASAGNA

SERVES 16

Lasagna is always a project. It's a perfect example of a recipe that you bookmark because it requires you to block out a significant chunk of time for it. If your freezer pantry is stocked with braised greens and béchamel, you will save yourself about an hour in making a lasagna to eat the same day. If you want to freeze the lasagna itself, then it's ideal to make your braised greens and béchamel fresh, rather than use previously frozen. (Why? So that you're not freezing and thawing these components more than once.) We like to bake the lasagna and then freeze it in individual portions, which eases the commitment of baking off an entire pan. This is especially helpful if you live in a household of one or two people.

●

Greens Filling

2 cups Braised Greens (page 134), thawed and at room temperature, finely chopped

2 cups Herbed Béchamel (page 120), thawed and at room temperature

Ricotta Filling

4 cups whole-milk ricotta cheese

4 large eggs

1 cup (4 ounces) finely grated Parmigiano-Reggiano cheese

1 teaspoon kosher salt

1 teaspoon freshly ground black pepper

Finely grated zest of 2 lemons

1 pound part-skim mozzarella cheese, shredded

1 pound aged provolone cheese, shredded

Kosher salt

1 pound dried lasagna pasta noodles

Olive oil, for drizzling

Preheat the oven to 375°F.

Make the greens filling: In a large bowl, stir together the greens and the béchamel, mixing well.

Make the ricotta filling: In a large bowl, stir together the ricotta, eggs, Parmigiano, salt, pepper, and lemon zest, mixing well.

In a large bowl, mix together the mozzarella and provolone.

Fill a large pot with water and salt it generously (it should taste salty like the ocean). Bring to a boil over high heat, add the lasagna noodles, and cook for 7 to 8 minutes, until just shy of al dente. Drain the noodles and drizzle some oil over them. Use your hands to coat them well to keep them from sticking.

To assemble the lasagna, scoop one-third of the greens filling into a deep 9 by 13-inch baking dish and spread it into an even layer. Follow with one-sixth of the cheese, and then a layer of the noodles, arranging them so they don't overlap and cutting them to the appropriate size if necessary. Follow the noodles with one-third of the ricotta filling, spreading it into an even layer. Sprinkle with one-sixth of the shredded cheese. Follow with a layer of noodles, again arranging them so they don't overlap and cutting them to the appropriate size if necessary. Use your palms to press the layers down evenly at this point.

Follow the noodle layer with one-third of the greens filling. Sprinkle with one-sixth of the shredded cheese. Follow with a layer of noodles, again arranging them so they don't overlap and cutting them to the appropriate size if necessary. Follow the noodles with one-third of the ricotta filling. Sprinkle with one-sixth of the shredded cheese. Follow with a layer of noodles, again arranging them so they don't overlap and cutting them to the appropriate size if necessary. Do another press-down move here with your hands.

Follow the noodle layer with the remaining third of the greens mixture. Sprinkle with one-sixth of the shredded cheese. Follow with a layer of noodles, again arranging them so they don't overlap and cutting them to the appropriate size if necessary. Follow the noodles with the remaining third of the ricotta mixture. Sprinkle with the remaining sixth of the shredded cheese. (You can freeze the unbaked lasagna at this point; see below.)

Cover the lasagna dish with tented aluminum foil and bake for 40 minutes. Remove the foil, rotate the dish 180 degrees, and bake an additional 20 minutes, until the center is hot and the lasagna is bubbling. The cheese on top should be melted and a little puffed. Let sit for 15 to 20 minutes before serving.

TO FREEZE UNBAKED LASAGNA: Wrap the assembled lasagna in two layers of plastic wrap, label and date, and freeze for up to 4 months.

TO COOK UNBAKED LASAGNA FROM FROZEN: Unwrap the baking dish, place in a cold oven, and set the oven to 375°F. When the oven reaches temperature, bake for 1½ hours, until the center is hot and the lasagna is bubbling.

TO FREEZE BAKED LASAGNA WHOLE: Let cool to 70°F, then transfer to the refrigerator and chill well. Wrap the baking dish in two layers of plastic wrap, label and date, and freeze for up to 4 months.

TO REHEAT THE WHOLE BAKED CASSEROLE FROM FROZEN: Unwrap the baking dish, place in a cold oven, and set the oven to 375°F. When the oven reaches temperature, bake for 1 hour, until hot throughout.

TO FREEZE BAKED LASAGNA IN INDIVIDUAL PORTIONS: Let cool to 70°F, then cut the lasagna into squares and place the squares on a rimmed baking sheet. Transfer to the freezer for 4 hours or up to overnight for a formative freeze (see page 31). Wrap each square in plastic wrap, transfer to a zip-top plastic bag, label and date, and freeze for up to 1 month.

TO REHEAT BAKED INDIVIDUAL LASAGNA PORTIONS FROM FROZEN: Place on a rimmed baking sheet in a preheated 375°F oven for 35 to 40 minutes, until hot throughout. Or place on a microwave-safe plate in a microwave, set the microwave on a medium setting (5 out of 10 on ours), and microwave in 3-minute increments.

PARM STOCK

MAKES 16 CUPS

If you operate a pizza restaurant, you find yourself with a surplus of Parmigiano rinds. Rather than throwing these flavor-packed ends away, we extract the flavor, transforming it into a liquid form that we can use to make soups, sauces, and more.

At home, it's harder to come by 2 pounds of Parmigiano rinds, but here's the good news: you can freeze the rinds as you go, storing them frozen until you have enough to make this stock.

•

2 pounds Parmigiano–
Reggiano rinds

8 quarts water

In a large stockpot over medium heat, combine the Parm rinds and water and bring to a vigorous simmer. Simmer for 90 minutes, until the liquid is reduced by half.

Strain through a fine-mesh strainer into a heatproof container and discard the solids. Let cool completely.

TO FREEZE: Divide into 2- or 4-cup portions in lidded plastic or glass containers, label and date, and freeze for up to 4 months.

TO THAW: Use the pull and thaw method (see page 43) or the cold water method (see page 43).

ITALIAN WEDDING SOUP

SERVES 8 TO 10

With the stock and meatballs already prepared, you can build a really lovely, light soup. The spring vegetables here are barely cooked; they get just a quick sauté and then continue cooking in the warm stock while you eat. It keeps them just a little bit crispy, showing off their freshness.

In fact, if you wanted to skip the meatballs and double up on the vegetables, you could, and the soup would still be great.

•

3 tablespoons extra virgin olive oil, plus more for garnish

1 cup minced yellow onion

1 cup minced celery

1 cup minced carrot

1 cup thinly sliced leeks, white and light green parts

2 cups ½-inch-long asparagus pieces

1 cup shelled English peas

Kosher salt

3 quarts Parm Stock (opposite page), thawed

24 to 28 Pork Meatballs (page 185), thawed

6 tablespoons cold unsalted butter

Finely grated zest and juice of 2 lemons

Freshly ground black pepper, for garnish

Finely chopped fresh chives, for garnish

Finely grated Parmigiano-Reggiano cheese, for garnish

In a large Dutch oven or other heavy pot over medium-high heat, warm the oil. Add the onion, celery, carrot, and leeks and cook, stirring occasionally, for about 5 minutes, until the vegetables soften. Add the asparagus and peas, season with salt, and cook for 1 minute. Transfer the vegetables to a plate and set aside.

Add the stock and meatballs to the pot and bring to a boil over high heat. Turn down the heat to a simmer and simmer for 5 minutes.

Turn off the heat. Stir in the butter, lemon zest and juice, and reserved vegetables. Ladle into bowls and garnish each serving with black pepper, chives, a drizzle of oil, and a dusting of Parmigiano.

TOMATO AND GREENS MINESTRONE

SERVES 10 TO 12

It's pretty incredible how much our Parm Stock mimics cream in this soup. It gives the soup a velvety, rich texture that most tomato-based soups can't achieve. This minestrone is a great lunch in the fall and spring, the shoulder seasons when the weather is unpredictable and you're never sure if you'll be hot or cold.

•

¼ cup extra virgin olive oil, plus more for garnish

1 large yellow onion, diced

4 large garlic cloves, pressed through a garlic press

1 tablespoon plus 1 teaspoon kosher salt

One 28-ounce can diced tomatoes with their juice

8 cups Parm Stock (page 128), freshly made or thawed

2 rosemary sprigs

¼ cup Dijon mustard

1 cup Braised Greens (page 134), freshly made or thawed

One 13-ounce can cannellini beans, drained and rinsed

Freshly ground black pepper

Shaved Parmigiano-Reggiano cheese, for garnish

In a medium Dutch oven or other heavy pot over medium heat, warm the oil. Add the onion and garlic and cook, stirring constantly, for 5 to 7 minutes, until softened. Add the salt and the tomatoes and their juice and bring to a simmer. Cook, stirring occasionally, for 5 minutes. Add the stock and rosemary, increase the heat to high, and bring to a boil. Turn down the heat to a simmer and cook for 20 minutes. Stir in the mustard, greens, and beans and simmer for 10 minutes to meld the flavors.

TO FREEZE: If the stock and greens weren't previously frozen, you can freeze the soup at this point. Let the soup cool to room temperature, then portion into quart-size lidded containers or vacuum pouches and refrigerate until chilled. Label and date and freeze for up to 3 months.

TO REHEAT: Thaw using the pull and thaw method (see page 43) or the cold water method (see page 43). Reheat in a saucepan or Dutch oven over medium heat.

To serve, ladle into bowls, garnish with black pepper and a drizzle of oil and a scattering of shaved Parmigiano.

8

Vegetables.

134 **BRAISED GREENS**

Braised Greens and Paneer • 136

Tea-Brined Pork Chops with Braised Greens
and Tomatoes • 137

140 **CHIMICHURRI / PESTO / SALSA VERDE**

Baked Feta with Roasted Peppers, Capers,
and Salsa Verde • 143

Kale and Broccoli Slaw with Pesto-Avocado
Dressing • 144

Pan-Roasted Salmon with Chimichurri • 147

148 **CARAMELIZED ONIONS**

Line Cook's Grilled Cheese • 149

Provençal Onion Tart (Pissaladière)
with Tomato-Olive Relish • 150

Roasted Beets with Chickpeas, Herbed Yogurt,
and Caramelized Onion Vinaigrette • 153

154 **MASHED POTATOES**

Harissa Lamb, Eggplant, and Potato Gratin • 155

Hot Dog Casserole • 158

Twice-Baked Mashed Potatoes • 159

Potato Pierogi • 161

BRAISED GREENS

MAKES ABOUT 4 CUPS

Every so often, we like to knock out a big batch of braised greens and freeze it to have on hand. Once wilted, the textural changes that come from freezing greens are less noticeable, especially when you mix the greens into other dishes.

We intentionally keep the door open to flavor these greens in a bunch of different directions by treating them to just a little bit of garlic, salt, and olive oil. So if you're making this recipe to eat immediately as a side, feel free to finish them with a squeeze of lemon juice, a splash of cider vinegar, or a sprinkle of red pepper flakes.

4 pounds braising greens (such as collards, kale, chard, or a mixture)

¼ cup neutral vegetable oil

2 garlic cloves, thinly sliced

Kosher salt

½ cup olive oil

Carefully wash the greens by soaking in a cold water bath in your sink and rinsing them a few times with fresh water. (Greens tend to carry lots of sand and dirt, so be diligent in this step. Let all of the dirt and silt sink to the bottom of your sink.) Separate the leaves from their stems by tearing or slicing off the leaves. Thinly slice the stems, discarding any woody ends. Cut the leaves into roughly 1½-inch squares.

In a large stockpot or Dutch oven over medium heat, warm the vegetable oil. Add the stems and cook, stirring, for about 5 minutes, until they begin to soften. Add the garlic and cook for 1 minute more. Add the leaves in batches by the handful, stirring constantly and letting each addition wilt down a bit before adding more. Once all of the greens have been added, cover and let steam for 5 minutes.

Uncover and season generously with salt. Add 1 tablespoon of the olive oil and stir to coat the greens. Continue to cook, stirring occasionally and adding the remaining olive oil 1 tablespoon at a time, waiting for the greens to absorb the oil before adding the next tablespoon. By the time you've added the entire ½ cup olive oil, the greens—both the leaves and the stems—should be wilted and tender. If you're eating the greens immediately, serve hot. Otherwise, let cool to room temperature for storage.

TO FREEZE: Chill the greens in the refrigerator, then divide into 2-cup portions. Transfer to quart-size zip-top plastic bags or vacuum pouches, label and date, and freeze for up to 4 months.

TO THAW: Use the pull and thaw method (see page 43) or the cold water method (see page 43).

TO REHEAT: Place the thawed greens in a skillet over medium heat and cook, stirring until steaming and hot. Alternatively, reheat the greens in a microwave on medium power (5 out of 10 on our microwave's settings).

BRAISED GREENS AND PANEER

SERVES 2

Kait's favorite takeout is Kebab and Curry, an Indian place right across from the North Carolina State campus. Its *palak paneer* feels like a hug.

But having braised greens in the freezer makes it nearly as easy to cook up a version of our own. It comes together in under 20 minutes and incorporates a mix of greens in place of the spinach that's standard for most Indian restaurants in America. You can puree the greens to your liking. We like them slightly pureed, so they still have a little bit of texture.

•

2 tablespoons neutral vegetable oil

1 yellow onion, chopped

½ teaspoon peeled and minced fresh ginger

3 garlic cloves, minced

1 green chile (such as serrano), stemmed, seeded, and minced

1 teaspoon garam masala

1 teaspoon ground coriander

1 teaspoon ground turmeric

½ teaspoon black mustard seeds

4 cups Braised Greens (page 134), thawed

1 cup heavy cream

Kosher salt

8 ounces paneer, cut into ¾-inch cubes (see Note)

Cooked basmati rice, for serving

In a large saucepan over medium heat, warm the oil. When it shimmers, add the onion and cook, stirring occasionally, for 5 to 7 minutes, until it softens and is translucent. Add the ginger, garlic, and chile and cook, stirring occasionally, for 3 to 4 minutes, until they soften and smell fragrant. Add the garam masala, coriander, turmeric, and mustard seeds and stir to coat the vegetables with the spices. Let the spices toast for 1 to 2 minutes, then add the greens and stir well. Pour in the cream, bring to a simmer, and simmer for 4 to 5 minutes; the cream will reduce slightly. Stir in 1 teaspoon salt, then taste and adjust with more if needed.

Use an immersion blender to puree some of the greens into the cream, leaving the texture uneven. Add the paneer and stir to coat. Bring the greens back to a gentle simmer and cook for 5 minutes more to heat the paneer and allow the flavors to meld.

Serve hot over rice.

NOTE

If paneer is unavailable, halloumi or panela cheese will work as well.

TEA-BRINED PORK CHOPS
with Braised Greens and Tomatoes

SERVES 4

Smoke, salt, fat, acidity, bitterness. This is the essence of what we want to eat during the summer months—something from the grill paired with the season's best tomatoes (here, grated into a fresh, coarse sauce) and anchored with rich, nutrient-dense braised greens.

In the dead of winter, the visuals of this dinner will carry us forward: One of us manning the cooking, one of us chilling down a bottle of rosé—both of us in T-shirts and sunglasses because the sun won't set until well past dinnertime. Dogs underfoot, smoke from the charcoal, the hum of an insect and a porch fan.

⬤

Pork Chops

¼ cup honey

2 tablespoons Lapsang souchong tea leaves (pinewood-smoked black tea)

2 rosemary sprigs

8 cups water

Kosher salt

4 bone-in pasture-raised pork chops, each 1¼ inches thick

Greens and Tomatoes

2 pounds tomatoes, cored and halved

Kosher salt

3 tablespoons olive oil

4 garlic cloves, thinly sliced

4 cups Braised Greens (page 134), thawed

¼ teaspoon red pepper flakes

Prepare the pork chops: In a medium saucepan over medium heat, warm the honey until it begins to bubble. Add the tea leaves and rosemary and swirl the pan until the tea becomes aromatic (it will smell a little like a campfire or smoked meat). Add the water, increase the heat to high, and bring to a boil. Stir in ½ cup salt and remove from the heat. Let the brine cool, then strain and discard the tea leaves.

Place the pork chops in a single layer in a high-sided dish and pour in the brine. The brine should be a minimum of ¼ inch higher than the pork chops. Cover and brine the pork in the refrigerator for 8 hours.

Remove the chops from the brine and pat dry with a towel.

Fire up your grill, creating one side with direct high heat and one side with indirect medium heat. Brush the grill grates clean and coat lightly with oil.

Season the sear side of each chop (this is the side that looks most plump and presentable) evenly with salt and place the chops, sear side down, on the hottest part of the grill. After 2 minutes, using tongs, rotate each chop 90 degrees counterclockwise (this creates those beautiful diamond-shaped grill marks and also gives us twice as much of the flavor that the caramelization from those marks creates). Let cook for 2 minutes more. Season the raw side facing up with kosher salt just as you seasoned the first side. Flip each chop so the raw side is now facing the grill grates, being sure to stay on the hottest part of the grill. After 2 minutes, rotate the chops 90 degrees counterclockwise and cook for 2 minutes more.

continued →

TEA-BRINED PORK CHOPS

continued

Move the pork chops to the cooler part of the grill and cook over indirect heat for 10 to 12 minutes more, until an instant-read thermometer inserted into the center (not touching bone) registers 135°F. Remove the chops from the grill and let rest for 10 to 15 minutes. The pork will continue to rise in temperature to 145° to 150°F.

Meanwhile, start the greens and tomatoes: Place a box grater over a shallow bowl. Grate the flesh side of a tomato half against the large holes of the grater—it will produce a tomato pulp and lots of juice— until you get to the skin; discard the skin. Repeat with the remaining tomato halves. Season the tomato pulp and juice with 1 teaspoon salt.

In a large skillet over medium heat, warm the oil. When it shimmers, add the garlic and cook for 1 minute, until it starts to smell lightly toasted. Add the tomato pulp and juice, stir to mix with the oil, and bring to a simmer. Add the greens and stir to combine. Sprinkle in the pepper flakes and cook, stirring occasionally, for 5 minutes more to let the flavors meld. Taste and adjust the seasoning to preference.

Slice the pork chops from the bone and then cut against the grain into ¼-inch-thick slices. Place a spoonful of the greens and tomatoes onto each plate and top with a sliced pork chop. Serve immediately.

CHIMICHURRI / PESTO / SALSA VERDE

This family of herb-based purees can be used as sauces, garnishes, marinades, and more. We are going to be honest and say that if you're thawing these to use in an uncooked component of a dish (such as in a relish or garnish), the previously frozen version won't be quite as good as a freshly made batch. However, when incorporated into a cooked finish product, such as a pasta sauce, the difference is minuscule. Either way, for convenience and ease, these are helpful tools to have in your frozen tool kit. One important technique note: Do blanch the herbs before pureeing if you plan to freeze; you'll get a higher textural quality upon thawing.

You also have lots of options for portioning and storage here. We provide our favorite method below, but you could portion the puree into ice-cube trays for the formative freeze, then pop out the frozen cubes and store them in a zip-top plastic bag, pulling them as needed. This method creates pretty small portions, however, as the typical volume of a well in an ice-cube tray is 1 ounce (2 tablespoons). If you prefer to store ½-cup or 1-cup portions in lidded plastic or glass containers, that works, too.

Remember to thaw these purees slowly; exposing them to heat in the thawing process will detract from their quality.

●

MAKES ABOUT 3½ CUPS

Leaves and stems from ½ bunch cilantro (about ¼ cup loosely packed)

¾ ounce fresh mint leaves (1 cup loosely packed)

1½ ounces fresh flat-leaf parsley leaves (2¼ cups loosely packed)

2 garlic cloves, minced

2 small to medium shallots

2 tablespoons plus 1 teaspoon kosher salt

2 tablespoons red pepper flakes

1 cup red wine vinegar

2 cups extra virgin olive oil

Chimichurri

Bring a large pot of water to a boil over high heat. Set a large bowl filled with ice water on the counter next to it. Working in two batches, put the cilantro, mint, and parsley into a fine-mesh strainer and blanch in the boiling water for about 10 seconds, then immediately shock them in the ice bath. Drain the leaves and squeeze out the excess moisture.

In a food processor, combine the garlic, shallots, salt, and pepper flakes and process until a paste forms. Add the vinegar and herbs and pulse a few times to mix. With the motor running, add the oil and process until a coarse puree forms.

To freeze, see directions on opposite page.

Pesto

4 ounces fresh basil leaves (about 6 cups loosely packed)

2 tablespoons pine nuts

1½ teaspoons kosher salt

1½ cups extra virgin olive oil

1 garlic clove

1 cup finely grated Parmigiano-Reggiano cheese

1 cup finely grated Pecorino Romano cheese

Bring a large pot of water to a boil over high heat. Set a large bowl filled with ice water on the counter next to it. Working in two batches, put the basil leaves into a fine-mesh strainer and blanch in the boiling water for about 10 seconds, then immediately shock them in the ice water. Drain the leaves and squeeze out the excess moisture.

In a blender, combine the pine nuts, salt, and ½ cup of the oil and blend to a puree. Add the basil, garlic, and the remaining 1 cup oil and blend until the puree looks creamy. Add the cheeses and blend just until mixed.

To freeze, see directions below.

Salsa Verde

2 ounces arugula, spinach, or similar dark, tender green (about 3 cups loosely packed)

4 oil-cured anchovy fillets

Finely grated zest of 2 lemons

½ cup dry-roasted almonds

6 garlic cloves

6 green onions, white and light green parts, chopped

1 tablespoon kosher salt

1½ cups extra virgin olive oil

Bring a large pot of water to a boil over high heat. Set a large bowl filled with ice water on the counter next to it. Working in two batches, put the greens into a fine-mesh strainer and blanch in the boiling water for about 10 seconds, then immediately shock them in the ice bath. Drain the leaves and squeeze out the excess moisture.

In a food processor, combine the anchovies, lemon zest, almonds, garlic, green onions, and salt and pulse until a coarse puree forms. Add the greens and pulse a few times to mix. With the motor running, add the oil and process until a smooth puree forms.

TO FREEZE CHIMICHURRI, PESTO, OR SALSA VERDE: Line a rimmed baking sheet with parchment paper, with an inch overhang on all sides. Pour the puree onto the parchment in an even layer, and transfer to the freezer for at least 4 hours or up to overnight for a formative freeze (see page 31). Turn the "sheet" out onto a cutting board and cut it into pieces. Transfer the pieces to a zip-top plastic bag, label and date, and freeze for up to 2 months.

TO THAW CHIMICHURRI, PESTO, OR SALSA VERDE: Thaw the portion that you need in a small bowl in the refrigerator (see page 43) or, if using immediately, on the countertop.

BAKED FETA

with Roasted Peppers, Capers, and Salsa Verde

SERVES 4

Feta isn't much of a melting cheese, so when it's baked, it holds its shape while softening into a creamier, more spreadable version of its typically crumbly self. Loading it up with our garlicky Salsa Verde, capers, and peppers creates a cheese-dip effect—perfect for smearing on crackers or pita.

●

½ cup Salsa Verde
(page 141), thawed

2 tablespoons
drained capers

½ cup roasted red
peppers

½ cup olive oil

One 8-ounce block
feta cheese

Crackers or pita,
for serving

Preheat the oven to 350°F.

In a medium bowl, mix together the salsa verde, capers, peppers, and oil. Place the feta in a small baking dish and pour the salsa verde mixture over the top.

Bake for 15 to 20 minutes, until the feta gives way easily when prodded with a knife.

Serve the feta warm in its baking dish with crackers on the side.

KALE AND BROCCOLI SLAW
with Pesto-Avocado Dressing

SERVES 8

This slaw is heavy on crunch, thanks to raw kale and broccoli. To keep it from being too much so, be sure to cut the vegetables quite finely. We usually advocate for cheese as a component of any salad but chose to show restraint here. The pesto is rich with Parmigiano and Pecorino Romano and provides that salty, briny note through its presence in the dressing.

●

2 bunches Lacinato kale

2 heads broccoli
(with stems)

1 medium red onion

Juice of 1 lemon

¼ cup extra virgin olive oil

1 teaspoon kosher salt

Dressing

2 ripe avocados, halved
and pitted

¼ cup sour cream

¼ cup mayonnaise

½ cup Pesto (page 141),
thawed

Kosher salt

Prepare the slaw: Separate the leaves from the stems. Thinly slice the leaves and put them into a large bowl. Trim any woody or tough ends from the stems, then finely chop and add to the bowl with the leaves.

Cut the broccoli florets from the stems. Finely dice the florets and add to the bowl with the kale. Use a vegetable peeler or knife to trim off the woody exterior from the stems, then trim off the tough ends. Finely dice the tender part of the stems and add to the bowl with the kale.

Cut the red onion in half through the stem end and thinly slice. Break up the slices into individual pieces and add to the bowl.

Drizzle the lemon juice and oil over the vegetables and then sprinkle with the salt. Massage the vegetables with your hands to mix everything together thoroughly. Let sit while you make the dressing.

Make the dressing: Scoop out the flesh of the avocados from the peel and drop into a food processor. Add the sour cream, mayonnaise, and pesto and process until smooth. Taste and season with salt if necessary (but remember that the salad is already seasoned with salt). You should have about 2 cups. The dressing will keep in a lidded container in the refrigerator for up to 3 days.

Add ½ cup of the dressing to the salad and toss to coat. Taste and add more if desired, then serve.

PAN-ROASTED SALMON

with Chimichurri

SERVES 2

We've blabbed on and on about how stocking your freezer makes for easier, quicker meals later on, and here's your proof. This pan-roasted salmon would be fine on its own, with just a spritz of lemon juice and the butter from the pan. But it is exceedingly more delicious with the addition of the chimichurri (in our opinion), and still clocks in under 15 minutes of cook time if you already have the sauce made. If you live for life hacks and productivity boosters, bookmark this page.

●

Two 6-ounce skinless salmon fillets

Kosher salt and freshly ground black pepper

2 tablespoons unsalted butter

¼ cup Chimichurri (page 140), thawed

Preheat the oven to 350°F.

Season the salmon fillets all over with salt and pepper. In a large oven-safe skillet over medium heat, melt the butter. When the foaming subsides, add the fillets to the pan. Cook undisturbed for 3 minutes, then flip the fillets and continue to cook for another 3 minutes. In the last minute, tilt the pan toward you, scoop up the brown butter in the pan, and spoon it over the fillets, basting them repeatedly for 30 seconds.

Transfer the pan to the oven and cook for another 5 minutes, just until the salmon is barely opaque all the way through.

To serve, place the salmon fillets on two plates and drizzle with the chimichurri.

CARAMELIZED ONIONS

**MAKES ABOUT
2½ CUPS**

Our friend (and a former editor of Kait's) Francis Lam likes to call bullshit on caramelized onion recipes that take less than a half hour. He's right to do so: the key factor in turning ordinary white or yellow onions into that rich, caramel-colored goo of sweet-savory flavor is time. Since we love cooking with caramelized onions but rarely have the patience to wait for them, freezing them for easier and more frequent use makes a ton of sense—in fact, caramelized onions were one of the first recipes we jotted down when dreaming of this cookbook.

This recipe is for a modest batch of 2½ cups; you should probably double it every time you make it. That way, you consolidate not only your time but also the tears you'll surely shed cutting this many onions.

●

5 pounds yellow onions, halved and thinly sliced (about 15 cups)

2 tablespoons kosher salt

¼ cup extra virgin olive oil

2 cups water

In a very large heavy pot or Dutch oven, combine the onions and the salt and let sit for 10 minutes. Add the olive oil, stir to coat, and place the pot over high heat until steam begins to rise from the pan. Lower the heat to medium, cover, and cook undisturbed for 20 minutes.

Now, uncover the pots. As you lift off the lids, lots of moisture will escape and you will see that the onions have begun to caramelize. Increase the heat to medium-high and cook, stirring constantly, for another 15 to 20 minutes, until the onions are a deep amber and are thick and sticky. If the onions begin to stick to the pan, deglaze with water, 1 tablespoon at a time. Remove from the heat and let cool to room temperature.

TO FREEZE: When completely cool, divide the onions into 1-cup portions and transfer to quart-size zip-top plastic bags or lidded plastic containers. Label and date and freeze for up to 3 months.

TO THAW: Use the pull and thaw method (see page 43) or the cold water method (see page 43).

LINE COOK'S GRILLED CHEESE

MAKES 1 SANDWICH

Why is this called a line cook's grilled cheese? Because the conditions are always right for making this sandwich after working a line shift at Poole's, our restaurant. Namely, there are always little nubbins and end pieces of really high-quality cheese (cheese-board cheese, as Ashley calls it) that you don't want to waste but also seem silly to save; there are always a couple of spoonfuls of caramelized onions at the bottom of the quart container; and there are always the exhaustion and appetite you've worked up after a long shift, for which a grilled cheese is a good fix.

This is delicious with an ice-cold Coca Cola, or a Martini.

•

2 slices sourdough bread

1 tablespoon mayonnaise

1 tablespoon whole-grain mustard

¼ cup Caramelized Onions (opposite page), thawed

4 ounces mixed "cheese-board cheese" (aged Cheddar, Gruyère, Jarlsberg, and so on), thinly sliced

2 tablespoons unsalted butter

Preheat the oven to 400°F.

Lay the bread slices on a cutting board. Spread the mayonnaise on 1 slice. Spread the mustard on the other slice. On the slice with the mayonnaise, arrange the caramelized onions in an even layer. On the side with the mustard, arrange the cheese in an even layer. Press the bread together, toppings facing in, to form a sandwich.

In a small skillet over medium-high heat, melt 1 tablespoon of the butter. When it melts, place the sandwich in the skillet and toast for about 4 minutes, until the bottom side of the bread is nicely golden brown. Lift the sandwich with a spatula and add the remaining 1 tablespoon butter to the skillet. When it melts, flip the sandwich so the browned side is now facing up. Toast for another 3 to 4 minutes, until the bottom side is nicely golden brown.

Transfer the sandwich to a small rimmed baking sheet and place in the oven. Bake for about 8 minutes, until the cheese is fully melted.

Slice the sandwich in half and serve.

PROVENÇAL ONION TART (PISSALADIÈRE)

with Tomato-Olive Relish

SERVES 12

If we ever needed convincing about the power of food photography (we don't, by the way—we're convinced), this recipe serves as a reminder. After flipping through Instagram and seeing a version of this French *pissaladière* posted on the account for King, a restaurant in New York City, Kait felt nearly compelled to get up and try making one. It was the perfect mix of social media bait: it conjured memories of a great meal in that restaurant, aspirations of sitting on a patio in the South of France while eating slices of this tart with a cold glass of Bandol, and confidence that we could easily make a version of it without too much fuss.

When we started scanning recipes and realized that caramelized onions were a key, if not main, component, you can imagine our relief that we had a container in our freezer, ready for just such inspiration to strike!

●

Make the tart: Preheat the oven to 425°F.

On a lightly floured work surface, roll out the puff pastry into a rectangle about 19 by 14 inches. Lay the puff pastry inside an 18 by 13-inch rimmed baking sheet, pushing the edges up the sides of the pan to form a rimmed crust. Dock the surface of the dough all over with a fork.

In a small bowl, mix together the onions, rosemary, and thyme. Arrange the onions in an even layer over the dough. Then arrange the anchovies in a crosshatch pattern over the onions.

Bake for about 20 minutes, until the crust is cooked through and golden brown. While the tart bakes, make the relish.

Make the relish: In a medium bowl, stir together all of the relish ingredients, mixing well.

Let the tart cool slightly, then cut into squares. Spoon some of the relish on top of each square and serve warm.

Tart

One 14-ounce sheet frozen puff pastry, thawed

2 cups Caramelized Onions (page 148), thawed

½ teaspoon chopped fresh rosemary

½ teaspoon chopped fresh thyme

20 oil-cured anchovy fillets

Relish

3 heirloom or beefsteak tomatoes, cored and finely diced

½ cup pitted black French olives, minced

¼ cup extra virgin olive oil

1 shallot, finely minced

ROASTED BEETS

with Chickpeas, Herbed Yogurt, and Caramelized Onion Vinaigrette

SERVES 4

Caramelized onions, thanks to their natural sugars, are almost jam-like in flavor and texture, and these attributes work really well with the acidity and punch of a vinaigrette.

We love the way the flavors of this vinaigrette meld against a roasted beet salad (a match for onions' earthy sweetness!), but it could be used on so much. Look for other ingredients that straddle that earthy-sweet line, like roasted winter squash or tomatoes.

1 pound medium beets, tops removed

One 13½–ounce can chickpeas

6 tablespoons extra virgin olive oil

Kosher salt and freshly ground black pepper

¼ cup firmly packed fresh mint leaves, chopped

¼ cup firmly packed fresh flat-leaf parsley leaves, chopped

2 tablespoons fresh cilantro leaves, chopped

1 cup full-fat plain Greek yogurt

Vinaigrette

½ cup Caramelized Onions (page 148), thawed

2 tablespoons sherry vinegar

1½ teaspoons Dijon mustard

1 cup neutral vegetable oil

Kosher salt and freshly ground black pepper

Preheat the oven to 400°F. Pour water to a depth of ¼ inch into a 9 by 13-inch baking dish. Add the beets and cover the dish securely with aluminum foil. Bake for 1 to 1½ hours, until a knife can be easily inserted into the beets.

Remove the beets from the oven. When cool enough to handle, rub off their skins with a paper towel. (The beets can be roasted up to 2 days ahead and stored in zip-top plastic bags in the refrigerator. Let come to room temperature before using.)

Meanwhile, drain and rinse the chickpeas and pat dry. Transfer to a rimmed baking sheet, drizzle with 2 tablespoons of the olive oil, and season with salt and pepper. Mix with your hands to make sure all of the chickpeas are coated. Transfer to the oven and roast, rotating the pan 180 degrees halfway through roasting, for about 20 minutes, until the chickpeas are bronze colored and crispy.

Reserve 1 teaspoon each of the mint, parsley, and cilantro for garnish and put the remainder into a medium bowl. Add the yogurt, ¼ teaspoon salt, and the remaining 4 tablespoons oil and mix well. Set aside.

Make the vinaigrette: In a food processor, combine half of the cara-melized onions, the vinegar, and the mustard. Pulse until the mixture forms a chunky paste. With the motor running, slowly add the vege-table oil and process until emulsified. Transfer the mixture to a bowl and stir in the other half of the caramelized onions. Season to taste with salt and pepper. You should have about 1⅔ cups. The vinaigrette will keep in a lidded container in the refrigerator for up to 1 week.

Cut the beets into bite-size wedges and transfer to a large bowl. Drizzle with ¼ cup of the vinaigrette and toss to coat.

Divide the yogurt among four bowls, spreading it around the base of each bowl. Pile the beets over the yogurt and top with the chickpeas. Garnish with the reserved herbs and serve.

MASHED POTATOES

**MAKES 2 QUARTS
PLUS 3 CUPS**

Mashed potatoes make the freezer pantry cut for a couple of reasons: Of course, they're delicious on their own, and a satisfying thing to be able to heat up and enjoy quickly. But more than that, they're great as an ingredient, too, and they transform into different dishes easily and successfully. They can act almost like a binder, as a filling (like in the pierogi on page 161), and as a base.

You'll get the best freezing and reheating results using vacuum sealing and sous vide as your packaging and reheating techniques. If you don't have access to these methods, you may want to reconstitute the potatoes with a little bit of warm milk to help achieve peak creaminess.

6 quarts water

6 tablespoons kosher salt

5 pounds Yukon gold potatoes, cut into 2-inch pieces

1 cup half-and-half

½ cup unsalted butter, cut into eight pieces

Fill a large pot with the water and add the salt. Add the potatoes and bring to a boil over high heat. Cook for 5 minutes, then lower the heat to medium and cook an additional 10 minutes, until tender when pierced with a knife. Drain the potatoes well, then transfer them to the bowl of a stand mixer fitted with the paddle attachment.

Add the half-and-half and the butter to the mixer. Turn on to medium-low speed and mix until smooth. Season additionally to your preference if needed.

If eating now, serve immediately while still hot.

TO FREEZE: Transfer the potatoes to a large rimmed baking sheet and spread them out into an even layer to cool faster. Once cooled to room temperature, divide the potatoes into 1-quart portions and put each portion into a vacuum pouch or zip-top plastic bag, spreading the potatoes into an even layer that can be stored flat. Label and date and freeze for up to 4 months.

TO THAW: Use the pull and thaw method (see page 43) or the cold water method (see page 43).

TO REHEAT: If stored in vacuum pouches, reheating from frozen using the sous vide method works well. Set the sous vide water bath to 145°F and drop in the pouch. It will take 1 hour to reach temperature. Otherwise, thaw first, then transfer the potatoes to a saucepan and reheat on the stove over medium-low heat. Add up to ¼ cup warm whole milk per quart of potatoes as needed to enhance creaminess.

HARISSA LAMB, EGGPLANT, AND POTATO GRATIN

SERVES 12

When working on this recipe, we couldn't quite decide if we wanted to make a version of moussaka (the eggplant casserole topped with béchamel) or shepherd's pie (the ground meat dish topped with mashed potatoes). Sometimes indecision is a good thing; this Franken-recipe is the best of both worlds.

We decided to layer the mashed potatoes on top (rather than just spooning them on) in a conquest for the perfect bite. That's what Ashley calls the bite that has every component of the dish represented. Most of the time, you have to make a perfect bite yourself, piling a small bit of each ingredient onto your fork. But here, that construction is architected for you: simply swoop your spoon through the layers and you're good to go.

This casserole freezes well if the mashed potatoes haven't previously been frozen.

2 small to medium globe eggplants (2 pounds total)

Kosher salt

4 tablespoons neutral vegetable oil

2 pounds ground lamb

2 cups diced yellow onion (about 1 large)

5 garlic cloves, minced

1 tablespoon dried mint

1 tablespoon dried oregano

½ teaspoon ground cumin

1 teaspoon sweet paprika

½ teaspoon ground cinnamon

1 tablespoon tomato paste

½ cup harissa paste

1 cup dry red wine

One 28-ounce can whole tomatoes, drained

2 cups beef stock or thawed Freezer Chicken Stock (page 204)

Thinly slice the eggplants into rounds about ⅛ inch thick. Put the slices into a colander, sprinkle with 1 tablespoon salt, and toss to coat evenly. Let sit for 1 hour, tossing the eggplant every 15 minutes. Pat the slices dry with a paper towel.

In a large Dutch oven or other heavy pot over medium heat, warm 2 tablespoons of the oil until it shimmers. Add the lamb and 1 teaspoon salt and cook, breaking it up with the back of a wooden spoon, for about 6 minutes, until no pink remains. Transfer the meat to a plate.

Add the remaining 2 tablespoons oil and the onion to the pot and cook, stirring occasionally, for 5 to 7 minutes, until softened and almost translucent. Stir in the garlic and cook, stirring, for 2 minutes more. Stir in the mint, oregano, cumin, paprika, and cinnamon and cook, stirring occasionally, for 2 to 3 minutes; the spices should be very fragrant. Add the tomato paste and harissa and cook for 5 to 6 minutes to caramelize the sugars in the paste a little bit. Pour in the wine and increase the heat to high. Bring the wine to a boil, lower the heat to a simmer, and reduce for 6 to 8 minutes, until almost completely evaporated.

Pour the tomatoes and their juices into a small bowl and use your hands to crush them up well. Add the reserved lamb and the tomatoes to the pot and stir to mix. Season with 1 tablespoon plus 2 teaspoons salt, then pour in the stock and bring to a simmer.

continued →

2 quarts Mashed Potatoes
(page 154), freshly made
or thawed

2 large eggs, beaten

1 cup finely grated
Parmesan cheese

8 ounces feta cheese,
crumbled

Chopped fresh mint and
flat-leaf parsley, for serving

Let simmer, stirring occasionally, for 25 minutes to meld the flavors and
let the stock reduce a bit. Turn down the heat to low and keep warm.

In a medium bowl, mix together the potatoes, eggs, half of the
Parmesan, and half of the feta. Set aside.

Preheat the oven to 350°F.

Ladle about 1 cup of the lamb sauce into a 9 by 13-inch baking dish
and spread it into an even layer. Follow with a layer of eggplant slices
and then a layer of about 1½ cups lamb sauce, then half of the mashed
potato mixture. Repeat the layers: 1½ cups sauce, a layer of eggplant,
1½ cups sauce, then the remaining half of the mashed potato mixture.
Sprinkle the remaining Parmesan and feta over the top. (If the potatoes
have not been previously frozen, you can freeze the unbaked gratin at
this point; see below.)

Bake for 55 to 60 minutes; the potato topping should take on some
golden brown color in spots, and the mixture should be bubbling. Let
rest for 10 minutes before serving. Garnish each portion with some
fresh mint and parsley.

TO FREEZE: If the mashed potatoes have not been previously frozen,
let the dish cool to room temperature, then refrigerate until well
chilled. Wrap the baking dish in two layers of plastic wrap, label and
date, and freeze for up to 3 months.

TO BAKE FROM FROZEN: Unwrap the baking dish and cover the
top with aluminum foil. Place in a cold oven and set the oven to 350°F.
When the oven reaches temperature, bake, removing the foil after
45 minutes, for 1½ hours, until a knife inserted into the center comes
out hot to the touch.

HOT DOG CASSEROLE

SERVES 8

This was one of Ashley's favorite dinners as a kid, made by her "Aunt" Marge, the mother of her godmother, Aunt Suze. Aunt Marge made it with classic beef hot dogs, but Ashley's mom, upon seeking out the recipe to placate requests from Ashley, decided to switch out the hot dogs in favor of kielbasas. However, the original name lives on and continues to inspire picky kids to eat their dinner.

Two 12-ounce packages kielbasas, diagonally sliced 1 inch thick

3 cups sauerkraut

2 quarts Mashed Potatoes (page 154), freshly made or thawed

2 large eggs

4 green onions, white and green parts, thinly sliced

1 tablespoon kosher salt

¼ teaspoon ground white pepper

1 pound sharp Cheddar cheese, grated

Preheat the oven to 350°F.

Place a large skillet over medium-high heat. When the pan is hot, add the kielbasas and sear on both sides. Transfer to a cutting board and let cool slightly.

Drain the sauerkraut and set aside. In a medium bowl, combine the potatoes. eggs, green onions, salt, white pepper, and half of the cheese and mix well.

In a 9 by 13-inch baking dish, arrange the kielbasa slices in an even layer. Top with the sauerkraut and then the potato mixture, spreading them both evenly. Layer the remaining cheese evenly over the top.

Bake for 20 to 25 minutes, until hot throughout and bubbly. Let sit for 5 minutes, then scoop heaping spoonfuls into bowls to serve.

TO FREEZE: If the mashed potatoes have not been previously frozen, let the dish cool to room temperature, then refrigerate until well chilled. Wrap the baking dish in two layers of plastic wrap, label and date, and freeze for up to 4 months.

TO REHEAT: Unwrap the dish, place in a cold oven, and set the oven to 400°F. Heat for 1 hour, until a knife inserted into the center comes out hot to the touch.

TWICE-BAKED MASHED POTATOES

SERVES 6 TO 8

Intersecting at the point where a loaded baked potato meets mashed potatoes, this dish is a major crowd-pleaser. We usually reserve it for a "steak house dinner," pairing it with a great steak, an iceberg wedge salad, and a side of Braised Greens (page 134). But don't let us close you off from other options. We wouldn't freeze this one; it's better to enjoy it on the same day you make it.

3 slices bacon (about 1 ounce), chopped

10 ounces sharp Cheddar cheese, grated

4 cups Mashed Potatoes (page 154), thawed

3 green onions, white and green parts, thinly sliced

1 tablespoon prepared horseradish

2 tablespoons sour cream

2 large eggs

1½ teaspoons kosher salt

½ teaspoon freshly ground black pepper

Preheat the oven to 400°F.

Put the bacon into a cold skillet, place over medium heat, and cook, stirring frequently, for 7 to 9 minutes, until crispy and the fat has rendered. Transfer the bacon to a paper towel–lined plate and reserve 2 tablespoons of the fat.

Divide the cheese in half. Put half into a large bowl and reserve the other half. Add the potatoes and green onions to the bowl and mix well with the cheese.

In a small bowl, whisk together the horseradish, sour cream, and eggs. Fold the horseradish mixture into the potato mixture, mixing well. Fold in the reserved bacon fat and crispy bacon pieces. Stir in the salt and black pepper.

Spoon the mixture into a 2-quart baking dish. Bake for about 20 minutes, then top with the remaining cheese and bake for an additional 12 to 15 minutes, until the cheese has melted and the casserole is bubbly. Let sit for 5 minutes, then scoop onto plates and serve.

POTATO PIEROGI

Our friend Lauren Ivey got us hooked on the idea of freezer pierogi. She has Polish-descended family on her dad's side and grew up eating pierogi with her grandparents, who live in Ohio. As they've gotten older, she has taken on the pierogi as her project, and she makes a big batch that she freezes before she goes to visit them so she can stock their freezer.

We've been the lucky recipients of a bag of Lauren's frozen potato pierogi a few times, and have relied on our stash to provide a quick meal more than once. They are mild and flexible enough to dress up however you like—with sour cream and apple butter, as written here, or with some sautéed mushrooms or spinach. Once we came across a pierogi Benedict on a restaurant brunch menu that featured pan-seared pierogi topped with a poached egg and hollandaise, and how could that ever be bad?

•

Dough

2 large eggs

1 cup water

¼ cup sour cream

4 cups all-purpose flour

1 tablespoon kosher salt

Filling

3 slices bacon (about 1 ounce), cooked until crispy and cooled

2 cups Mashed Potatoes (page 154), thawed

1 cup farmer cheese or ricotta cheese, drained

2 tablespoons Caramelized Onions (page 148), thawed (optional)

2 large egg yolks

1 tablespoon all-purpose flour

½ teaspoon freshly ground black pepper

½ teaspoon kosher salt

Make the dough: In a medium bowl, whisk together the eggs, water, and sour cream. In a food processor, combine about 3½ cups of the flour and the salt and pulse a few times to mix. With the motor running, add the wet ingredients, stopping the machine as soon as the mixture comes together into a dough.

Turn the dough out onto a well-floured work surface and form into a ball. Knead the dough a few times with the base of your palm, adding more of the flour as needed until a smooth dough forms that does not stick to your hand or the work surface. Press the dough into a thick disk, wrap in plastic wrap, and let rest at room temperature for 1 hour.

Meanwhile, make the filling: Chop the cooled bacon into small bites. In a medium bowl, combine the bacon, potatoes, cheese, onions, egg yolks, flour, and pepper and mix well. Stir in the salt and set aside.

Assemble the pierogi: Line a rimmed baking sheet with parchment paper. Cut the dough into quarters. On a well-floured work surface, roll out one-fourth of the dough about ⅛ inch thick. Using a 5-inch round pastry or biscuit cutter, cut out as many rounds as possible (set dough scraps aside). To shape the pierogi, stretch each round slightly as if you were stretching a tiny pizza. Holding the round in your open palm, spoon about 2 teaspoons of the filling onto the center of each round. Then, using your fingers or a pastry brush, moisten the edge of the round with the egg, fold the round in half over the filling, and press the edges together to form a half-moon. Crimp the curved edge with the tines of a fork to help seal. As the pierogi are ready, transfer

continued →

POTATO PIEROGI

continued

To Assemble and Serve

1 large egg, beaten

Kosher salt

½ cup unsalted butter

¼ cup neutral vegetable oil

Sour cream, for serving

Apple butter, for serving

them to the prepared pan. Repeat with the remaining dough quarters and filling. Pull together the dough scraps and form into a ball. Roll out ⅛ inch thick and cut out as many rounds as possible. Repeat with filling and shaping.

TO FREEZE: Place the baking sheet of uncooked pierogi in the freezer for at least 4 hours or up to overnight for a formative freeze (see page 31). Slide them into a zip-top plastic bag, label and date, and freeze for up to 4 months.

TO COOK AND SERVE: Bring a large pot of salted water to a boil. Working in batches of ten pierogi, lower the pierogi into the water and boil for 2 to 3 minutes (or 3 to 4 minutes if boiling from frozen), until the dough is cooked through and the filling is hot. Using a wire skimmer, transfer the pierogi to a paper towel–lined plate to dry slightly.

Meanwhile, in a large skillet over medium heat, melt the butter with the oil. Once the foaming subsides, stir the butter until it begins to brown and smell nutty. When all of the pierogi are cooked, add them to the pan and gently fold them into the brown butter for 2 to 3 minutes.

Transfer the pierogi to a serving plate and drizzle the brown butter over the top. Serve with the sour cream and apple butter on the side.

Freezer-
FRIENDLY
DISHES

PART THREE

This section holds the dishes that you were probably envisioning when you picked up a "freezer" cookbook. It contains recipes for fully composed dishes that you can eat now or freeze for later. Looking to cook something for a homebound friend? Seeking meals to make ahead of time for a busy week? This is your section.

At our house, we typically try to plan ahead for two or three of the week's meals, using fully prepped dishes (like the ones in this chapter) from our freezer. The other four or five days of the week are more of an improv, guided by what we're in the mood for and leaving space for a night out.

This approach works great, assuming your freezer is already stocked with these items. But building up your inventory will take time. We suggest that every time you decide to cook one of the dishes in this section, consider doubling the recipe. Instead of one dish of Tex-Mex Cheese Enchiladas (page 211), make two. Stock up on cookie dough by knocking out both cookie recipes (pages 225 and 226) in one day. If you've already committed to spend time cooking in your kitchen one day, double down on the time spent. It won't take double the time (usually), and you'll be saving yourself future labor by loading up the freezer.

But don't forget to make a freezer inventory that you can maintain and update, so you're eating this bounty at the same rate you're cooking it. Get into a rhythm: every time you open your freezer to put something into it, make a plan to take something out and eat it. This will save you from winding up with a freezer stuffed with out-of-date food.

Breakfast and brunch dishes.

Egg, Potato, and Cheddar
Breakfast Burritos • 168

Cheesy Sausage and Sage Waffles • 170

Pistachio Croissant French Toast
with Orange Blossom Soft Cream • 173

Tortilla Breakfast Pie • 175

Chocolate Chia Pudding • 178

EGG, POTATO, AND CHEDDAR BREAKFAST BURRITOS

MAKES 4 BURRITOS

To stash your freezer with delicious, homemade breakfast burritos is to give a gift to your future hungover self. It's one of our favorite forms of self-care. We came up with this recipe to remedy the morning after one of those impromptu nights that go just a little bit longer than you're expecting. It checks every box for those days when you need to be a grown-up and get out of bed, but you really don't want to.

Adding cottage cheese to scrambled eggs helps to "freezer-proof" them—they retain a better, fluffier texture. The microwave is our favorite way to heat up burritos, but you can also do it in the oven.

●

12 ounces Yukon gold potatoes (about 3 medium)

1 teaspoon olive oil

1 teaspoon kosher salt

8 large eggs

½ cup full-fat cottage cheese

2 tablespoons unsalted butter

1 cup shredded cheese (see Note)

½ cup Salsa Verde (page 141), thawed (optional)

4 extra-large flour tortillas

Preheat the oven to 400°F.

Poke the skin of each potato several times with the tines of a fork. Coat the potatoes lightly with the oil and then season them with ¼ teaspoon of the salt. Place on a rimmed baking sheet and bake for about 40 minutes, until fork-tender. Let cool completely.

Meanwhile, in a blender, combine the eggs, cottage cheese, and ¼ teaspoon of the salt and blend on low speed until smooth. Let rest in the blender for 10 minutes. Pulse on low speed for 30 seconds.

In a medium skillet over medium heat, melt the butter. Add the egg mixture and, using a heat-resistant spatula, stir constantly, being sure to move the spatula across the bottom of the pan and bring the thin cooked layers to the top. Cook for about 5 minutes, until the eggs are done but still have a creamy texture. Remove the pan from the heat and transfer the eggs to a cool container to stop the cooking. Let cool completely.

Dice the cooled potatoes into ½-inch pieces, transfer to a medium bowl, and season with the remaining ½ teaspoon salt. Add the eggs, cheese, and salsa verde and mix together.

Lay a tortilla on a work surface. Spoon one-fourth of the egg mixture in a cylindrical mound horizontally along the center of the tortilla, leaving about 3 inches uncovered on both sides. Fold the bottom half of the tortilla over the mixture, then fold in each side of the tortilla, and finally roll the whole thing up over itself, forming the burrito. Set aside seam side down. Repeat with the remaining tortillas and filling.

TO FREEZE: Place each burrito on a sheet of parchment paper and wrap it in the parchment the same way you wrapped the tortilla around the filling: fold the bottom over the burrito, fold in the sides, and then roll up to the top. Tape the parchment to secure it. Repeat with the remaining burritos. Transfer the wrapped burritos to a zip-top plastic bag, label and date, and freeze for up to 3 months.

TO HEAT FROM FROZEN IN THE MICROWAVE: Remove the parchment from the burrito. Wrap a lightly dampened paper towel around the burrito (this will create steam in the microwave that will help resoften the tortilla) and place on a microwave-safe plate. Place in the microwave, set the microwave on a medium-high heat setting (6 or 7 out of 10 on ours), and microwave for about 2 minutes. Flip the burrito and microwave for another 2 minutes, until hot throughout.

TO HEAT FROM FROZEN IN THE OVEN: Place the burrito on a small rimmed baking sheet, place in a cold oven, and set the oven to 400°F. Heat for 20 to 25 minutes, until hot throughout.

NOTE

Ashley likes to use a mix of sharp Cheddar and Monterey Jack cheeses, but this is all about personal preference, so run with it.

CHEESY SAUSAGE AND SAGE WAFFLES

MAKES 8 WAFFLES

We're not waffle-ordering people.* We prefer the cheesy, sausage-loaded thing on any given breakfast menu. But waffles make *great* freezer pastries, so we have chosen to hop on the bandwagon of this breakfast of champions.

Here's our best attempt to stay true to ourselves while embracing the freezer breakfast lifestyle: a waffle dressed up as the cheesy, sausage-loaded thing. This waffle batter is studded with shredded mozzarella and crumbled pork sausage. When heated, the cheese crisps up, creating a nearly crunchy waffle exterior. Dipped in maple syrup, it's a case study for the merits of sweet-savory flavor pairings.

•

1 pound loose breakfast sausage

1¾ cups all-purpose flour

2 teaspoons baking powder

¼ teaspoon baking soda

1 tablespoon sugar

½ teaspoon kosher salt

3 large eggs

½ cup unsalted butter, melted and cooled

1½ cups full-fat buttermilk

2 cups shredded mozzarella cheese

½ cup shredded Parmesan cheese

4 fresh sage leaves, minced

Pure maple syrup, for serving

In a large skillet over medium heat, cook the sausage, breaking it up with the back of a wooden spoon, for 8 to 10 minutes, until crumbled and no pink remains. Transfer to a paper towel–lined plate and let cool completely.

In a medium bowl, whisk together the flour, baking powder, baking soda, sugar, and salt. In a small bowl, whisk together the eggs, butter, and buttermilk. Add the wet ingredients to the dry ingredients and fold together with a rubber spatula just until mixed. Fold in the sausage, mozzarella, Parmesan, and sage.

Preheat a waffle maker. If your waffle maker has heat settings, set it to medium. Spray the grids with nonstick cooking spray. Ladle some of the batter onto the bottom grid (about ¾ cup for a standard 7- to 8-inch round waffle), close the lid, and cook for about 4 minutes, until cooked through and golden brown. Transfer to a wire rack to cool. Repeat with the remaining batter.

TO FREEZE: Let the waffles cool completely at room temperature. Wrap each waffle individually in plastic wrap and carefully place the waffles in a zip-top plastic bag. Label and date and freeze for up to 3 months.

TO REHEAT FROM FROZEN: Pull a waffle from the plastic bag and unwrap it. Toast in a toaster on medium-high heat until warm and crispy throughout. Alternatively, preheat the oven to 350°F, place the waffle on a rimmed baking sheet, and heat for about 15 minutes, until warm and crispy throughout.

Drizzle with maple syrup and serve.

● **CHEFFIN' IT UP**

Cut into quarters, these waffles also make elegant party snacks. Top with a dollop of crème fraîche and a spoonful of caviar.

* The notable exception to this generalization is, of course, the pecan waffle at Waffle House.

PISTACHIO CROISSANT FRENCH TOAST

with Orange Blossom Soft Cream

SERVES 12

To make a good croissant is a real labor of love. But even the best ones begin to lose their luster pretty quickly—on day two, they're just not as delicious. This recipe started as a "how to use up days-old croissants" idea when Ashley brought Kait home some beautiful but slightly stale croissants from Du Pain et des Idées in Paris. It's basically a bread pudding, so you could use cubed brioche or even plain old white bread if you don't have any leftover croissants lying around. (That said, check with your local bakery or coffee shop at the end of the day. Often times, they have leftover pastries they can't sell the next day and are looking to find homes for.)

When we freeze these, we like to portion them in single servings. That means you can enjoy a fancy breakfast even if it's just you.

1 cup pistachios

4 large eggs

4 cups half-and-half

1½ cups firmly packed light brown sugar

¾ teaspoon pure vanilla extract

1 teaspoon kosher salt

Finely grated zest of 1 small orange

4 large croissants, cut into 1-inch cubes

Orange Blossom Soft Cream, for serving (recipe follows)

Preheat the oven to 350°F.

Spread the pistachios on a rimmed baking sheet and toast, stirring the nuts and rotating the pan 180 degrees after 3 minutes to ensure even toasting, for 6 minutes, until they are fragrant and have taken on some color. Set aside.

In a large bowl, whisk the eggs until blended. Add the half-and-half, sugar, vanilla, salt, and orange zest and whisk until incorporated.

Coat a 9 by 13-inch glass baking dish with butter or nonstick cooking spray. Transfer the croissant cubes and the pistachios to the baking dish. Shake the dish gently so the cubes fit in the dish and level out. Ladle the egg mixture over the cubes, being sure to cover all of them. Once all of the egg mixture is in the dish, lay a piece of parchment paper or plastic wrap over the surface and, using your palms, apply gentle pressure to submerge all of the cubes in the liquid. Let the dish sit at room temperature for 1 hour, repeating the pressing step every 15 minutes or so.

Remove the parchment or plastic wrap and cover the dish with aluminum foil. Bake for 30 minutes. Remove the foil, rotate the dish 180 degrees, and bake for about 15 minutes longer, until the custard is set and the surface is golden brown.

If serving immediately, remove from the oven and let cool for 15 minutes, then cut into squares and serve each square topped with a dollop of the soft cream.

continued →

173

PISTACHIO CROISSANT FRENCH TOAST

continued

TO FREEZE: Let cool to room temperature. Flip the casserole out onto a cutting board and cut into twelve equal squares. Arrange the squares on a rimmed baking sheet and freeze for at least 4 hours or up overnight for a formative freeze (see page 31). Wrap each square in plastic wrap and put the squares into a zip-top plastic bag or lidded plastic container. Label and date and freeze for up to 6 months.

TO REHEAT FROM FROZEN: Coat a rimmed baking sheet with nonstick cooking spray or butter and arrange the desired number of squares on it. Place in a cold oven and set the oven to 350°F. Reheat for 30 to 45 minutes, until warm throughout. Serve warm with a dollop of the soft cream on each square.

MAKES 2 CUPS

Orange Blossom Soft Cream

1 cup cold heavy cream

1 tablespoon sugar

1 tablespoon finely grated orange zest

1 teaspoon orange blossom water

In a medium bowl, whisk the cream until soft peaks form. Add the sugar, orange zest, and orange blossom water and whisk for a few minutes more, until all of the ingredients are incorporated and the cream has stiffened a bit. It should still be softer than a full whip.

Cover and refrigerate until ready to use. It will keep for up to 2 days in a lidded container in the fridge.

TORTILLA BREAKFAST PIE

Here's the promise that this breakfast pie can make to you: That Saturday morning, not too far from now, when you wake up craving something hearty and delicious, you'll weigh the option of cooking something involved. But you'll be dissuaded—not enough time, kids to entertain, bed feels too comfy to dismiss. Freezer-ready chilaquiles-inspired tortilla pie to the rescue. For the small work required to fry a few eggs and chop a few radishes, you get a breakfast that combines something rich and plentiful with something fresh, crunchy, and zippy. It's a no-brainer!

There are two different potential points at which you can stop and freeze in this recipe: the chile sauce and the assembled dish. It just depends on how far ahead you're trying to get.

●

Chile Sauce

4 Roma tomatoes

Neutral vegetable oil, for charring the vegetables

1 poblano chile, stemmed and quartered lengthwise

½ jalapeño chile, stemmed and seeded if you'd like less heat

½ yellow onion

2 garlic cloves

1 teaspoon sea salt

Tortilla Pie

3 cups chile sauce, thawed if frozen

7 ounces blue corn tortilla chips (about 11 cups)

8 ounces panela cheese, crumbled

8 ounces Chihuahua cheese, grated

Make the sauce: Cut the tomatoes in half across the equator. Using a paper towel, wipe a thin layer of oil over the bottom of a cast-iron skillet and set over high heat. When the skillet is hot, add the tomato halves, cut side down, along with the chiles, onion (cut side down), and garlic. Cook everything for about 4 minutes, until charred on the underside. Flip everything and cook for about 2 minutes, until the chiles are cooked all the way through. Transfer the vegetables and garlic to a small saucepan and add water until just barely covered.

Bring to a boil over high heat, then turn down the heat to low and simmer gently, adding additional water if needed to prevent the vegetables from sticking to the bottom, for 45 minutes to 1 hour, until the vegetables are very broken down and soft. Remove from the heat and let cool briefly.

Transfer the contents of the pan to a blender, add the salt, and puree until the mixture is a smooth, pourable sauce (add more water if it's too thick); you should have about 3 cups.

If you like, you can freeze the sauce at this point. Let cool completely, transfer to a lidded container, label and date, and freeze for up to 6 months. To thaw, use the pull and thaw method (see page 43) or the cold water method (see page 43).

Make the pie: In a large saucepan over medium heat, bring the sauce to a simmer. In small handfuls, add the chips and stir in. Once all of the chips are in the sauce, stir gently, working from the bottom of the pan to the top. Then simmer, stirring and coating the chips, for about 5 minutes, until the chips are softened and lose some of their volume. Remove from the heat and let sit for 10 minutes.

continued →

TORTILLA BREAKFAST PIE

continued

To Serve

6 tablespoons neutral vegetable oil

6 large eggs

Kosher salt and freshly ground black pepper

8 radishes, thinly sliced

½ cup loosely packed fresh cilantro leaves

2 ripe avocados, halved, pitted, peeled, and diced

1 green onion, white and light green parts, thinly sliced

Juice of 1 lime

Sour cream, for serving

Spray a 9-inch pie pan with nonstick cooking spray. Arrange half of the chip mixture in the bottom of the pan. Sprinkle half of the panela cheese and then half of the Chihuahua cheese over the chip mixture in an even layer. Repeat with the remaining chip mixture, followed by the remaining panela and Chihuahua cheeses.

TO FREEZE: Let the pie cool to room temperature. Transfer to the refrigerator to chill completely. Wrap the pie pan in two layers of plastic wrap. Label and date and freeze for up to 4 months.

TO BAKE FROM FROZEN: Unwrap the pie. Place the pan in a cold oven and set the oven to 350°F. When the oven reaches temperature, bake for 45 minutes, until bubbling.

TO BAKE FROM ROOM TEMPERATURE: Preheat the oven to 350°F and bake for 15 to 18 minutes, until bubbling.

TO SERVE: While the tortilla pie bakes, fry the eggs. In a nonstick skillet over medium-low heat, warm 2 tablespoons of the oil. Carefully crack 2 of the eggs into the skillet, taking care not to break the yolks or let the eggs overlap. Sprinkle the eggs with salt and pepper. Let cook for about 2 minutes, until the whites are beginning to set on the bottom. With a spatula, flip each egg and cook for another 2 to 3 minutes, depending on desired doneness. Transfer the eggs to a plate and repeat with the remaining eggs, two at a time, and oil.

In a medium bowl, combine the radishes, cilantro, avocados, and green onion. Season with ¼ teaspoon salt and half of the lime juice and stir gently to mix. Taste and add more salt and lime juice if needed.

Divide the tortilla pie into six portions and spoon each portion onto a plate. Top each portion with a dollop of sour cream and a fried egg and set a spoonful of the radish salad alongside. Serve warm.

CHOCOLATE CHIA PUDDING

SERVES 6

Chia pudding would be easy to mock if Kait didn't love it so much. Dairy-free, gluten-free, and vegan, it's no wonder why it's Instagram famous in the wellness community. But what you may not know is that chia pudding can be frozen!

Once we figured this out—thanks, internet—it was game on, and Kait has made chia pudding variations part of her breakfast rotation. This chocolate version is a favorite because it's reminiscent of a Mounds bar, but you can opt for a million different flavor combinations.

One important note: The pudding needs to be properly and patiently thawed, preferably in a refrigerator for 24 hours. Do not expose it to heat in an attempt to speed up the process. Heat messes with the delicate consistency in not-so-delicious ways.

•

Two 13½-ounce cans coconut milk, shaken well (see Note)

½ cup chia seeds

½ cup natural cocoa powder

⅔ cup pure maple syrup

1 teaspoon kosher salt

1 teaspoon pure vanilla extract

Toasted coconut flakes, granola, or chopped nuts (such as pecans or almonds), for serving

In a medium bowl, whisk together the coconut milk, chia seeds, cocoa powder, maple syrup, salt, and vanilla, mixing well. Cover the bowl and transfer to the refrigerator to set the pudding. Pull it out and give it a stir every 30 minutes. It will take about 4 hours to thicken to a pudding texture.

TO FREEZE: Divide the pudding into individual portion-size containers (8-ounce glass jars with silicone-coated lids are great for this). Label and date and freeze for up to 1 month.

TO THAW: Use the pull and thaw method (see page 43) or the cold water method (see page 43). Do not expose to heat.

Serve cold, topped with coconut flakes or other toppings of your choice.

NOTE

For extra-smooth pudding, whirl the coconut milk in a blender or food processor for 1 minute before proceeding with the recipe.

Snacks and bites.

Roasted Jalapeño Poppers
with Sausage and Tomatoes • 183

Curried Cheddar and Olive Bites • 184

Pork Meatballs • 185

Ham and Swiss Cheese Rolls • 186

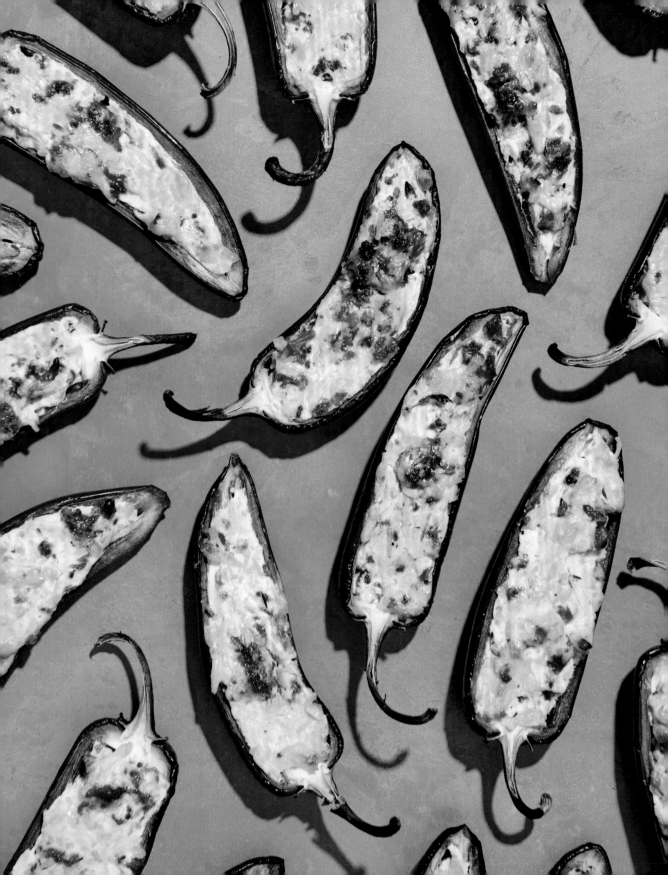

ROASTED JALAPEÑO POPPERS
with Sausage and Tomatoes

MAKES 30 POPPERS

When it comes to sports, we're lackadaisical. Kait is a lapsed Packers fan; Ashley will get excited about the occasional North Carolina State game. But we can always get excited about a sports snack, which is why we love this recipe.

It's nothing like the battered and fried sports-bar poppers. Those have their place, but we're not interested in making them at home. Instead, these are roasted and open-faced, which allows the flavor of the pepper to really shine while still satisfying a cheesy, gooey craving. Having a bag of these in your freezer comes in handy for late-night snacking, too. Rather than steering the Lyft driver to the drive-through ('fess up, we've all done it), head home and stick a few of these in the oven.

8 ounces loose country sausage (see Note)

¾ cup shredded sharp Cheddar cheese

¾ cup shredded Parmesan cheese

Juice of 1 lemon

5 dashes of hot sauce, such as Tabasco

¾ cup diced fresh tomatoes, or ½ cup drained diced canned tomatoes

½ teaspoon fresh thyme leaves

8 ounces cream cheese, at room temperature

Kosher salt

15 small to medium jalapeño chiles, stemmed, halved lengthwise, and seeds and ribs removed

In a large, nonstick skillet over medium heat, cook the sausage, breaking it up with the back of a wooden spoon, for 8 to 10 minutes, until crumbled and no pink remains. Transfer to a paper towel–lined plate and let cool completely.

In a medium bowl, combine the Cheddar, Parmesan, lemon juice, hot sauce, tomatoes, thyme, and cream cheese and stir until well mixed. Fold in the sausage and season to taste with salt.

Fill each jalapeño half with 1 to 1½ teaspoons of the cream cheese filling; the chile half should be full but not heaping, or the filling will overflow when cooked.

TO FREEZE: Arrange the jalapeño halves, filling side up, on a rimmed baking sheet and freeze for at least 4 hours or up to overnight for a formative freeze (see page 31). Transfer to a zip-top plastic bag, label and date, and freeze for up to 6 months.

TO COOK: Preheat the oven to 375°F. Arrange the peppers, filling side up, on a wire rack set over a rimmed baking sheet. Bake for 15 to 18 minutes if cooking immediately after preparing, or for 22 to 25 minutes if cooking from frozen, until the chiles are slightly shriveled and the filling is browned in spots. Let cool slightly before serving.

NOTE

For the sausage in these poppers, we prefer Neese's Country Sausage.

CURRIED CHEDDAR AND OLIVE BITES

MAKES 72 BITES

Kait's mom, Lisa, is a freezer-season queen and inspired more than a few of our freezer moves that ended up in this book. Her freezer is always stocked with balls of homemade cookie dough and English toffee, as well as these little appetizers. This recipe is a riff on one that Lisa's mom (Kait's nana) used to make, which she called English muffin hors d'oeuvres. We changed the name for two reasons: we're not fancy enough to serve anyone hors d'oeuvres, and while these are indeed built on English muffins, the original name belied the punchy, bold flavors that come to play in these bite-size snacks.

2 cups finely grated sharp Cheddar cheese

1 cup mayonnaise

1½ cups chopped black olives

1 bunch green onions, white and light green parts only, sliced

1 teaspoon curry powder

¾ teaspoon kosher salt

6 English muffins

In a medium bowl, combine the Cheddar, mayonnaise, olives, green onions, curry powder, and salt and mix well.

Split the English muffins in half horizontally. Divide the cheese mixture evenly among the muffin halves, spreading it evenly; you want a thick layer. Cut each half into six pie-shaped wedges.

TO FREEZE: Arrange the bites on a rimmed baking sheet and freeze for at least 4 hours or up to overnight for a formative freeze (see page 31). Slide the bites into a zip-top plastic bag, label and date, and freeze for up to 6 months.

TO COOK: Preheat the oven to 375°F. Arrange your desired amount of bites on a rimmed baking sheet and bake for 13 to 15 minutes if cooking immediately after preparing, or for 18 to 20 minutes if cooking from frozen, until bubbly.

Serve hot.

PORK MEATBALLS

MAKES 24 MEATBALLS

These pork meatballs are the home kitchen–friendly versions of the recipe we developed for Poole'side Pies, our Neapolitan-inspired pizza joint. We had a lot of friends who acted as our meatball gurus and helped us on our journey, among them Tandy Wilson (chef and owner of City House in Nashville) and Sarah Grueneberg (chef and owner of Monteverde in Chicago). Sarah suggested that we add *soppressata*, a spicy Italian salami, to the mix, giving it a little touch of heat. Then Ashley decided to use mortadella, an emulsified Italian bologna, to lend a great texture.

But when we tried making the recipe with the mortadella that's available at the grocery store, we weren't happy with the results. Enter the hot dog, the everyman's emulsified bologna. Don't worry. These meatballs aren't overwhelmed with hot dog flavor. We use just enough to help nail that tender texture.

You could leave these meatballs undressed for a simple finger food or dress them up with your favorite tomato sauce and plenty of Parmesan cheese.

2 slices white bread, cubed

½ cup whole milk

2 ounces beef hot dog, chopped

2 ounces soppressata, chopped

1 pound ground pork

¼ cup minced yellow onion

1 garlic clove, minced

1½ teaspoons minced fresh oregano

2 large eggs

1 teaspoon kosher salt

Put the bread into a medium bowl, pour in the milk, and let sit for 1 hour. Scoop the bread into a fine-mesh strainer and use your hands to press the bread and force out as much of the liquid as possible. Transfer the bread to a food processor and puree until a smooth paste forms. Transfer the bread paste to a large bowl and wipe out the food processor.

Add the hot dog and soppressata to the food processor and pulse until finely ground. Add to the bowl with the bread along with the pork, onion, garlic, oregano, eggs, and salt. Use your hands to mix all of the ingredients together until just combined; do not overmix. Cover the bowl and place in the fridge for at least 1 hour or up to overnight.

To shape each meatball, scoop up about 2 tablespoons of the pork mixture and shape into a ball between your palms.

TO FREEZE: Arrange the meatballs on a parchment paper–lined rimmed baking sheet and freeze for at least 4 hours or up to overnight for a formative freeze (see page 31). Transfer the balls to a zip-top plastic bag, label and date, and freeze for up to 6 months.

TO COOK: Preheat the oven to 375°F. Arrange the meatballs on a rimmed baking sheet and bake for 13 to 15 minutes if cooking immediately after preparing, or for 20 to 22 minutes if cooking from frozen, until browned and cooked through.

Serve hot.

HAM AND SWISS CHEESE ROLLS

MAKES 12 ROLLS

The Hawaiian slider roll is a pretty great freezable vehicle, and Ashley's mom, Lynn, has perfected one of the most beloved appetizer versions for this ingredient—the ham and Swiss roll—to a science. We've become loyal fans.

The main difference between making these for the freezer and making them to eat right now is the butter. The classic recipe calls for melting the butter, but when freezing the rolls, mixing softened butter with the other ingredients works better. That way, the butter doesn't melt into the bread until you bake it, which concentrates that delicious sweet-salty-punchy flavor.

●

Compound Butter

½ cup unsalted butter, at room temperature

2 tablespoons Worcestershire sauce

2 tablespoons light brown sugar

2 tablespoons poppy seeds

2 tablespoons minced yellow onion

2 tablespoons Dijon mustard

One 12-pack Hawaiian slider rolls

½ cup mayonnaise

8 ounces thinly sliced deli ham

8 ounces shredded Swiss cheese (about 2 cups)

Make the compound butter: In a small bowl, combine the butter, Worcestershire sauce, sugar, poppy seeds, onion, and mustard and mix well. Set aside.

Assemble the rolls: Break the pack of rolls into individual squares, then cut each square in half horizontally. Place the bottom halves, cut side up, on a work surface. Spread evenly with the mayonnaise. Divide the ham evenly among the roll bottoms, tearing or cutting the slices into pieces as needed to fit the roll (you don't want too much overhang). Divide the cheese evenly among the roll bottoms, arranging it on the ham. Cover with the roll tops, cut side down. Arrange the rolls on a rimmed baking sheet, spacing them a few inches apart, and spread the compound butter on the top of each roll, dividing it evenly.

TO FREEZE: Place the baking sheet in the freezer for at least 4 hours or up to overnight for a formative freeze (see page 31). Transfer the rolls to a lidded plastic or glass container, label and date, and freeze for up to 1 month.

TO COOK: Preheat the oven to 350°F. Arrange the desired number of rolls on a rimmed baking sheet. Bake for 10 minutes if cooking immediately after preparing, or for 18 to 20 minutes if cooking from frozen, until the cheese is melted and the rolls are hot throughout.

Serve hot.

● **CHEFFIN' IT UP**

Honestly, we don't tend to mess with this one because the classic version is so perfect. That said, you could use this compound butter on a bunch of different stuff and get some really lovely results. Can you imagine it melted and drizzled over popcorn? We can.

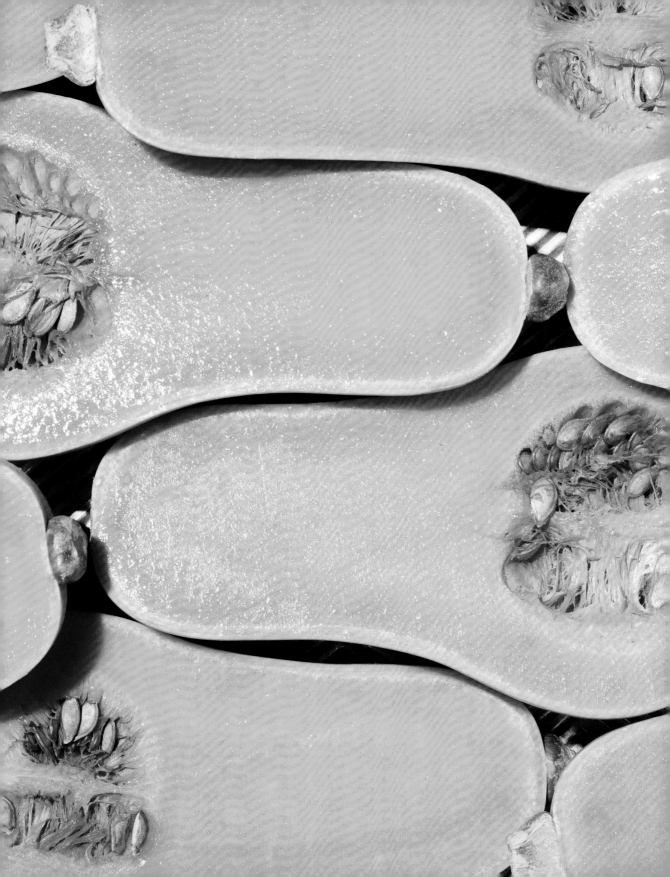

11

Soups and saucy things.

Basic Butternut Squash Soup • 191

Turkey Chili with White Beans • 195

Chilled Tomato and Cucumber Soup • 197

Tomato-Dijon Bisque • 199

New Manhattan Chowder • 200

Chicken and Kale Tortilla Soup • 203

FREEZER CHICKEN STOCK • 204

Penne alla Vodka • 206

BASIC BUTTERNUT SQUASH SOUP

**MAKES 4 QUARTS
(1 QUART SERVES
2 OR 3)**

4 large butternut squash
(about 10 pounds total)

Olive oil, for rubbing

Kosher salt

24 thyme sprigs

2 fresh bay leaves

1 tablespoon black
peppercorns

¼ cup neutral vegetable oil

4 large yellow onions,
thinly sliced (about 8 cups)

2 cups dry white wine

4 cups water

½ cup honey

This squash soup recipe isn't revolutionary. It's just about letting
the squash do its thing, with some aromatics to give it a little lift.
But having this soup ready to go in your freezer for any manner of
upgrade or creative repurposing? That's the exciting part. Check
out the variations at the end to see how Ashley chefs it up.

•

Preheat the oven to 375°F.

Split each squash in half through the stem end and scoop out the seeds
and fibers. Arrange the halves, cut side up, on one large rimmed baking
sheet (or two if necessary). Rub the cut surface of each squash half
with about 1 tablespoon olive oil and season generously with salt. Bake
for 35 to 40 minutes, until the flesh is fork-tender. Let cool slightly.

Cut a medium-size square of cheesecloth. Put the thyme, bay leaves,
and peppercorns on the center of the square, then bring the edges
together and tie securely with kitchen string to form a sachet. In a
large pot or Dutch oven over medium heat, warm the vegetable oil.
Add the onions and sauté for about 20 minutes, until softened and
light amber (about halfway to caramelized). Add the herb sachet and
cook, stirring, for 4 minutes. Add the wine, increase the heat to high,
and cook for about 8 minutes, until reduced by half.

Scoop the squash flesh from its skin and add it to the pan. Add
the water and bring to a boil. Turn down the heat to medium and
simmer, stirring frequently, for 30 minutes. Stir in 2 tablespoons
plus 2 teaspoons salt and the honey and simmer for 5 minutes more.
Remove from the heat and let cool for 10 minutes.

Remove and discard the sachet. Working in small batches, transfer
the soup to a blender and puree until smooth. You can also use an
immersion blender, but it won't be quite as smooth. Taste and season
to your preference.

TO FREEZE: Let the soup cool to under 70°F. Transfer to the fridge
to chill. Transfer the soup to your preferred freezer vessel. We split
it among four quart-size lidded plastic containers, but zip-top plastic
bags or vacuum pouches will also work. Label and date and freeze
for up to 9 months.

TO REHEAT: Use your preferred reheat method. You can thaw first,
using the pull and thaw method (see page 43) or the cold water
method (see page 43), and then transfer to a medium pot and bring
to a simmer. Or you can use the microwave, Instant Pot, or sous vide
method (see page 40) to reheat directly. For sous vide, set the water

continued →

BASIC BUTTERNUT SQUASH SOUP

continued

bath temperature to 145°F and drop in a pouch. It will take about 1 hour to reach temperature.

Ladle into bowls and serve hot.

● **CHEFFIN' IT UP**

Here are two ways to reinvigorate this soup that will take you 20 minutes or less. Each preparation serves two.

Miso-Ginger Butternut Squash Soup

Reheat 1 quart Butternut Squash Soup. In a medium saucepan over medium heat, warm 2 tablespoons neutral vegetable oil. Add 1 teaspoon peeled and finely chopped fresh ginger and 1 tablespoon chopped green onion (white and light green parts) and cook, stirring, for about 3 minutes, until fragrant. Stir in 1 tablespoon white or red miso paste followed by 1 teaspoon each soy sauce and toasted sesame oil. Pour in the soup, increase the heat to medium-high and bring to a boil, stirring occasionally. Turn down the heat to a simmer and cook, whisking frequently, for 5 to 8 minutes. Taste and season to your preference. Ladle into bowls.

Seared Scallops with Butternut Squash, Apples, and Parsley

In a medium saucepan over medium heat, add 2 cups of the soup and bring to a simmer. Cook, stirring occasionally, for about 8 minutes, until the soup reduces by one-third. Keep warm.

Have 8 large scallops (U/10 size) ready. Put ¼ cup Wondra flour into a small, shallow dish. In a medium skillet over medium-high heat, warm 2 tablespoons neutral vegetable oil. One at a time, dip one side of each scallop into the flour and then place, flour side down, into the skillet. Cook for about 2 minutes, until the edges of the scallops touching the pan are turning a beautiful golden brown and look almost pleated. Add 1 tablespoon unsalted butter to the pan and tilt the pan to swirl it around evenly. Cook for 1 minute more, then flip the scallops. Tilt the pan toward you and, using a spoon, baste the scallops repeatedly with the brown butter for 2 minutes. Transfer the scallops to a paper towel–lined plate.

Cut ½ apple into matchsticks, transfer to a small bowl, and add ¼ cup loosely packed fresh flat-leaf parsley leaves. Add 1 teaspoon extra virgin olive oil, ½ teaspoon fresh lemon juice, and a sprinkle of kosher salt and mix together gently.

To serve, ladle about ⅔ cup of the reduced soup into each bowl. Arrange 4 scallops on the soup in each bowl, then top with half of the apple-parsley mixture.

TURKEY CHILI

with White Beans

MAKES 7 QUARTS
(1 QUART SERVES
2 OR 3)

Everyone needs a good house chili recipe, and ours is a lighter, more nuanced take on the version of Texas chili that Kait grew up on.

This is a frequent flyer in our house. We keep a healthy stash in the freezer and pull from it often when in need of a quick, hearty, and relatively healthy dinner.

Last note: If "chili" means something very specific to you that does not resemble this, feel free to call it a ground turkey stew—or whatever you need to tell yourself to move forward with making it.

¼ cup canola or olive oil

3 large yellow onions, chopped

Kosher salt

2 tablespoons dried oregano

2 tablespoons ground cumin

4 pounds ground turkey

2 tablespoons tomato paste

½ cup chili powder

4 dried bay leaves

2 tablespoons Dutch-processed cocoa powder

1 tablespoon smoked paprika

½ teaspoon ground cinnamon

Four 28-ounce cans diced tomatoes with their juice

8 cups turkey stock or thawed Freezer Chicken Stock (page 204)

Two 8-ounce cans tomato sauce

Six 15-ounce cans small white beans, rinsed and drained

In a large Dutch oven or other heavy pot over high heat, warm the oil. Add the onions and ½ teaspoon salt and cook, stirring occasionally, for about 10 minutes, until the onions are tender and have taken on just a bit of color. Add the oregano and cumin and stir for 1 minute. Turn down the heat to medium-high, add the turkey, and cook, breaking it up with the back of a wooden spoon, for 10 to 12 minutes, until no pink remains. Stir in the tomato paste, chili powder, bay leaves, cocoa powder, paprika, cinnamon, and ¼ cup plus 2 tablespoons salt. Add the tomatoes with their juices, breaking them up with the back of the spoon. Pour in the stock and tomato sauce, stir well, and bring to a boil. Turn down the heat to a simmer and simmer uncovered, stirring occasionally, for 45 minutes.

Add the beans to the pot and simmer for about 10 minutes longer to blend the flavors. Discard the bay leaves.

TO FREEZE: If you are not using previously frozen ingredients, you can freeze this chili. Let the chili cool to under 70°F on the stove or counter. Because this is a large batch of chili, you may want to use an ice bath to help cool it in less than 2 hours. To do this, plug your sink and fill with ice water to a depth of a few inches. Set the pot in the sink and stir occasionally to help the chili cool faster.

Transfer the chili to the fridge to chill. Transfer the chili to your preferred freezer vessel. We split it among seven quart-size lidded plastic containers, but zip-top plastic bags or vacuum pouches will also work. Label and date and freeze for up to 4 months.

TO REHEAT: Use your preferred reheat method. You can thaw first, using the pull and thaw method (see page 43) or the cold water

continued →

TURKEY CHILI

continued

method (see page 43), and then transfer to a medium saucepan and bring to a simmer. Or you can use the microwave, Instant Pot, or sous vide method (see page 40) to reheat directly. For sous vide, set the water bath temperature to 145°F and drop in a pouch. It will take about 1 hour to reach temperature.

Taste and season to your preference. Ladle into bowls and serve.

● **CHEFFIN' IT UP**

Here are two variations for serving the chili. Each preparation serves two.

Turkey Chili with Spiced Basmati Rice, Fried Shallots, and Yogurt

Reheat 1 quart chili; keep warm while you make the rice and shallots. Slice 3 shallots across the equator and separate into rings. In a large skillet over medium heat, warm ¼ cup canola oil until shimmering. Add the shallot rings and fry gently for about 6 minutes, until crispy and golden. Transfer to a paper towel–lined plate and sprinkle with kosher salt. Return the pan with the oil to medium heat. Add 1 teaspoon each coriander seeds and cumin seeds and ½ teaspoon freshly ground black pepper. When the seeds begin to sizzle and smell fragrant, add 1 cup basmati rice and stir to coat the grains with the oil. Add 2 cups water and 1 teaspoon kosher salt and bring to a boil. Cover, turn down the heat to the lowest heat setting, and cook for 12 minutes. Remove from the heat and let stand, covered, for another 10 minutes. Remove the lid and fluff the rice. Spoon some rice into two bowls and ladle the chili over the rice. Top each serving with a healthy spoonful (about ¼ cup) of plain Greek yogurt and a generous sprinkling of fried shallots.

Turkey Chili with Goat Cheese and Chimichurri

Reheat 1 quart chili. Thaw ¼ cup Chimichurri (page 140), give it a whisk, and season to taste with kosher salt and freshly ground pepper if it needs it. Crumble about 2 ounces chèvre. Ladle the chili into two bowls and top each serving with half of the chèvre and a generous drizzle of the chimichurri.

CHILLED TOMATO AND CUCUMBER SOUP

**MAKES 2 QUARTS BASE;
SERVES 4 TO 6**

Once you've had this soup, you might forsake all other pureed tomato soups for good. It's a little labor intensive, but it's worth it. (Make sure to plan accordingly because you need to start the day before.)

The trick to freezing this recipe is to stop and freeze before the final step. Emulsifications don't hold up well in the freezer, but the tomato-cucumber pulp will freeze just fine. Once thawed, the base is emulsified with the olive oil right before serving.

Base

6 quarts ice water

6 tablespoons kosher salt

6 pounds Roma tomatoes (25 to 28 tomatoes), cored and cut into quarter-size pieces

2 pounds cucumbers, cut into quarter-size pieces

To Finish

2 teaspoons sherry vinegar

3 cups extra virgin olive oil

4 teaspoons kosher salt

Make the base: In a large pot or other container, combine the ice water and salt and stir until the salt dissolves completely. Add the tomatoes and cucumbers, cover, and refrigerate overnight. The next day, pour the contents of the pot into a colander set in the sink.

Working in batches, transfer the tomatoes and cucumbers in the colander to a food processor and process until the mixture looks like a fine pulp. Pass the mixture through a tamis (drum sieve) or food mill; a fine-mesh strainer is too fine. You want a little bit of pulp to pass through. If using a tamis, scrape back and forth with a bowl scraper or a wooden spoon to push through all of the juice. Discard any remaining pulp. Repeat until all of the tomatoes and cucumbers are processed. This is your base. If you are freezing the soup, this is where you stop and freeze.

TO FREEZE THE BASE: Transfer the base to your preferred freezer vessel. We split it between two quart-size lidded plastic containers, but zip-top plastic bags or vacuum pouches will also work. Label and date and freeze for up to 4 months.

TO THAW THE BASE: Because this is a cold soup, we prefer the pull and thaw method (see page 43) or the cold water method (see page 43). Applying heat can alter the taste of the finished soup.

TO FINISH THE SOUP: Put half of the base (1 quart) into a blender or food processor. Turn on the motor and process until the mixture lightens slightly in color. With the motor running, add 1 teaspoon of the vinegar and then slowly drizzle in 1½ cups of the oil. Add 2 teaspoons of the salt, taste, and season additionally to preference. Repeat with the remaining quart of base. Ladle into bowls and serve cold.

● CHEFFIN' IT UP

This soup recipe loves to be paired with rich shellfish: poached shrimp, lobster, or crab in the bottom of the bowl is a dreamy addition that'll upgrade this dish.

TOMATO-DIJON BISQUE

**MAKES 4 QUARTS
(1 QUART SERVES
2 OR 3)**

Ashley has a long-standing love of all things tomato, but tomato soup in particular satisfies a specific childhood craving. As a kid, her dad would make a lunch of Campbell's tomato soup and grilled cheese for her and her brother, Zak. But he'd swap out the water for milk to give it more body and flavor, and that touch of dairy informed this take on the classic, which she originally came up with for our former coffee shop, Joule Coffee + Table.

This soup is a bisque, but we like to leave the texture a bit chunkier than what is typical. Of course, you could puree this to velvety smoothness à la Campbell's if you like. We won't stop you.

•

¼ cup neutral vegetable oil

2 large yellow onions, finely diced (about 4 cups)

12 thyme sprigs, cut in half and tied in a cheesecloth sachet

6 large garlic cloves, pressed through a garlic press

3 tablespoons kosher salt

2½ cups dry white wine

Three 28-ounce cans diced tomatoes with their juice

4 cups water

¼ cup Dijon mustard

4 cups organic tomato juice

3 cups heavy cream

2 teaspoons freshly ground black pepper

Finely grated Parmesan cheese and extra virgin olive oil, for serving

In a large, heavy stockpot over medium heat, warm the oil. Add the onions and cook, stirring constantly, for about 5 minutes, until slightly tender. Add the thyme sachet and garlic and stir until both are aromatic. Stir in 1 tablespoon of the salt.

Increase the heat to high and add the wine. Allow to boil vigorously for about 10 minutes, until the liquid is reduced by two-thirds. Add the tomatoes and their juice and the water and bring the contents of the pot back to a boil. Turn down the heat to a simmer and simmer, stirring occasionally, for 1 hour, until all of the solids have broken down and the mixture has thickened slightly.

Turn down the heat to low and, using an immersion blender, lightly pulse the contents of the pot until a coarse puree forms. Stir in the mustard, tomato juice, cream, the remaining 2 tablespoons salt, and the pepper and bring to a low simmer. Simmer, stirring occasionally, for 20 minutes to blend the flavors. Remove from the heat.

TO FREEZE: Let the soup cool to under 70°F on the stove or counter. Transfer to the fridge to chill. Transfer the soup to your preferred freezer vessel. We split it among four quart-size lidded plastic containers, but zip-top plastic bags or vacuum pouches will also work. Label and date and freeze for up to 6 months.

TO REHEAT: Use your preferred reheat method. You can thaw first, using the pull and thaw method (see page 43) or the cold water method (see page 43), and then transfer to a medium saucepan and bring to a simmer. Or you can use the microwave, Instant Pot, or sous vide method (see page 40) to reheat directly. For sous vide, set the water bath temperature to 145°F and drop in a pouch. It will take 1 hour to reach temperature. Taste and season to your preference.

Ladle into bowls, sprinkle with Parmesan, and drizzle with olive oil. Serve hot.

NEW MANHATTAN CHOWDER

**MAKES 3 QUARTS BASE;
SERVES 8 TO 10**

If you're the type of person who struggles to decide what to order at restaurants and would often be tempted to order two things instead of one, welcome to our club. Why choose when you don't have to, right? This soup is the embodiment of that mantra: it takes two competing versions of clam chowder and blends them into one particularly delicious dish.

The base of this chowder can be made ahead and frozen; you add the clams just before you're ready to serve. Do not freeze this soup after the clams have been added.

•

Base

4 medium thyme sprigs

½ fresh bay leaf

1 garlic clove, smashed

1 teaspoon black peppercorns

½ cup neutral vegetable oil

2 cups diced yellow onions (in small dice)

1 cup sliced celery (stalks halved lengthwise, then sliced crosswise ¼ inch thick)

Sea salt

1 cup dry white wine

Two 12-ounce cans crushed tomatoes

2 cups bottled clam juice

3 cups heavy cream

2 tablespoons Dijon mustard

2 cups diced Yukon gold potatoes (in ⅜-inch dice)

Freshly ground black pepper

Make the base: Cut a small square of cheesecloth. Put the thyme, bay leaf, garlic, and peppercorns on the center of the square, then bring the edges together and tie securely with kitchen string to form a sachet.

In a heavy 4-quart pot over medium heat, warm the oil until it shimmers. Add the onions, celery, and sachet, season lightly with salt, and stir continuously for 6 to 8 minutes, until the vegetables are translucent and the herbs are fragrant. Add the wine and cook until the liquid reduces by half. Add the tomatoes and simmer for 10 minutes. Add the clam juice, cream, and mustard, stir well, and bring to a simmer. Add the potatoes and cook for about 12 minutes, until tender (but not falling apart). Once the potatoes are tender, turn down the heat to low and season to taste with salt and pepper. This is your base. If you are freezing your chowder, this is where you stop and remove the chowder from the heat. Otherwise, proceed to the serving instructions.

TO FREEZE: Let the base cool to under 70°F on the stove or counter. Transfer to the fridge to chill. Transfer the base to your preferred freezer vessel. We suggest a gallon-size zip-top plastic bag. Label and date and freeze for up to 6 months.

TO THAW: Use your preferred thawing method. We recommend the pull and thaw method (see page 43) or the cold water method (see page 43).

TO FINISH: Place the clams in a bowl and cover with cold water. Let soak for 30 minutes; drain the clams and cover with fresh cold water. Let soak for another 30 minutes. Drain once more and set aside.

continued →

NEW MANHATTAN CHOWDER

continued

To Finish

36 to 48 littleneck clams, scrubbed

3 cups whole milk

4 tablespoons cold unsalted butter

Sea salt and freshly ground black pepper

Lemon wedges, for garnish

Sliced fresh chives, for garnish

Put the base into a large, heavy pot and bring to a simmer over medium heat. Stir in the milk and bring back to a simmer. Add the butter 1 tablespoon at a time, stirring after each addition until melted. Once all of the butter has been incorporated, add the clams and stir gently for about 8 minutes, until they open (discard any clams that fail to open after 10 minutes).

Season the chowder to taste with salt and pepper (don't do this before all of the clams open, as they will likely add a noticeable amount of salt to the soup). Ladle into high-sided bowls and garnish with lemon wedges and chives.

● **CHEFFIN' IT UP**

Instead of clams, add crabmeat or lobster meat for a shellfish chowder.

CHICKEN AND KALE TORTILLA SOUP

SERVES 6 TO 8

Ashley could live on soup. Seriously, there's hardly ever a day where "soup" doesn't sound like a good option. In fact, the only thing that's probably keeping her from a steady diet of soup is Kait, who would rather eat a bowl of pasta.

Sometimes we meet in the middle (soup with pasta in it?), but on days when Ashley wins out in the "what to make for dinner" battle, her soup approach is usually about using up whatever is in the fridge or pantry. This is where a solid frozen stock is crucial.

To that end, the "freezer" part of this recipe is actually just the stock. And we know there are about a trillion chicken stock recipes out there, so by all means feel free to switch this one out for your favorite. Even with boxed grocery-store stock, you could do worse than the end result here.

8 cups Freezer Chicken Stock (page 204), thawed

10 blue corn tortilla chips

8 full cilantro sprigs

2 tablespoons neutral vegetable oil

2 garlic cloves, crushed with the side of a knife

1 bunch Lacinato kale or other hearty greens, tender stems and leaves coarsely chopped

Kosher salt

1 ripe medium tomato, diced

¼ cup extra virgin olive oil

3 cups pulled Chicken Confit (page 94), thawed and drained, or shredded cooked chicken

1 tablespoon cold unsalted butter

2 limes

In a medium saucepan, combine the stock and tortilla chips and bring to a boil over high heat. Turn down the heat to a low simmer and simmer for 15 minutes, until the chips have completely softened and started to disintegrate (being careful not to reduce the stock). Add half of the cilantro sprigs (stems and all), remove from the heat, and let cool for a few minutes. Transfer to a blender and buzz until smooth.

Place the empty saucepan on the stove over medium heat until the surface of the pot is dry. Add the vegetable oil and garlic and cook, stirring occasionally, about 2 minutes, until the garlic is aromatic and lightly toasted. Add the greens and cook, stirring often, for about 6 minutes, until tender. Season lightly with salt, then add the contents of the blender and bring to a simmer.

While the soup is heating, in a small bowl, season the tomato lightly with salt and let sit until the juice starts to collect in the bottom of the bowl. Add the olive oil and stir to mix. Set aside.

Add the chicken meat to the simmering soup and simmer until heated through. Once everything is warm, cut the heat and add the butter and the juice from 1 lime. Stir to emulsify, then season to taste with salt.

To serve, cut the remaining lime into wedges. Divide the soup among bowls and garnish with the tomato relish, the leaves from the remaining cilantro sprigs, and the lime wedges.

FREEZER CHICKEN STOCK

MAKES 8 CUPS

The key takeaway of this recipe, which is not an original idea on our part, is about storing odds and ends in your freezer until you have enough in quantity and enough time to make stock. We keep a "stock bag" in the freezer and add to it the backs of chickens we've spatchcocked and roasted, the green parts of leeks, the trimmings of carrots, the stems of mushrooms and herbs, and the ends and extras of celery stalks. All of this stuff can go into stock after it has been stored in the freezer. It's like frozen compost except the compost is liquid gold.

4 pounds chicken bones and bone-y pieces (such as necks, backs, wings, and the like)

8 ounces alliums (such as yellow onions, leeks, shallots, and green onions), cut into chunks

8 ounces aromatic vegetables (such as carrots, celery, and herbs), cut into chunks

Anything else you want to throw in

8 quarts water

In a large stockpot, combine the chicken, alliums, aromatic vegetables, your "anything else," and the water and bring to a boil over medium-high heat. Turn down the heat to a simmer and skim off any scrum from the surface. Let simmer gently for about 90 minutes, until the liquid is reduced by half.

Remove from the heat and strain through a fine-mesh strainer into a large bowl or other container. Discard the solids. Return the stock to the stockpot, place over medium heat, bring to a simmer, and simmer for about 45 minutes, until reduced again by half. You should have 8 cups stock. Remove from the heat.

TO FREEZE: Let the stock cool to under 70°F on a counter. Transfer to the fridge to chill. Transfer the stock to your preferred freezer vessel. We split it between two quart-size lidded plastic containers, but zip-top plastic bags or vacuum pouches will also work. Label and date and freeze for up to 1 year.

TO THAW: Use your preferred thawing method. We recommend the pull and thaw method (see page 43) or the cold running water method (see page 43). Taste and season to your preference, then use as desired in recipes.

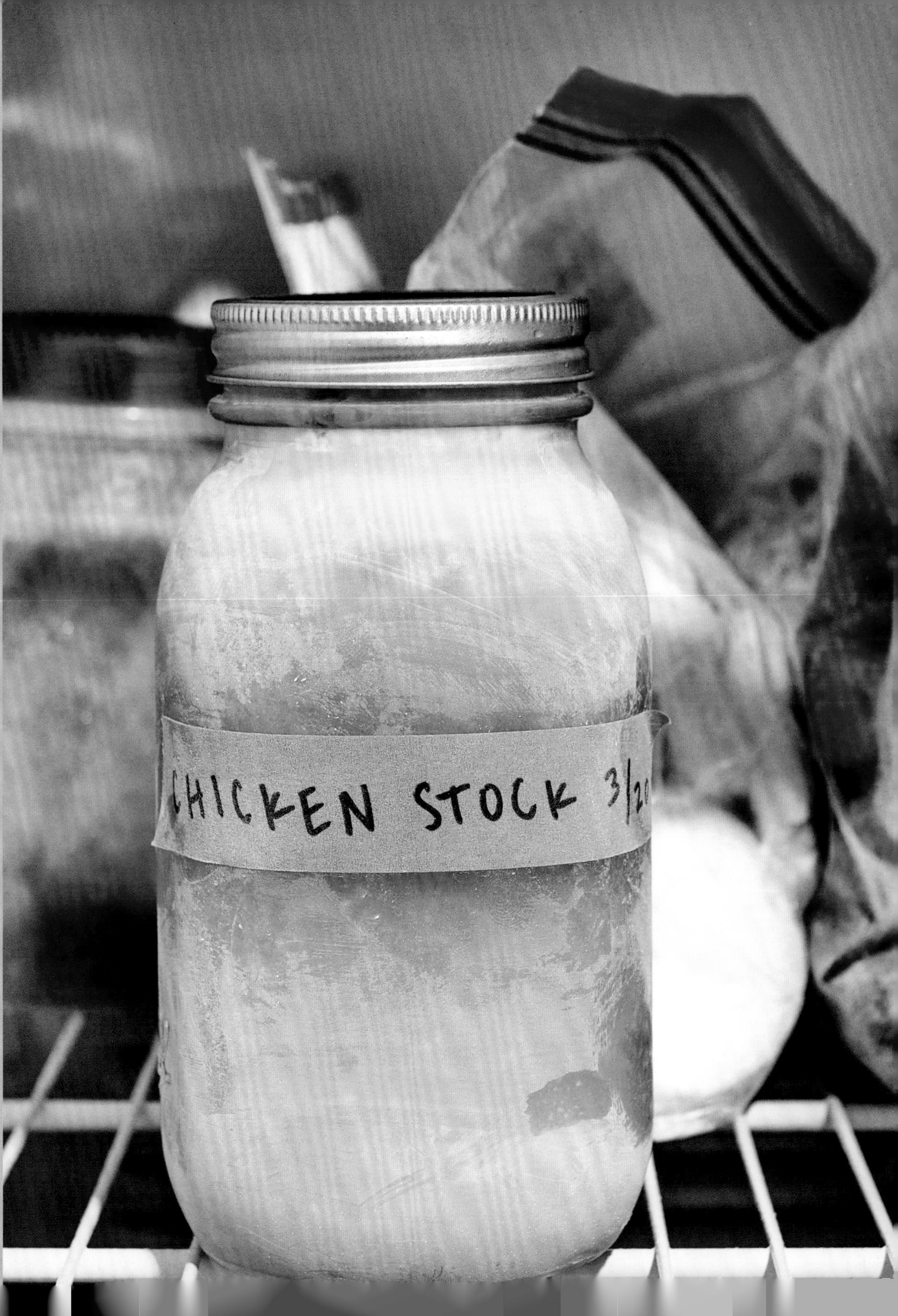
CHICKEN STOCK 3/20

PENNE ALLA VODKA

SERVES 8

This *alla vodka* sauce is a love language at our house. Kait's ultimate comfort food is a bowl of pasta, and Ashley has an uncanny intuition as to when to pull a pint of this sauce from the freezer (examples: during marathon cookbook-writing sessions; after very busy weeks at work; when we've been on the road just a little too long; when one of us is a little bit blue). If you're feeling in any way depleted, this vodka sauce is like a hug.

A note about portioning: The sauce recipe makes about 4 pints; each pint feeds about two people.

•

Make the sauce: In a medium Dutch oven or other heavy pan over medium-high heat, warm the oil until it shimmers. Add the onions and cook, stirring constantly, for about 6 minutes, until softened and starting to turn translucent. (The onions will release a lot of moisture, which will create lots of steam, making stirring constantly important.) Add the garlic and salt and cook, still stirring constantly, for 4 minutes more. The mixture will have started to take on a hint of color and smell very fragrant.

Next, add the pepper flakes and tomato paste and stir to incorporate into the onion mixture. Turn down the heat to medium and cook for 10 minutes, still stirring constantly. The mixture will be very dry and begin to caramelize in spots.

Remove from the heat and move the pan away from any open flame. Add the vodka, stir it into the mixture, and then use a stick lighter to ignite the vodka. Return the pan to medium heat and cook for 6 minutes more, stirring constantly. The flame will go out quickly and the mixture will continue to caramelize.

Add the water and stir to incorporate. Then add the cream and stir to incorporate. Turn down the heat to low and cook for 10 minutes more, stirring constantly. The mixture should release steam, but it should not bubble, simmer, or boil. The texture of the sauce should be thick and creamy. Remove from the heat.

TO FREEZE: Cool the sauce over an ice bath to room temperature. Transfer to the fridge to chill. Transfer to four pint-size lidded plastic containers; zip-top plastic bags or vacuum pouches will also work. Label and date and freeze for up to 3 months.

TO THAW: Use the pull and thaw method (see page 43) or the cold water method (see page 43).

Sauce

¾ cup extra virgin olive oil

4 cups minced yellow onions

6 garlic cloves, pressed through a garlic press

2 tablespoons kosher salt

1 teaspoon red pepper flakes, finely chopped

2 cups tomato paste

1 cup vodka

1 cup water

3 cups heavy cream

To Serve

Kosher salt

2⅔ pounds dried penne rigate (⅔ pound for each pint of sauce)

8 ounces Parmesan cheese, finely grated (2 ounces for each pint of sauce), plus more for finishing

16 fresh basil leaves, minced (4 leaves for each pint of sauce)

TO SERVE: Fill a large pot with water and salt it generously (it should taste salty like the ocean). Bring to a boil over high heat, add the desired amount of pasta, and cook for 2 to 3 minutes less than the package instructions say, usually 8 or 9 minutes. Drain the pasta, reserving 1 cup of the pasta water for every pint of sauce you are using.

Return the pot to the stove over medium heat and add the vodka sauce. When it begins to simmer gently, add the pasta. Cook, stirring constantly, for 5 to 6 minutes, adding a little bit of the pasta water every few minutes; the sauce will begin to cling to the pasta as the pasta finishes cooking in the sauce. Stir in the cheese, a little bit at a time, letting it completely incorporate into the sauce after each addition. Taste to make sure the pasta is fully cooked.

Spoon into pasta bowls, sprinkle with the basil, and finish with more Parmesan. Serve immediately.

12

Casseroles and bakes.

Tex-Mex Cheese Enchiladas • 211

Charred Corn, Squash, and Onion Gratin • 215

Pimento Mac and Cheese Custard • 217

Deviled Crab Rigatoni • 221

TEX-MEX CHEESE ENCHILADAS

SERVES 4 TO 6

To re-create the cheese enchiladas they would eat around Christmas when visiting family in Dallas, Kait and her mom reverse engineered the recipe. They went back and forth tweaking and revising it, developing the recipe as a way to chase a memory (a quixotic quest if there ever was one), and now it's at a place where the whole family feels like it's close enough to stop futzing.

You can freeze both the chile sauce and the chile gravy or the entire assembled dish. We usually make this ahead and freeze it, then bring it out as a supplemental meal around the holidays. It's a great dinner for the "eve" of whatever the big occasion might be—Thanksgiving Eve, Christmas Eve, birthday eve, you name it.

•

Guajillo Sauce

7 guajillo chiles, stemmed and seeded

2 dried árbol or ancho chiles, stemmed

1 yellow onion, chopped

One 8-ounce can chopped tomatoes, drained

2 cups water

Chile Gravy

¼ cup chipotle or ancho chile powder

4 teaspoons ground cumin

2 teaspoons garlic powder

1 teaspoon dried oregano

2 teaspoons kosher salt

1 teaspoon freshly ground black pepper

½ cup neutral vegetable oil

½ cup all-purpose flour

4 cups beef or vegetable stock (see Note)

Make the guajillo sauce: In a medium saucepan, combine the guajillo chiles, árbol chiles, onion, tomatoes, and water and bring to a boil over high heat. Turn down the heat to low and simmer gently, adding water if needed to prevent sticking, for about 15 minutes, until the chiles are softened. Remove from the heat and let cool for 15 minutes.

Transfer the contents of the saucepan to a blender or food processor and puree on high speed until liquefied. Add more water if needed to achieve the consistency of a sauce. Set aside; keep warm if assembling the enchiladas the same day. (The sauce can be stored in a lidded container in the refrigerator for up to 1 week or in the freezer for up to 6 months.)

Make the chile gravy: In a small bowl, mix together the chile powder, cumin, garlic powder, oregano, salt, and pepper. Set aside. In a medium Dutch oven or high-sided saucepan over medium-high heat, warm the oil. When it shimmers, stir in the flour and continue stirring for 3 to 4 minutes, until a light brown roux forms. Add the reserved spice mixture and cook, stirring and blending the ingredients, for 1 minute. Add the stock slowly and stir until the gravy thickens a little. Lower the heat to a simmer and cook for 15 minutes, stirring occasionally. Add water to adjust the thickness. It needs to be the consistency of gravy—a little thick but pourable. Keep warm while you assemble the enchiladas. (The gravy can be stored in a lidded container in the refrigerator for up to 5 days or in the freezer for up to 6 months. Rewarm on the stove before using.)

continued →

TEX-MEX CHEESE ENCHILADAS

continued

Enchiladas

12 very fresh corn tortillas (see Note)

5 to 6 cups finely shredded cheese (such as Cheddar or Mexican cheese blend)

1 white onion, chopped (optional)

Sour cream, for serving

Assemble the enchiladas: If baking and eating now, preheat the oven to 375°F. Pour the warm guajillo sauce into a shallow bowl.

Dip a tortilla into the guajillo sauce, covering it completely. Let any excess drip off; you want the tortilla to soften but not so much that it tears. Place the tortilla inside a 9 by 13-inch baking dish. Sprinkle 2 to 3 tablespoons cheese in a line down the center of the tortilla, then fold the tortilla over to form a cylinder with the cheese in the middle. Place the enchilada, seam side down, along the short edge of the dish. Repeat with the remaining tortillas, nestling them side by side, until the dish is full. Pour the warm chile gravy over the top of the enchiladas.

TO FREEZE THE ASSEMBLED DISH: Prepare according to the directions and reserve the remaining cheese for when you're ready to bake. Let cool completely to room temperature, then chill uncovered in the refrigerator for 1 hour. Press a piece of plastic wrap directly onto the surface of the enchiladas, almost like you would when making a custard. This will help prevent freezer burn. Tightly wrap the entire dish in plastic wrap and then tightly wrap in aluminum foil. Label and date and freeze for up to 4 months.

TO BAKE FROM FROZEN: Place the wrapped enchiladas in a cold oven and set the oven to 375°F. When the oven reaches temperature, bake for 1 hour, then remove the foil and plastic wrap. Bake for another 30 minutes to 1 hour, until hot in the center and bubbling. Sprinkle the remaining cheese and the onion evenly over the surface for the last 20 minutes of baking.

TO BAKE FROM ROOM TEMPERATURE: Sprinkle the surface of the assembled dish evenly with the remaining cheese and the onion. Bake for about 20 minutes, until bubbling and the cheese is melted.

Serve warm, with a dollop of sour cream atop each serving.

NOTE

To keep the recipe vegetarian, use vegetable stock in the chile gravy. Make sure the tortillas are very fresh. If they are stale, they'll fall apart!

CHARRED CORN, SQUASH, AND ONION GRATIN

SERVES 4 TO 6

At the farmers' market in Raleigh, from late June to mid-September, every single stand sags under the weight of three prolific crops: corn, summer squash, and tomatoes. The beauty of these ingredients, at that time of year, is that you hardly need to do anything to them to enjoy them. Case in point: corn with a little bit of compound butter (see page 112); thinly sliced zucchini with mint, feta, and hazelnuts; a tomato sandwich on white bread.

But when the heat hasn't zapped the energy out of you, and there's enough time in the day to do something slightly more elaborate, make this gratin. Make two—one for now, one to freeze and enjoy after these ingredients have disappeared from farm stands.

A freezer note: Typically mayonnaise-based custards don't hold up as well in the freezer as egg-based ones. By pureeing some of the corn into the custard and baking it beforehand, you're stabilizing things enough to prevent the mayonnaise from doing anything weird, like breaking.

●

8 ears corn

Neutral vegetable oil, for rubbing

Kosher salt and freshly ground black pepper

4 zucchini or other summer squash

4 Vidalia onions

2 pounds tomatoes (such as beefsteak or heirloom)

1 cup mayonnaise

2 tablespoons Dijon mustard

2 tablespoons prepared horseradish

½ cup whole milk

½ cup heavy cream

2 teaspoons chopped fresh thyme

12 fresh basil leaves

8 ounces sharp white Cheddar cheese, shredded

8 ounces chèvre

Prepare a fire in a charcoal or gas grill for direct cooking over high heat.

Remove the husks and silk from the corn and rub each ear with a small amount of oil. Season with salt and pepper. Slice the zucchini in half lengthwise, rub with a small amount of vegetable oil, and season with salt and pepper. Halve each onion across the equator, rub with a small amount of oil, and season the cut sides with salt and pepper.

Grill the vegetables: Place the corn on the grates directly over the fire and grill, rotating the ears every 3 to 4 minutes, until there is a nice spattering of golden brown and amber. Place the zucchini, cut side down, on the grates directly over the fire and grill, undisturbed, for 4 to 5 minutes, until deeply golden brown on the underside. Flip the zucchini and repeat on the other side. Place the onions, cut side down, on the grates and grill for 6 to 8 minutes, until the surface is well charred. Flip the onions and cook for another 3 to 4 minutes. Transfer all of the vegetables to a rimmed baking sheet and let cool until they can be handled.

Preheat the oven to 350°F.

continued →

CHARRED CORN, SQUASH, AND ONION GRATIN

continued

Cut the corn kernels from the cobs. Cut the zucchini into ¼-inch-thick half-moons. Thinly slice the onions, keeping the slices intact as much as you can. Set aside all of the vegetables.

Core the tomatoes and cut into ¼-inch-thick slices. Lay them in a single layer, not overlapping, on a rimmed baking sheet and sprinkle with salt and pepper. Let sit for 10 minutes; the salt will leach out some of their juices. Working in batches, transfer the slices to a salad spinner and carefully spin the tomatoes to remove excess juice.

In a blender, combine the mayonnaise, mustard, horseradish, milk, cream, thyme, basil, and one-fourth of the corn kernels. Blend to make a smooth custard.

In a shallow 2½ to 3-quart gratin dish or a 9 by 13-inch baking dish, build the gratin: Arrange one-third of the tomato slices in an even layer, followed by half each of the zucchini, onion, and corn. Top with half each of the Cheddar and chèvre (you can just pinch off small nubs of the chèvre and dot them across the surface evenly). Repeat the layers with half of the remaining tomato slices and all of the remaining zucchini, onion, corn, chèvre, and Cheddar. Finish with a final layer of tomato slices. Pour the custard evenly over the layers.

Bake the gratin, rotating the dish 180 degrees halfway through baking, for 40 minutes, until bubbling. If eating immediately, cut into portions and serve hot.

TO FREEZE: Let the gratin cool to room temperature on a counter, then refrigerate until well chilled. Wrap the baking dish in two layers of plastic wrap, label and date, and freeze for up to 3 months.

TO REHEAT FROM FROZEN: Unwrap the baking dish, place in a cold oven, and set the oven to 350°F. When the oven reaches temperature, bake for about 40 minutes, until hot throughout and bubbling. Cut into portions and serve hot.

PIMENTO MAC AND CHEESE CUSTARD

SERVES 8

No, sorry. You can't make and freeze the Poole's mac au gratin. The dish for which Ashley (and our first restaurant, Poole's) is best known is a creamy, gooey version of the classic, covered with a brûléed lid of crispy cheese to boot. But it won't be worth a damn if you try to stick it into a freezer—all cheese and cream, nothing to hold it together.

However, there is a way to have your macaroni fix in the freezer: a custard-style baked mac 'n' cheese, like the one that we serve at Beasley's, our restaurant dedicated to fried chicken and other classic Southern dishes. Instead of a cream-based sauce, this one uses eggs *and* béchamel to help bind a very cheesy filling with the noodles. We also stud the bake with pimentos, which help to cut the richness with a little bit of acidity.

●

2 quarts water

Kosher salt

8 ounces elbow macaroni

8 ounces white Cheddar cheese, shredded

4 ounces aged Cheddar cheese, shredded

4 ounces Parmesan cheese, grated

1 cup jarred pimentos, chopped

2 tablespoons all-purpose flour

6 large eggs

2 tablespoons hot sauce, such as Tabasco

One 12-ounce can evaporated milk

1 cup half-and-half

8 cups Herbed Béchamel (page 120), freshly made or thawed

Preheat the oven to 350°F. Grease a 9 by 13-inch baking dish with nonstick cooking spray.

Fill a large pot with the water and add 2 tablespoons salt. Bring to a boil over high heat, add the macaroni, and cook for about 5 minutes, until just shy of al dente. Drain and set aside.

In a medium bowl, mix together the white and aged Cheddars and the Parmesan. Remove and reserve one-fourth of the cheese mix for the top. To the bowl with the rest of the cheese mix, add the macaroni, pimentos, and flour and mix well to combine. Pour the mixture into the prepared baking dish.

In a large bowl, whisk the eggs until blended, then whisk in the hot sauce, evaporated milk, half-and-half, and 2 teaspoons salt, mixing well. While whisking constantly, slowly add the béchamel to create a custard. Pour the custard evenly over the noodle mixture.

Cover with a layer of plastic wrap and a layer of aluminum foil and bake for 50 minutes, rotating the dish 180 degrees halfway through baking. Uncover the dish. If you plan to eat the mac and cheese right away, sprinkle the reserved cheese on top. If you plan to freeze the dish, do not add the cheese. Continue to bake, uncovered, for 15 to 20 minutes, until set, golden, and bubbling. Remove from the oven and let sit for 5 minutes before serving.

continued →

PIMENTO MAC AND CHEESE CUSTARD

continued

TO FREEZE: Let cool to room temperature, then refrigerate until well chilled. Wrap the baking dish in two layers of plastic wrap, label and date, and freeze for up to 3 months.

TO THAW: You can reheat this dish from frozen, or you can thaw it using the pull and thaw method (see page 43).

TO REHEAT: If reheating from frozen, unwrap the dish, place in a cold oven, and set the oven to 350°F. When the oven reaches temperature, bake for 1½ hours, then sprinkle the surface with the remaining cheese mix and bake for 15 minutes longer, until bubbling. If reheating after thawing, cut the cook time to 30 to 45 minutes.

DEVILED CRAB RIGATONI

SERVES 8

This baked rigatoni is a showstopper, and as far as seafood pastas go, it clocks in as way sexier than tuna noodle casserole. We love it because it transforms a creamy à la minute pasta into a make-ahead dish that's still packed with flavor. From the sherry and garlic–enhanced leeks to the addition of Dijon and Worcestershire, every step of this dish is well seasoned.

In North Carolina, we have access to very fresh blue crabmeat most of the year. But if it's hard for you to find good crabmeat, you can definitely use peeled and deveined shrimp, cut into ½-inch pieces.

●

Kosher salt

8 ounces rigatoni

¼ cup olive oil

3 tablespoons unsalted butter

4 leeks, white part only, cleaned and thinly sliced

4 garlic cloves, finely chopped

½ cup sweet sherry

2 cups heavy cream

4 large eggs, lightly beaten

¼ cup Dijon mustard

1 tablespoon Worcestershire sauce

¼ teaspoon cayenne pepper

Freshly ground black pepper

8 ounces lump crabmeat, picked over for shell fragments

Chopped fresh flat-leaf parsley, for garnish

Butter an 8 by 11-inch baking dish.

Fill a large pot with water and salt it generously (it should taste salty like the ocean). Bring to a boil over high heat, add the rigatoni, and cook 11½ minutes, just shy of al dente. Drain well and let cool slightly.

In a large skillet over medium heat, warm the oil and butter. When the butter melts, add the leeks and cook, stirring frequently, for 10 to 12 minutes, until softened and translucent. Add the garlic, season with 1 teaspoon salt, and cook, stirring occasionally, for 4 to 5 minutes, until the garlic has softened. Add the sherry and reduce, stirring often, for about 5 minutes, until most of the liquid has evaporated. Let cool.

In a large bowl, whisk together the cream, eggs, Dijon, Worcestershire sauce, and cayenne. Add 2 to 3 teaspoons black pepper, 2 teaspoons salt, the crabmeat, leeks, and rigatoni. Stir to coat and distribute everything evenly. Pour into the prepared dish.

TO FREEZE THE ASSEMBLED DISH: Wrap the baking dish in two layers of plastic wrap, label and date, and freeze for up to 3 months.

TO BAKE FROM FROZEN: Unwrap the baking dish and cover with foil. Place in a cold oven and set the oven to 350°F. Bake for 1 hour, then remove the foil. Bake for another 15 to 20 minutes, until the surface is browned in spots and the custard is set.

TO BAKE FROM ROOM TEMPERATURE: Preheat the oven to 350°F. Cover the baking dish with foil and bake for 20 minutes. Remove the foil and bake, uncovered, another 10 minutes, until the surface is browned in spots and the custard is set.

After removing from the oven, let rest for 5 minutes. Serve onto plates and garnish with a sprinkle of parsley.

13

Sweets.

Zucchini–Poppy Seed Bread • 224

Tahini–Brown Butter Chocolate Chip Cookies • 225

Malted Coffee Toffee Cookies • 226

Salty Dog Icebox Pie • 228

Frozen Cheesecake Cookie Sandwiches • 230

Miso-Caramel Shortbread • 232

Spiced Pumpkin Pudding Cakes • 235

223

ZUCCHINI-POPPY SEED BREAD

MAKES 1 LOAF

More than any other type of loaf cake, zucchini bread holds the nostalgia candle in our house. For Ashley, zucchini bread was a fixture in the house growing up—an easy use for the abundance of squash that flourished in her dad's garden each summer. This is her mom's recipe, with a few small tweaks from us.

We like to freeze individual slices so we can reheat only what we need, rather than the entire loaf. This helps preserve the loaf and avoids that situation in which it gets dry before you can finish it.

●

1½ cups all-purpose flour

1 teaspoon ground cinnamon

2 teaspoons kosher salt

½ teaspoon baking soda

⅛ teaspoon baking powder

2 teaspoons poppy seeds

½ cup extra virgin olive oil

2 large eggs, lightly beaten

1 cup sugar

1½ teaspoons pure vanilla extract

2 cups coarsely shredded zucchini (about 12 ounces)

Unsalted butter, for toasting

Flaky sea salt, for serving

Preheat the oven to 375°F. Butter an 8½ by 4½-inch loaf pan, then coat with sugar, tapping out the excess.

In a large bowl, whisk together the flour, cinnamon, salt, baking soda, baking powder, and poppy seeds. In a medium bowl, whisk together the oil, eggs, sugar, and vanilla. Add the zucchini to the oil mixture and stir to mix. Then stir the wet ingredients into the dry ingredients until well mixed.

Pour the batter into the prepared pan. Bake for about 65 minutes, until a toothpick inserted into the center comes out clean. Let the zucchini bread cool completely in the pan on a wire rack before turning it out to serve or prepare for freezing.

TO FREEZE: Slice the loaf and lay the slices in a single layer on a rimmed baking sheet. Freeze for 2 to 3 hours, or until hard, for a formative freeze (see page 31). Transfer the slices to a zip-top plastic bag, label and date, and freeze for up to 6 weeks.

TO THAW: You could thaw and reheat the slices in the microwave or the oven, but we prefer to pull and thaw (see page 43) the slices the day before and reheat on the stove top.

TO REHEAT: When ready to serve, melt 1 tablespoon unsalted butter in a small skillet over medium-high heat. Add the thawed slice and toast for about 5 minutes, until slightly crispy on the underside. Sprinkle the toast with flaky salt and enjoy.

TAHINI-BROWN BUTTER CHOCOLATE CHIP COOKIES

MAKES 20 COOKIES

Do you remember the time before tahini was the ubiquitously beloved, accessible, popular ingredient in the States that it is today? We thank the chefs and cookbook writers such as Adeena Sussman, Michael Solomonov, and Yotam Ottolenghi for helping to popularize this staple of Middle Eastern cuisine with a new audience. Silky textured, not as intensely flavored as a nut butter, rich with just a mild bitterness, easily shifts between savory and sweet applications—we're in love.

Tahini chocolate chip cookies have proliferated since the paste's rise to power, but that couldn't stop us from putting our own version out there. We like to brown the butter beforehand to match that nutty flavor from the tahini. It's an extra, slightly tedious step, but worth it.

1 cup unsalted butter, at room temperature

2¼ cups all-purpose flour

1¼ teaspoons kosher salt

1¼ teaspoons baking soda

¾ cup tahini

1 cup granulated sugar

½ cup plus 2 tablespoons firmly packed light brown sugar

2 large eggs

1½ teaspoons pure vanilla extract

2½ cups semi-sweet chocolate chips

In a medium saucepan over medium heat, melt the butter. Stir frequently; after it stops foaming, it will slowly start to darken and smell nutty. Continue stirring until it smells very toasty, and turns almost nut-brown in color. Then remove from the heat and pour into a heatproof measuring cup; it may not quite measure 1 cup. Refrigerate for 1 to 2 hours, until solidified.

Sift the flour, salt, and baking soda into a medium bowl. In a stand mixer fitted with the paddle attachment, mix together the browned butter, tahini, and both sugars on medium speed until barely combined. Add the eggs and vanilla and mix until partly combined. Add the dry ingredients and mix until the batter is lumpy but not completely combined. Add the chocolate chips and mix just until combined.

Line a large rimmed baking sheet with parchment paper. Using a 2-ounce scoop (about ¼ cup), scoop the cookies onto the prepared pan, spacing them about 2 inches apart. If baking without first freezing, cover and refrigerate overnight. If freezing immediately, skip the refrigeration.

TO FREEZE: Place the baking sheet in the freezer for at least 4 hours or up to overnight for a formative freeze (see page 31). Transfer the cookies to a zip-top plastic bag, label and date, and freeze for up to 9 months.

TO BAKE: Preheat the oven to 400°F. Bake the cookies for 12 to 15 minutes if the dough is refrigerated, or 15 to 18 minutes if it is frozen, until the edges are golden brown. Transfer to a wire rack and let cool for a few minutes before serving. The cookies will keep in a zip-top plastic bag at room temperature for 5 days.

MALTED COFFEE TOFFEE COOKIES

MAKES 20 COOKIES

Living up to the stereotype of most savory chefs, Ashley's not much for making dessert. Kait likes to bake, but doesn't get to do it very much. That means when people come over for dinner at our house, we're pretty disappointing in our dessert offerings—a few pieces of sliced fruit and some chunks of good chocolate are about as elaborate as it gets.

That is until Kait started making cookie dough and keeping it in the freezer. It's something her mom always did, and it's a perfect way to have a little sweet in the house without committing to eating an entire batch before it goes bad.

Now, post-meal, Kait can bake off some fresh cookies by just grabbing a few different balls of dough from the freezer. You'd be surprised at how excited people get over the prospect of a freshly baked cookie. This particular cookie has a lot going on, with a great ratio of sweet to salty to bitter. Ashley isn't a fan of overly sweet desserts, so we've taken the sugar down a bit.

2¼ cups all-purpose flour

1¼ teaspoons kosher salt

1¼ teaspoons baking soda

1 tablespoon ground coffee (not instant!)

1¼ cups unsalted butter, at room temperature

¾ cup granulated sugar

¾ cup firmly packed light brown sugar

2 large eggs

1½ teaspoons pure vanilla extract

2 tablespoons malted milk powder

2½ cups chopped English-style toffee

Sift together the flour, salt, baking soda, and coffee into a medium bowl. In a stand mixer fitted with the paddle attachment, mix together the butter and both sugars on medium speed until barely combined. Add the eggs and vanilla and mix until partly combined. Add the sifted dry ingredients and the malted milk powder and mix until the batter is lumpy but not completely combined. Add the toffee and mix just until combined.

Line a large rimmed baking sheet with parchment paper. Using a 2-ounce scoop (about ¼ cup), scoop the cookies onto the prepared pan, spacing them about 2 inches apart. If baking without first freezing, cover and refrigerate overnight. If freezing immediately, skip the refrigeration.

TO FREEZE: Place the baking sheet in the freezer for at least 4 hours or up to overnight for a formative freeze (see page 31). Transfer the cookies to a zip-top plastic bag, label and date, and freeze for up to 9 months.

TO BAKE: Preheat the oven to 375°F. Bake the cookies for 12 to 15 minutes if the dough is refrigerated, or 15 to 18 minutes if it is frozen, until the edges are golden brown. Transfer to a wire rack and let cool for a few minutes before serving. The cookies will keep in a zip-top plastic bag at room temperature for 5 days.

SALTY DOG ICEBOX PIE

SERVES 8

For a period of three or four years, Ashley's cocktail of choice was the Greyhound—vodka and fresh-squeezed grapefruit juice.

She might switch it up at the bar these days, but we both continue to love the flavor of grapefruit and wanted to showcase it in a freezer-ready dessert: icebox pie. We use saltines for the crust, which offsets the sweet-bitter custard with a bit of salt (a Greyhound with a salt rim is called a Salty Dog, hence the name). For the filling, fresh grapefruit juice makes a simple, delicious curd.

This pie should be kept in the freezer and served frozen. The curd alone, stored in a lidded container in the freezer, will keep well for 6 months.

●

Make the crust: Preheat the oven to 350°F.

Using your hands or a food processor, crush the crackers into fine crumbs. Transfer to a medium bowl. Add the butter and sugar and mix together with a rubber spatula until the crumbs stick together when you press some between your fingers.

Pour the crumb mixture into a 9-inch pie pan and use your hands to press it onto the bottom and up the sides in an even layer. Bake for 15 to 17 minutes, until golden brown. Let cool completely on a wire rack.

Make the filling: In a medium saucepan over medium heat, bring the grapefruit juice to a simmer and simmer for about 15 minutes, until reduced by half. Let cool to room temperature.

In a medium saucepan, whisk together the eggs, egg yolks, and sugar until blended. Whisk in the reduced grapefruit juice and set over medium heat. Cook, stirring constantly, for about 10 minutes, until slightly thickened. It should be the consistency of a melted smoothie. Turn off the heat and add the butter a cube at a time, stirring after each addition until fully incorporated before adding the next piece. The curd should be thick enough to coat a spoon; it will continue to thicken as it cools. Transfer to a heatproof bowl and press a piece of plastic wrap directly onto the surface to prevent a skin forming. Let cool to room temperature.

Transfer the curd to the pie shell and spread into an even layer.

TO FREEZE: Place a fresh piece of plastic wrap on the surface of the filling and freeze the pie for at least 4 hours or up to overnight for a formative freeze (see page 31). Remove the plastic layer on the surface, and wrap the entire pie with two layers of plastic wrap, label and date, and freeze for up to 2 weeks.

To serve, unwrap the pie, cut into slices, and serve frozen.

Crust

1 sleeve saltine crackers (about 4 ounces or 40 crackers)

½ cup unsalted butter, melted

3 tablespoons sugar

Filling

1½ cups fresh grapefruit juice, strained

2 large eggs

4 large egg yolks

¾ cup sugar

6 tablespoons unsalted butter, cut into 6 cubes

FROZEN CHEESECAKE
COOKIE SANDWICHES

MAKES 16 SQUARES

If you ask Ashley what inspired this recipe, she'd say "Creamy Burger." If you ask Kait, she'd say "It's-It." Each is a regional version of an oatmeal cookie ice cream sandwich. We've kept the main selling points—oatmeal cookie shell, chocolate coating—but have matured things from the original with a crème fraîche–laden cheesecake filling. This whole thing is a no-bake dessert, making it a great recipe to save for those hot summer days when you'd rather do anything than turn on the oven.

●

Cookie Crust

1 cup all-purpose flour

¾ teaspoon kosher salt

¼ teaspoon ground cinnamon

6 tablespoons unsalted butter

¾ cup firmly packed dark brown sugar

½ cup granulated sugar

1 cup neutral vegetable oil

1 teaspoon pure vanilla extract

3 cups old-fashioned rolled oats

Filling

4 ounces cream cheese, at room temperature

½ cup confectioners' sugar

½ teaspoon kosher salt

2 teaspoons pure vanilla extract

½ cup crème fraîche

½ cup heavy cream

Make the cookie crust: Sift together the flour, salt, and cinnamon into a medium bowl. In a stand mixer fitted with the paddle attachment, cream together the butter and brown and granulated sugars on medium speed for 4 minutes, until light and fluffy. Add the vegetable oil and vanilla and beat until well mixed. On low speed, add the flour mixture in two batches alternately with the oats in two batches, beginning with the flour mixture and beating after each addition until incorporated.

Line the bottom and two opposite sides of two 8-inch square pans with parchment paper, allowing the parchment to overhang the sides by about 2 inches. Divide the dough evenly between the two pans, pressing it into an even layer. Place in the refrigerator to chill while you make the filling.

Make the filling: In a stand mixer fitted with the whisk attachment, beat together the cream cheese and confectioners' sugar on high speed until smooth. Beat in the salt and vanilla, then add the crème fraîche and continue to beat on high speed for a few seconds, until well mixed and smooth. Add the cream and beat on high speed for about 1 minute, until the mixture holds stiff peaks.

Remove the pans from the refrigerator. Spread the filling evenly over one of the cookie crusts. Using the parchment overhang of the second cookie crust, lift the crust out of the pan and flip it on top of the filling. Remove the parchment and press down firmly and evenly on the top crust. Freeze, uncovered, for 2 hours or up to overnight.

Place a wire rack on a rimmed baking sheet. Using the parchment overhang, lift the frozen filled square from the pan and set on a cutting board. Using a sharp knife cut into 16 uniform squares. Place the squares on the wire rack and place the baking sheet in the freezer while you prepare the chocolate shell.

Chocolate Shell

1 cup dark chocolate chips

3 tablespoons refined coconut oil

Pinch of sea salt

1 tablespoon Dutch-processed cocoa powder

1 teaspoon pure vanilla extract

Make the chocolate shell: In a microwave-safe bowl, combine the chocolate and coconut oil and place in a microwave. Set the microwave on medium heat (5 out of 10 on ours) and microwave in 30-second increments, stirring after each increment, until the chocolate is melted and smooth. Stir in the salt, cocoa powder, and vanilla.

Working quickly, dip each sandwich into the chocolate mixture to coat. You can do a full coat or only a half coat—it's up to you. As each sandwich is dipped, return it to the wire rack to dry. (If you aren't speedy in this process, the sandwiches will start to melt, so stay focused.)

TO FREEZE: Return the baking sheet to the freezer for about 1 hour, until the chocolate has hardened. Then wrap the sandwiches individually in plastic wrap, slide them into a zip-top plastic bag, label and date, and freeze for up to 3 months.

MISO-CARAMEL SHORTBREAD

MAKES 16 COOKIES

A good shortbread should be a paradox. Every bite should be both salty and sweet, both chewy and crumbly. Miso, the fermented soybean paste, is the essence of savory, which means that it plays beautifully with sugar. For this recipe, we use white miso (aka blond miso), which is the mildest in flavor, in both the shortbread dough and the caramel.

•

Shortbread

1 cup cold unsalted butter, cut into ½-inch pieces

½ cup confectioners' sugar

¼ cup firmly packed light brown sugar

2 heaping tablespoons white miso

1 teaspoon pure vanilla extract

2¼ cups all-purpose flour

1 teaspoon kosher salt

Caramel

¾ cup granulated sugar

¼ cup water

½ cup heavy cream

1 tablespoon white miso

Make the shortbread: Preheat the oven to 350°F.

In a stand mixer fitted with the paddle attachment, cream together the butter, confectioners' and brown sugars, miso, and vanilla on medium speed for 1 to 2 minutes, until light and fluffy. On low speed, add the flour and salt and beat until a crumbly dough forms.

Line the bottom and two opposite sides of an 8-inch square pan with parchment paper, allowing the parchment to overhang the sides by about 2 inches. Press the dough onto the bottom of the pan in an even layer. Dock the surface with a fork. Bake for 18 to 20 minutes, until the surface is beginning to turn golden brown. Let cool in the pan on a wire rack for 10 minutes, then, using the parchment overhang, lift the shortbread from the pan and set on a cutting board. While the shortbread is still warm, cut it into 16 uniform squares. Let cool to room temperature.

Make the caramel: In a heavy medium saucepan over medium-high heat, stir together the sugar and water just until all of the sugar is wet. Without additional stirring, bring the mixture to a boil and boil for 5 to 7 minutes, until it turns a deep golden brown and wisps of smoke just start to form or it reaches 350°F on a candy thermometer, then immediately remove from the heat.

Once off the heat, carefully pour in the cream, which will cause the caramel to bubble. Stir to mix well. If the caramel seizes up and hardens with the addition of the cream, put the pan back over low heat and stir until the caramel is liquid again. Whisk in the miso, then allow to cool slightly.

Drizzle each shortbread square with some of the caramel. Place the shortbread in the refrigerator to chill and set.

TO FREEZE: Transfer the shortbread squares to a rimmed baking sheet and freeze for at least 4 hours or up to overnight for a formative freeze (see page 31). Transfer the squares to a lidded container, label and date, and freeze for up to 3 months.

TO THAW: Pull the shortbread out and let sit at room temperature for 15 to 20 minutes.

SPICED PUMPKIN PUDDING CAKES

MAKES 24 CAKES

Unfortunately, superlight, fluffy cakes with a great crumb and creamy frosting layers don't do well in the freezer. There's the tradition of freezing some of your wedding cake to eat on your anniversary, but anyone who has actually done that will agree: the cake just doesn't hold up.

Luckily, we have a workaround for those who love cake: the sticky gooey pudding-style cake. We're referring to the Old English version of pudding here—think sticky toffee pudding or persimmon pudding. These are basically custards, but they are bound with just enough flour to fortify them against time spent in the freezer.

These pumpkin pudding cakes are sort of a cross between sticky toffee and persimmon puddings. We bake them in muffin pans to have individual cakes, but you could also bake the batter in a 9 by 13-inch baking dish and then cut the finished cake into squares.

•

1 cup Medjool dates (about 5 ounces), pitted

1 cup boiling water

1¾ teaspoons baking soda

1¾ cups all-purpose flour

1 teaspoon baking powder

½ teaspoon salt

½ teaspoon freshly grated nutmeg

1 teaspoon ground cinnamon

One 15-ounce can pumpkin puree

1 cup sugar

½ cup unsalted butter, melted

1 cup heavy cream

1 cup evaporated milk

2 large eggs, lightly beaten

1 teaspoon peeled and finely grated fresh ginger

Sweetened whipped cream and freshly grated nutmeg, for serving

Preheat the oven to 325°F. Grease the molds of two 12-cup muffin pans with butter or nonstick spray (do not use paper liners).

Put the dates into a heatproof medium bowl and cover them with the boiling water. Stir in ¾ teaspoon of the baking soda and let sit for 15 minutes. Transfer the dates and their soaking water to a food processor or blender and puree until smooth.

Sift together the flour, baking powder, salt, nutmeg, cinnamon, and the remaining 1 teaspoon baking soda into a medium bowl. In a large bowl, whisk together the pumpkin, sugar, butter, cream, milk, eggs, and ginger until well mixed. Stir in the date puree. Add the dry ingredients to the wet ingredients and mix well.

Divide the batter evenly among the muffin cups. Bake for about 45 minutes, until a knife inserted into the center of a muffin comes out clean. Let cool in the pan on a wire rack for 10 minutes, then carefully remove the cakes from the pan.

TO FREEZE: Let the cakes cool to room temperature. Arrange on a rimmed baking sheet and place in the freezer for at least 4 hours or up to overnight for a formative freeze (see page 31). Transfer the cakes to a zip-top plastic bag, label and date, and freeze for up to 6 months.

TO REHEAT: Place the frozen cakes on a microwave-safe plate and cover with a dampened paper towel. (This will create steam in the microwave that will help resoften the cakes.) Place in the microwave, set the microwave on a medium-low setting (3 out of 10 on ours), and microwave for 5 minutes, until hot throughout.

Serve warm with whipped cream and a sprinkle of nutmeg.

14

Beverages.

Multitasker Smoothie • 238

Margarita Slush • 239

Boulevardier Slushie • 240

Three Sheets • 242

Watermelon Juice • 245

Chai Concentrate • 246

Jalapeño-Ginger Syrup • 248

Strawberries for Morning and Evening • 249

MULTITASKER SMOOTHIE

MAKES 1 SMOOTHIE

As the name would suggest, this smoothie is your move when you're so busy that you need your breakfast and your coffee in the same glass. Ashley started drinking these while she was training for the Chefs Cycle bike ride benefiting Share Our Strength. Riding bikes for multiple miles has the tendency to deplete you, especially in the humidity of North Carolina, and she'd come back from a morning ride experiencing equal parts hunger, thirst, and coffee headache. These smoothies were the quickest way to solve all three, short of an IV drip.

The lengthy bike rides are less frequent, but the smoothie has stayed on in our rotation as a Hall of Famer because it hits that sweet spot on the matrix of delicious (more milkshake than smoothie) and convenient. Plus, it has the added bonus of being a way to use up brown bananas.

●

1 very ripe banana (ripe to the point of mostly brown), peeled and frozen (see Note)

¾ cup unsweetened almond milk

¼ cup cold brew coffee concentrate or room-temperature espresso

¼ cup almond butter

2 teaspoons agave nectar

½ cup ice cubes

Pinch of sea salt

Combine the banana, almond milk, coffee, almond butter, agave nectar, ice, and salt in a blender and blend until smooth. Pour into a chilled glass and serve with a straw.

NOTE

Banana bread is the classic vehicle for overripe bananas, but if you're not in a baking mood, you can still extend the life of this all-too-common banana state: freeze 'em! Peel the bananas and place them on a waxed paper–lined rimmed baking sheet. Place in the freezer overnight, then transfer the bananas to a zip-top plastic bag or vacuum-sealed pouch, label and date, and return to the freezer for up to 6 months.

MARGARITA SLUSH

**MAKES ABOUT
20 COCKTAILS**

We are major margarita people. So much so that Ashley bought Kait a frozen-drink machine for her thirtieth birthday. We also served frozen margaritas at our wedding. To put it mildly, we come to this recipe with a lot of practice, and a lot of opinions. Having finely crafted our recipe over several years, we believe that the key to the right acidity and texture involves a mixture of three different citrus juices. Sorry, purists, we won't be dissuaded here.

Although you can make a decent frozen margarita in a blender, making it in the freezer like a slushie creates an even better texture. It uses a similar technique to the Boulevardier Slushie (page 240), and since Derby Day and Cinco de Mayo often coincide, you could do an entire week of slushie drinks and stay right on brand.

1⅓ cups sugar

4⅓ cups water

2 cups fresh orange juice, strained

2 cups fresh lime juice, strained

2 cups fresh grapefruit juice, strained

4 cups blanco tequila

½ cup Cointreau

In a medium saucepot, stir together the sugar and 1⅓ cups of the water. Place over medium heat and cook, stirring occasionally, until the sugar has completely dissolved, 5 to 7 minutes. Let cool.

In a large bowl, combine all of the remaining ingredients and the reserved simple syrup and mix well. Divide the mixture between two shallow baking dishes; the liquid should be no more than 1 inch deep. (Two 9 by 13-inch baking dishes work well.)

Carefully transfer the baking dishes to the freezer and freeze the mixture for about 4 hours, until mostly solid, scraping the surface of the mixture every hour or so with the tines of a fork to create a granita-like consistency.

Spoon into cups and serve with spoons and straws.

NOTE

To make this slush in batches in a blender, omit the 3 cups water and skip the freezer step. Pour 1½ cups of the mixture into a blender and add 2 cups ice cubes. Blend until you reach the desired consistency. Repeat with the remaining mix in batches.

BOULEVARDIER SLUSHIE

**MAKES ABOUT
8 COCKTAILS**

This slush was born during an annual ski trip in Colorado. We take a week each winter to hole up in the mountains in a big house with a bunch of friends. It's equal parts skiing, lounging around in sweatpants, eating snacks, and drinking drinks. Every meal has assigned "captains," and because three meals a day just aren't enough, there are also captains for après-ski, a glorified happy hour.

Kait made this slush one afternoon as her entry for après-ski. Pair it with a snack of some salty potato chips and olives.

·

½ cup sugar

2 cups water

1 cup bourbon

1 cup Campari

1 cup sweet vermouth

2 cups fresh orange juice, strained

To make a simple syrup, in a small saucepan over medium heat, combine the sugar and 1 cup of the water and heat, stirring, until the sugar dissolves. Remove from the heat and add the remaining 1 cup water. Let cool to room temperature.

In a large pitcher or other container, combine the diluted simple syrup, the bourbon, Campari, vermouth, and orange juice and stir well. Pour the mixture into a large, shallow baking dish; the liquid should be no more than 1 inch deep. (A 9 by 13-inch baking dish works well.)

Carefully transfer the baking dish to the freezer and freeze the mixture for about 4 hours, until it is mostly solid, scraping the surface of the mixture every hour or so with the tines of a fork to create a granita-like consistency.

Spoon into cups and serve with a spoon and a straw.

THREE SHEETS

You know that bottle of vodka that you keep in your freezer (next to your cash)? This is the same idea but better. The freezing point of alcohol (−17°F) is lower than water, and lower than the temperature in your freezer. This means that you can bottle booze-forward cocktails—think Negronis, Martinis, and other spirit-heavy drinks. Pulling a frosty bottle of batched cocktails is a sophisticated party move. Pair any of these with one of the freezer snacks in this book and you'll never need another happy hour outside of your own kitchen.

●

Kait's Negroni

MAKES 8 COCKTAILS

1 cup London dry gin
1 cup sweet vermouth
1 cup Campari
Ice cubes, for serving

In a pitcher, stir together the gin, sweet vermouth, and Campari. Pour into a bottle, cap tightly, and freeze for up to 1 month.

For each cocktail, pour 3 ounces into an ice-filled rocks glass.

The Vesper

MAKES 4 COCKTAILS

1½ cups gin
½ cup vodka
¼ cup Lillet Blanc
1 ounce cold filtered water
Lemon peel twists, for garnish

In a pitcher, stir together the gin, vodka, and Lillet. Pour into a bottle, cap tightly, and freeze for up to 1 month.

For each cocktail, pour 4½ ounces mix into a chilled Martini glass along with ¼ ounce of the filtered water. Garnish with a lemon twist.

Vieux Carre

MAKES 9 COCKTAILS

¾ cup rye
¾ cup Cognac
¾ cup sweet vermouth
5 tablespoons Bénédictine
Pimento bitters, for serving
Maraschino cherries or lemon peel twists, for garnish

In a pitcher, stir together the rye, Cognac, vermouth, and Bénédictine. Pour into a bottle, cap tightly, and freeze for up to 1 month.

For each cocktail, pour 2½ ounces into a chilled cocktail glass along with a splash of cold water and a dash of pimento bitters. Garnish with a cherry.

WATERMELON JUICE

MAKES 6 QUARTS

Watermelon juice is one of our preservation priorities during the summer. It's all you need to achieve what feels like a "fancy" cocktail. Our favorite way to enjoy it is in the form of a Collins made with vodka or gin, a touch of lemon juice, and soda. Throw some mint or basil in the shaker if you'd like an herbaceous profile.

●

½ large seedless watermelon (about 6 pounds)

Cut the watermelon half into manageable chunks and cut away the rind. Place the chunks into a very large bowl.

Rest a fine-mesh strainer on a second large bowl and set the bowl near the first bowl. Using your hands, crush the watermelon into a puree. As juice accumulates, pour it off through the strainer into the second bowl.

When all of the flesh is crushed, work in batches to transfer the flesh to the strainer and push out as much juice as possible. Discard any solids remaining in the strainer.

TO FREEZE: Portions matter here. If you think you'll be using watermelon juice in larger batches, freeze in quart-size portions. Otherwise, freeze in 1-cup portions, either in small zip-top plastic bags or smaller glass or plastic lidded containers. For single-cocktail servings, freeze the juice in ice-cube trays for at least 4 hours or up to overnight for a formative freeze (see page 31), then pop out the cubes and slide them into a zip-top plastic bag. Label and date the container and freeze for up to 3 months.

TO THAW: Don't expose watermelon juice to heat! Use only the pull and thaw method (see page 43) or the cold water method (see page 43).

MAKES 1 COCKTAIL

Watermelon Collins

2 ounces vodka or gin

1 ounce fresh lemon juice

2 ounces Watermelon Juice, fresh or thawed

Ice cubes, for shaker and glass

Club soda, for topping off

Small mint sprig, for garnish

In a cocktail shaker, combine the vodka, lemon juice, and watermelon juice. Fill the shaker with ice, cover, and shake well. Strain into an ice-filled Collins glass, top off with soda to the rim, and stir once. Garnish with the mint.

CHAI CONCENTRATE

**MAKES ENOUGH FOR
16 CHAI LATTES**

When Kait was growing up, chai with milk was one of her very favorite "grown-up" indulgences.

But somewhere along the way in adulthood, she abandoned chai as a regular thing. Then just this past year, while visiting some friends in the California desert, she was offered a mug of hot chai with steamed oat milk. It was fragrant and warming and reminded her of how much she loved it.

You can certainly buy chai concentrate, but the finished drink is much more satisfying (and makes your house smell *delicious*) if you make the concentrate yourself with whole spices. We freeze the concentrate in cubes so we can quickly thaw a cube or two and just add milk.

10 green cardamom pods

2 cinnamon sticks, about 3 inches long, each broken into a few pieces

4 star anise pods

12 black peppercorns

10 whole cloves

½ cup loose black tea (such as Assam)

1½-inch piece fresh ginger, sliced into coins

4 cups boiling water

½ cup firmly packed dark brown sugar

½ cup coconut palm sugar

In a dry skillet over medium heat, combine the cardamom, cinnamon, star anise, peppercorns, and cloves and toast, shaking the skillet back and forth to prevent scorching, for about 2 minutes, until very fragrant. Transfer the spices to a mortar and crush gently with a pestle. You're not trying to grind them, just break them up a bit.

In a heatproof medium bowl, combine the tea and ginger. Pour in the boiling water and let sit for 5 minutes. Add the crushed spices and let steep for 10 minutes. Strain the contents of the bowl through a fine-mesh strainer placed over a small saucepan. Place over medium-high heat, bring to a boil, and boil for about 8 minutes, until reduced by half. Stir in both sugars and continue to stir until dissolved. Remove from the heat and let cool completely.

TO FREEZE: Divide into 1- or 2-ounce portions (2- or 4-tablespoon portions); ice-cube trays work well. Place in the freezer for at least 4 hours or up to overnight for a formative freeze (see page 31). Pop the cubes out of the trays and slide them into a zip-top plastic bag. Label and date, then freeze for up to 6 months.

TO THAW: Place the desired number of portions in a vessel and let thaw at room temperature for 10 to 15 minutes.

● **CHEFFIN' IT UP**

Spiced Chai Latte

In a milk steamer or in a small saucepan on the stove, heat 2 ounces (¼ cup) thawed chai concentrate with 8 ounces (1 cup) milk of your preference. In India, chai is made with extra-high-in-fat milk, so half-and-half would be pretty close. Or try the concentrate with a nondairy option, such as oat milk or coconut milk. Pour into a mug and enjoy.

JALAPEÑO-GINGER SYRUP

MAKES 4 CUPS

Pro tip: You can freeze simple syrup. It may not be necessary to preserve the plain-Jane simple syrup you have in your fridge right now, but keep this wisdom in mind for when you make an infused simple syrup that you can't use up and don't want to toss.

This jalapeño-spiked ginger syrup is a slight tweak of the regular ginger syrup we make for Moscow Mules at our restaurants. Paired with soda and some fresh herbs (both mint and basil work wonders), it makes a refreshing mocktail. Add vodka to make it a cocktail.

6 ounces fresh ginger, peeled and coarsely chopped

2 ounces jalapeño chiles, stemmed, half of the seeds removed, and sliced

2½ cups sugar

2½ cups water

In a medium saucepan, combine all of the ingredients and bring to a boil over high heat, stirring to dissolve the sugar. Lower the heat and simmer gently, stirring occasionally, for 15 minutes. Remove from the heat and let sit for 30 minutes.

Strain through a fine-mesh strainer and discard the solids. Let cool completely before using. The syrup will keep in a lidded container in the refrigerator up to 1 week.

TO FREEZE: Portion into 1- or 2-cup jars or containers, label and date, and freeze for up to 3 months.

TO THAW: Use the pull and thaw method (see page 43) or the cold water method (see page 43).

STRAWBERRIES FOR MORNING AND EVENING

Strawberries and daylight saving time click in around the same time every year, hardly a coincidence in our minds. Just like an extra hour of sunlight, strawberries lift the moods in our house, reminding us that the era of braises and root vegetables is closing, and this, too, shall pass.

Because strawberries are first in the lineup of sexy, pretty-colored produce, we overindulge. We buy too much; we go on a strawberry baking and cooking bender; we walk around with strawberry seeds in our teeth for most of April.

This puree (strained of those pesky seeds) speaks to these over-excitable first days of spring, when warm-weather produce is a promise, not the given that it will end up becoming by September. You can use this puree during every meal part, and if you're like us, you will: in your breakfast smoothie or your evening spritz; on vanilla ice cream or pound cake.

●

MAKES 3 CUPS

2 pounds ripe to overripe fresh strawberries, hulled, rinsed, patted dry, and halved

1 cup sugar

Strawberry Puree

Put the strawberries and sugar into a medium bowl and toss to coat well. Let sit for 30 minutes. The strawberries will macerate and release their juices, which will dissolve the sugar.

Transfer to a blender or food processor and process until smooth. Strain the puree through a fine-mesh strainer.

TO FREEZE: Portion into ice-cube trays for use in drinks (the standard tray well holds 1 ounce, or 2 tablespoons) and/or in one or more zip-top plastic bags. Label and date, and freeze for up to 6 months.

TO THAW: Use the pull and thaw method (see page 43) or the cold water method (see page 43).

continued →

STRAWBERRIES FOR MORNING AND EVENING

continued

MAKES 1 SMOOTHIE

¼ cup Strawberry Puree (page 249)

1 cup full-fat plain Greek yogurt

¼ cup granola

½ cup unsweetened almond milk

1½ cups ice cubes

Morning

In a blender, combine the strawberry puree, yogurt, granola, almond milk, and ice and puree until smooth. Pour into a glass and serve.

MAKES 1 COCKTAIL

2 ounces Strawberry Puree (page 249)

2 ounces white rum

½ ounce Aperol

1 ounce fresh lemon juice

Ice cubes, for shaker

Splash of sparkling wine

Evening

In a cocktail shaker, combine the strawberry puree, rum, Aperol, and lemon juice. Fill the shaker with ice, cover, and shake well. Strain into a coupe. Gently pour the wine over the back of a spoon held just above the surface of the cocktail so it floats on top.

Resources.

APPLIANCES AND TOOLS

Anova Precision Cooker

Our favorite immersion circulator for reheating via sous vide, available at a reasonable price point.
Williams-Sonoma.com

Breville Microwave

Breville makes a few different microwaves that increase in price and capability. We like the middle of the road option, which provides an impressive amount of control and even cooking in its settings.
Williams-Sonoma.com

Cabela's 15-inch Vacuum Sealers

If you want a vacuum sealer with a larger width and more power, consider one of these entries—a step up in price, but with more space to seal wider bags.
Cabelas.com

Geryon Vacuum Sealer

A basic, entry-level countertop vacuum sealer. Limited to 12-inch-wide bags.
Amazon.com

Instant Pot

This cult appliance provides a shortcut to thawing and reheating liquid substances like stocks, soups, and stews.
Instantpot.com

Thermapen Probe Thermometers

These super-accurate, quick-read probe thermometers can help you gauge internal temps as you cool down and reheat food.
Thermoworks.com

TruTemp Fridge/ Freezer Thermometer

Keep one of these analog thermometers in your freezer to determine the temperature and make sure it's cold enough.
Amazon.com

FREEZER PACKAGING

18-inch Foodservice Film Roll

We don't have a specific brand allegiance, but we do *highly* suggest buying a roll of plastic wrap that is 18 inches wide (rather than the standard grocery store film that comes in 12-inch-wide rolls). It makes it much easier to properly wrap full dishes for the freezer.
Amazon.com or **webstaurant.com**

Disposable Aluminum Containers

Use disposable pie tins, baking dishes, and other containers for the freezer so that your regular dishes aren't pulled out of rotation.
Webstaurant.com

Extreme Freeze Plastic Quart and Pint Containers

Known as "delis" in restaurants, these workhorse containers are excellent for a number of applications and durable enough to use for freezer food storage. This line is specifically made for freezing.
Amazon.com

Rubbermaid Glass Food Storage Containers

These glass containers come in a variety of sizes and have silicone-lined lids for an airtight seal.
Amazon.com

UltraSource

Our resource for vacuum bags. Also sells commercial vacuum sealing machines for those who vacuum pack in large quantities.
Ultrasourceusa.com

Ziploc Freezer Bags

We use this brand of freezer bags in quart and gallon sizes.
Amazon.com

LABELING

Masking Tape and Tape Dispenser

We follow the lead of most kitchens and use brightly colored masking tape (like painter's tape) to label our containers. We have a tape dispenser that we keep on the counter, in easy reach of our cooking space.
Amazon.com or any hardware store

Waterproof Labels

If you prefer adhesive labels, try waterproof white film labels.
Avery.com

Acknowledgments.

The creation of a cookbook, even in the best of times, is always a team effort. And we're lucky to have such an amazing team because this cookbook was written, photographed, and edited during a particularly tumultuous time in our lives. We truly could not have done it without the help of so many incredible folks, especially the following.

David Black. Thank you for fighting to make this the book we wanted, and for always looking out for us! You are a champion for your clients, and thoughtful and caring friend.

Lauren V. Allen. You are such a talent and one of the most professional, easygoing, and dedicated people we've ever worked with. Your work on the photos of this book went above and beyond, and we are so grateful for your flexibility, patience, and dedication.

Charlotte Coman. The engine behind our recipe writing and testing machine! Your preparation, diligence, and focus made recipe testing for this book a breeze. Thank you for being such a boss, always.

Kate Bolen. A thank you, and an apology! You put so much into making this book successful, from your whip-smart edits to your support for our creative vision. On top of that, you had the unfortunate job of keeping us on track to get to the finish line, which, in the year of 2020, was no small feat. We are super grateful that we have you in our corner.

Kelly Snowden. You helped us take a broad idea and distill it down into this book with such warmth and insight. Thank you for bringing clarity and structure to our vision; this is a far better cookbook than we could have hoped to make without your contributions in its earliest stages.

Betsy Stromberg. It's always pretty magical to go from a Word doc to the first pages of a layout, when a book's identity really comes into focus. Thank you for creating a design that helped to bring these recipes and ideas to life!

Jenny Wapner. Thank you for introducing us into the Ten Speed fold and for setting our bar for editor-author relationships so high! The incredible experience we had with you in writing the Poole's book was instrumental in shaping this book as well.

Kristin Perrakis, Jean Armstrong, and the Williams-Sonoma team. Thank you for the support, and for bridging the space between the professional restaurant kitchen and the stoves of passionate home cooks everywhere.

About the authors.

ASHLEY CHRISTENSEN is the chef and owner of five restaurants in Raleigh, North Carolina: Poole's, Beasley's Chicken + Honey, Fox Liquor Bar, Death & Taxes, and Poole'side Pies. Ashley has received the James Beard Award for Best Chef: Southeast and for Outstanding Chef, and was named Chef of the Year by Eater. Her work has been featured in *Bon Appétit*, *Gourmet*, the *New York Times*, *Southern Living*, and *Garden & Gun*, and she has appeared on Food Network's *Iron Chef America* and MSNBC's *Your Business*. Her first cookbook is *Poole's: Recipes and Stories from a Modern Diner*.

KAITLYN GOALEN is a writer, editor, and cook, and she is the executive director of AC Restaurants, the hospitality group founded and owned by Ashley Christensen in Raleigh, North Carolina. She co-founded the Short Stack Editions series of single-subject, digest-size cookbooks and co-authored the full-length *Short Stack Cookbook*. She has also co-authored *Cook Like a Local*, *Poole's*, and *The Craft Cocktail Party*. She has contributed to a variety of national publications, including *Garden & Gun*, *Southern Living*, and *Food & Wine*.

Index.

See also "Recipes Organized by Course" on pages 6–7.

A

Almond Rice Pudding with Rhubarb-Apricot Jam, 71
aluminum containers, 253
anchovies
  freezing, 17, 24
  Provençal Onion Tart (Pissaladière) with Tomato-Olive Relish, 150
  Salsa Verde, 141
Aperol
  Strawberries for Evening, 251
apples
  Apple Pie, 73–74
  Cabbage Salad with Crispy Pork Shoulder, Apples, and Maple-Cider Vinaigrette, 86
  freezing, 24
  Seared Scallops with Butternut Squash, Apples, and Parsley, 192
appliances, 253
Apricot Jam, Rhubarb-, 71
avocados
  Pesto-Avocado Dressing, 144
  Potato Pork Cakes with Marinated Peppers, Summer Squash, and Avocado, 90–93
  Tortilla Breakfast Pie, 175–76

B

bacon
  freezing, 17, 24
  Potato Pierogi, 161–62
  Quiche Lorraine, 78
  Twice-Baked Mashed Potatoes, 159
bananas
  Banana Cream Profiteroles, 67
  freezing, 24, 238
  Multitasker Smoothie, 238
basil
  Pesto, 141
beans
  Chicken Niçoise Salad, 96
  freezing, 24
  Green Bean Casserole, 125
  Roasted Beets with Chickpeas, Herbed Yogurt, and Caramelized Onion Vinaigrette, 153

Tomato and Greens Minestrone, 130
Turkey Chili with White Beans, 195–96
Béchamel, Herbed, 120
beef
  Beef and Coconut Stew with Root Vegetables, 106
  Braised Short Ribs, 102
  Braised Short Ribs with Cauliflower Fonduta, 105
  freezing, 17, 24, 36
  Short Rib Stroganoff with Egg Noodles, 103
  Stuffed Peppers with Short Ribs and Rice, 109
Beets, Roasted, with Chickpeas, Herbed Yogurt, and Caramelized Onion Vinaigrette, 153
bell peppers. See peppers
berries
  freezing, 24
  See also individual berries
beverages
  Boulevardier Slushie, 240
  Chai Concentrate, 246
  Kait's Negroni, 242
  Margarita Slush, 239
  Spiced Chai Latte, 246
  Strawberries for Evening, 251
  The Vesper, 242
  Vieux Carre, 242
  Watermelon Collins, 245
  Watermelon Juice, 245
  See also smoothies
biscuits
  Biscuit Dumplings or "Gnocchi," 57
  Blueberry-Ginger Cobbler, 59
  Buttermilk Biscuits, 56–57
  Chicken and Dumplings, 60
  freezing, 25, 32
  Orange Biscuits, 57
  Sausage and Cheese Biscuits, 57
  Sausage Gravy with Buttermilk Biscuits, 122
Blueberry-Ginger Cobbler, 59
bourbon
  Boulevardier Slushie, 240

bread
  freezing, 25
  Zucchini–Poppy Seed Bread, 224
  See also Cornbread; sandwiches
broccoli
  Broccoli Cheddar Chicken Bake, 101
  freezing, 24
  Kale and Broccoli Slaw with Pesto-Avocado Dressing, 144
Buffalo Chicken Dip, 100
Burritos, Egg, Potato, and Cheddar Breakfast, 168–69
butter
  compound, 112
  freezing, 15–16, 25
  Pimento Cheese Butter, 113
  Preserved Lemon–Garlic Butter, 116
Buttermilk Biscuits, 56–57

C

Cabbage Salad with Crispy Pork Shoulder, Apples, and Maple-Cider Vinaigrette, 86
cakes
  freezing, 25
  Spiced Pumpkin Pudding Cakes, 235
Campari
  Boulevardier Slushie, 240
  Kait's Negroni, 242
Carnitas Tacos, 85
casseroles, freezing, 25, 32
Cauliflower Fonduta, Braised Short Ribs with, 105
chai
  Chai Concentrate, 246
  Spiced Chai Latte, 246
cheese
  Baked Feta with Roasted Peppers, Capers, and Salsa Verde, 143
  Braised Greens and Paneer, 136
  Braised Short Ribs with Cauliflower Fonduta, 105
  Broccoli Cheddar Chicken Bake, 101
  Buffalo Chicken Dip, 100
  Charred Corn, Squash, and Onion Gratin, 215

Cheesy Sausage and Sage
Waffles, 170
Cornbread Panzanella with
Watermelon, Cucumber, and
Za'atar Vinaigrette, 53
Curried Cheddar and Olive
Bites, 184
Egg, Potato, and Cheddar
Breakfast Burritos, 168–69
Four-Cheese and Greens
Lasagna, 126–27
freezing, 15, 25
Frozen Cheesecake Cookie
Sandwiches, 230–31
Ham and Swiss Cheese Rolls, 186
Harissa Lamb, Eggplant, and
Potato Gratin, 155–56
Hot Dog Casserole, 158
Line Cook's Grilled Cheese, 149
Parm Stock, 128
Penne alla Vodka, 206–7
Pesto, 141
Pimento Cheese Butter, 113
Pimento Cheese Hand Pies, 77
Pimento Mac and Cheese
Custard, 217–18
Poole's Three-Cheese
Gougères, 63
Pork Reuben on Rye with Swiss,
Kraut, and Russian Dressing, 89
Potato Pierogi, 161–62
Quiche Lorraine, 78
The Quickest Risotto
Parmigiano, 69
Roasted Jalapeño Poppers with
Sausage and Tomatoes, 183
Sausage and Cheese Biscuits, 57
Tex-Mex Cheese
Enchiladas, 211–12
Tortilla Breakfast Pie, 175–76
Turkey Chili with Goat Cheese
and Chimichurri, 196
Twice-Baked Mashed Potatoes, 159
Chia Pudding, Chocolate, 178
chicken
Broccoli Cheddar Chicken
Bake, 101
Buffalo Chicken Dip, 100
Chicken and Dumplings, 60
Chicken and Kale Tortilla
Soup, 203

Chicken Confit, 94
Chicken Niçoise Salad, 96
Chicken Piccata Farfalle with
Sweet Potato, 99
Chicken Rillettes, 95
Freezer Chicken Stock, 204
freezing, 17, 24, 36
Pan-Roasted Chicken Breast
with Preserved Lemon–Garlic
Butter, 119
Chickpeas, Roasted Beets with
Herbed Yogurt, Caramelized
Onion Vinaigrette, and, 153
chiles
Chile Gravy, 211
Chile Sauce, 175
Guajillo Sauce, 211
Jalapeño-Ginger Syrup, 248
Roasted Jalapeño Poppers with
Sausage and Tomatoes, 183
chili
Turkey Chili with Goat Cheese
and Chimichurri, 196
Turkey Chili with Spiced Basmati
Rice, Fried Shallots, and
Yogurt, 196
Turkey Chili with White
Beans, 195–96
Chimichurri, 140, 141
chocolate
Chocolate Chia Pudding, 178
Frozen Cheesecake Cookie
Sandwiches, 230–31
Tahini–Brown Butter Chocolate
Chip Cookies, 225
Chowder, New
Manhattan, 200–202
Churros, 64
clams
New Manhattan
Chowder, 200–202
Seafood Stuffies, 54
Cobbler, Blueberry-Ginger, 59
coconut milk
Beef and Coconut Stew with
Root Vegetables, 106
Chocolate Chia Pudding, 178
coffee
Malted Coffee Toffee
Cookies, 226
Multitasker Smoothie, 238

Cognac
Vieux Carre, 242
cold water thawing, 43–44
condiments, freezing, 18
Confit, Chicken, 94
cookies
freezing dough for, 25, 32
Frozen Cheesecake Cookie
Sandwiches, 230–31
Malted Coffee Toffee
Cookies, 226
Miso-Caramel Shortbread, 232
Tahini–Brown Butter Chocolate
Chip Cookies, 225
corn
Charred Corn, Squash, and Onion
Gratin, 215
Chicken and Dumplings, 60
freezing, 24
Cornbread, 50–51
Cornbread Crumbs, 51
Cornbread Panzanella with
Watermelon, Cucumber, and
Za'atar Vinaigrette, 53
Lynn's Thanksgiving Dressing, 55
Seafood Stuffies, 54
countertop thawing, 43
crab
Deviled Crab Rigatoni, 221
freezing, 17, 24
Seafood Stuffies, 54
Croissant French Toast, Pistachio,
with Orange Blossom Soft
Cream, 173–74
cucumbers
Chilled Tomato and Cucumber
Soup, 197
Cornbread Panzanella with
Watermelon, Cucumber, and
Za'atar Vinaigrette, 53

D
dairy
freezing, 15–16
frozen food lifespan for, 25
dates
Spiced Pumpkin Pudding
Cakes, 235
Deviled Crab Rigatoni, 221
Dip, Buffalo Chicken, 100
dough, freezing, 25

Doughnuts, Pâte à Choux, 64
Dressing, Lynn's Thanksgiving, 55
dumplings
    Biscuit Dumplings or "Gnocchi," 57
    Chicken and Dumplings, 60
    Potato Pierogi, 161–62

E

eggplant
    freezing, 24
    Harissa Lamb, Eggplant, and
        Potato Gratin, 155–56
eggs
    Chicken Niçoise Salad, 96
    Egg, Potato, and Cheddar
        Breakfast Burritos, 168–69
    freezing, 16–17, 25
    Quiche Lorraine, 78
    Tortilla Breakfast Pie, 175–76
Enchiladas, Tex-Mex Cheese, 211–12
expiration guidelines, 12, 21–22,
    24–25

F

fish
    freezing, 17, 24
    Pan-Roasted Salmon with
        Chimichurri, 147
    See also anchovies
Fonduta, Cauliflower, 105
freezer
    inventory, 22–23
    organizing, 22–23
    as pantry, 5, 47
    temperature of, 28
freezer burn, 15, 22, 27, 32, 35, 113
freezing
    advantages of, 1–2, 5, 11, 47
    cooling food before, 28–29
    expiration guidelines for, 12,
        21–22, 24–25
    food decay and, 9, 27–29
    labeling and, 36, 254
    packaging and, 32, 34–36,
        253–54
    portioning and, 29, 31–32
    successfulness of, by food
        type, 12, 15–18
    textural changes and, 12
French Toast, Pistachio Croissant,
    with Orange Blossom Soft
    Cream, 173–74

Fritters, Savory, 64
fruits
    blanching, 15
    freezing, 12, 15
    frozen food lifespan for, 24
    See also individual fruits

G

gin
    Kait's Negroni, 242
    The Vesper, 242
    Watermelon Collins, 245
ginger
    Blueberry-Ginger Cobbler, 59
    Jalapeño-Ginger Syrup, 248
    Miso-Ginger Butternut Squash
        Soup, 192
glass containers, 34, 254
Gougères, Poole's Three-Cheese, 63
grains
    freezing, 17–18
    frozen food lifespan for, 25
    See also individual grains
grapefruit
    Margarita Slush, 239
    Salty Dog Icebox Pie, 228
gravy
    Chile Gravy, 211
    Sausage Gravy with Buttermilk
        Biscuits, 122
greens
    Braised Greens, 134
    Braised Greens and Paneer, 136
    Four-Cheese and Greens
        Lasagna, 126–27
    freezing, 24
    Salsa Verde, 141
    Tea-Brined Pork Chop with
        Braised Greens and
        Tomatoes, 137–38
    Tomato and Greens
        Minestrone, 130
    See also individual greens

H

Ham and Swiss Cheese Rolls, 186
Harissa Lamb, Eggplant, and
    Potato Gratin, 155–56
Herbed Béchamel, 120
hot dogs
    Hot Dog Casserole, 158
    Pork Meatballs, 185

I

ice cream, 16, 25, 36
Instant Pot, reheating with, 40, 253
Italian Wedding Soup, 129

J

Jam, Rhubarb-Apricot, 71

K

Kait's Negroni, 242
kale
    Chicken and Kale Tortilla
        Soup, 203
    Kale and Broccoli Slaw with
        Pesto-Avocado Dressing, 144

L

labeling, 36, 254
lamb
    freezing, 17, 36
    Harissa Lamb, Eggplant, and
        Potato Gratin, 155–56
lasagna
    Four-Cheese and Greens
        Lasagna, 126–27
    freezing, 32
lemons
    Preserved Lemon–Garlic
        Butter, 116
    Preserved Lemons, 116
lettuce
    Chicken Niçoise Salad, 96
Lillet Blanc
    The Vesper, 242
limes
    Margarita Slush, 239
Line Cook's Grilled Cheese, 149
Lynn's Thanksgiving Dressing, 55

M

Mac and Cheese Custard,
    Pimento, 217–18
Malted Coffee Toffee Cookies, 226
Manhattan Chowder,
    New, 200–202
Maple-Cider Vinaigrette, 86
Margarita Slush, 239
meat
    freezing, 17, 36
    frozen food lifespan for, 24
    See also individual meats

meatballs
    freezing, 32
    Pork Meatballs, 185
microwave, thawing and reheating
    with, 40–41, 253
Minestrone, Tomato and Greens, 130
miso
    Miso-Caramel Shortbread, 232
    Miso-Ginger Butternut Squash
      Soup, 192
Multitasker Smoothie, 238
mushrooms
    Green Bean Casserole, 125
    Quiche Lorraine, 78
    The Quickest Risotto
      Parmigiano, 69
    Short Rib Stroganoff with Egg
      Noodles, 103

N

Negroni, Kait's, 242
Niçoise Salad, Chicken, 96
noodles. *See* pasta and noodles
nuts
    freezing, 17–18
    See also individual nuts

O

oats
    Frozen Cheesecake Cookie
      Sandwiches, 230–31
olives
    Chicken Niçoise Salad, 96
    Curried Cheddar and Olive
      Bites, 184
    Tomato-Olive Relish, 150
onions
    Caramelized Onions, 148
    Caramelized Onion
      Vinaigrette, 153
    Charred Corn, Squash, and
      Onion Gratin, 215
    freezing, 24
    Provençal Onion Tart
      (Pissaladière) with Tomato-
      Olive Relish, 150
Orange Blossom Soft Cream, 174
oranges
    Boulevardier Slushie, 240
    Margarita Slush, 239
    Orange Biscuits, 57
    oven, reheating with, 40

Oysters, Roasted, with Pimento
    Cheese Butter, 115

P

packaging, 32, 34–36, 253–54
Panzanella, Cornbread, with
    Watermelon, Cucumber, and
    Za'atar Vinaigrette, 53
Parm Stock, 128
parsley
    Chimichurri, 140, 141
pasta and noodles
    Chicken Piccata Farfalle with
      Sweet Potato, 99
    Deviled Crab Rigatoni, 221
    Four-Cheese and Greens
      Lasagna, 126–27
    Penne alla Vodka, 206–7
    Pimento Mac and Cheese
      Custard, 217–18
    Short Rib Stroganoff with Egg
      Noodles, 103
Pâte à Choux, 62
    Banana Cream Profiteroles, 67
    Pâte à Choux Doughnuts, 64
    Poole's Three-Cheese
      Gougères, 63
pears, freezing, 24
peas
    freezing, 24
    Italian Wedding Soup, 129
peppers
    Baked Feta with Roasted
      Peppers, Capers, and Salsa
      Verde, 143
    Marinated Peppers, 93
    Pimento Cheese Butter, 113
    Pimento Cheese Hand Pies, 77
    Pimento Mac and Cheese
      Custard, 217–18
    Potato Pork Cakes with
      Marinated Peppers, Summer
      Squash, and Avocado, 90–93
    Stuffed Peppers with Short Ribs
      and Rice, 109
    See also chiles
Pesto, 141
    Pesto-Avocado Dressing, 144
Pierogi, Potato, 161–62
pies
    Apple Pie, 73–74
    freezing, 32

Piecrust, 72
    Pimento Cheese Hand Pies, 77
    Salty Dog Icebox Pie, 228
    Tortilla Breakfast Pie, 175–76
pimentos. *See* peppers
Pissaladière (Provençal Onion
    Tart), 150
Pistachio Croissant French Toast
    with Orange Blossom Soft
    Cream, 173–74
plastic bags, 34–35, 254
plastic containers, 34, 254
plastic wrap, 35, 253
Poole's Three-Cheese Gougères, 63
pork
    Cabbage Salad with Crispy Pork
      Shoulder, Apples, and Maple-
      Cider Vinaigrette, 86
    Carnitas Tacos, 85
    freezing, 17, 24, 36
    Italian Wedding Soup, 129
    Pork Meatballs, 185
    Pork Reuben on Rye with
      Swiss, Kraut, and Russian
      Dressing, 89
    Potato Pork Cakes with
      Marinated Peppers, Summer
      Squash, and Avocado, 90–93
    Pulled Pork Shoulder, Mike's
      Way, 82–83
    Tea-Brined Pork Chop with
      Braised Greens and
      Tomatoes, 137–38
    See also bacon; ham; sausage
portioning, 29, 31–32
potatoes
    Chicken and Dumplings, 60
    Egg, Potato, and Cheddar
      Breakfast Burritos, 168–69
    Harissa Lamb, Eggplant, and
      Potato Gratin, 155–56
    Hot Dog Casserole, 158
    Mashed Potatoes, 154
    New Manhattan
      Chowder, 200–202
    Potato Pierogi, 161–62
    Potato Pork Cakes with
      Marinated Peppers, Summer
      Squash, and Avocado, 90–93
    Twice-Baked Mashed
      Potatoes, 159
Profiteroles, Banana Cream, 67

Provençal Onion Tart (Pissaladière) with Tomato-Olive Relish, 150
puddings
    Almond Rice Pudding with Rhubarb-Apricot Jam, 71
    Chocolate Chia Pudding, 178
puff pastry
    Provençal Onion Tart (Pissaladière) with Tomato-Olive Relish, 150
pull and thaw method, 43
Pumpkin Pudding Cakes, Spiced, 235

Q

quiche
    freezing, 32
    Quiche Lorraine, 78
quinoa
    Broccoli Cheddar Chicken Bake, 101

R

refrigerator
    cooling food in, before freezing, 28–29
    thawing food in, 43
reheating
    advantages of, 39
    methods for, 40–41
    thawing vs., 41
Relish, Tomato-Olive, 150
Reuben, Pork, on Rye with Swiss, Kraut, and Russian Dressing, 89
Rhubarb-Apricot Jam, 71
rice
    Almond Rice Pudding with Rhubarb-Apricot Jam, 71
    Beef and Coconut Stew with Root Vegetables, 106
    freezing, 25
    The Quickest Risotto Parmigiano, 69
    Risotto, 68
    Stuffed Peppers with Short Ribs and Rice, 109
    Turkey Chili with Spiced Basmati Rice, Fried Shallots, and Yogurt, 196
Rillettes, Chicken, 95
Risotto, 68
    Almond Rice Pudding with Rhubarb-Apricot Jam, 71

The Quickest Risotto Parmigiano, 69
Rolls, Ham and Swiss Cheese, 186
rum
    Strawberries for Evening, 251
Russian Dressing, 89
rutabagas
    Beef and Coconut Stew with Root Vegetables, 106
rye whiskey
    Vieux Carre, 242

S

salad dressings and vinaigrettes
    Caramelized Onion Vinaigrette, 153
    Maple-Cider Vinaigrette, 86
    Pesto-Avocado Dressing, 144
    Russian Dressing, 89
    Za'atar Vinaigrette, 53
salads
    Cabbage Salad with Crispy Pork Shoulder, Apples, and Maple-Cider Vinaigrette, 86
    Chicken Niçoise Salad, 96
    Cornbread Panzanella with Watermelon, Cucumber, and Za'atar Vinaigrette, 53
    Kale and Broccoli Slaw with Pesto-Avocado Dressing, 144
    Roasted Beets with Chickpeas, Herbed Yogurt, and Caramelized Onion Vinaigrette, 153
salmon
    freezing, 17, 24
    Pan-Roasted Salmon with Chimichurri, 147
salsas. See sauces and salsas
Salty Dog Icebox Pie, 228
sandwiches
    Line Cook's Grilled Cheese, 149
    Pork Reuben on Rye with Swiss, Kraut, and Russian Dressing, 89
sauces and salsas
    Chile Sauce, 175
    Chimichurri, 140, 141
    freezing, 18
    frozen food lifespan for, 25
    Guajillo Sauce, 211
    Herbed Béchamel, 120
    Penne alla Vodka, 206–7

Pesto, 141
    Salsa Verde, 141
sauerkraut
    Hot Dog Casserole, 158
    Pork Reuben on Rye with Swiss, Kraut, and Russian Dressing, 89
sausage
    Cheesy Sausage and Sage Waffles, 170
    freezing, 17, 24
    Hot Dog Casserole, 158
    Pork Meatballs, 185
    Roasted Jalapeño Poppers with Sausage and Tomatoes, 183
    Sausage and Cheese Biscuits, 57
    Sausage Gravy with Buttermilk Biscuits, 122
Scallops, Seared, with Butternut Squash, Apples, and Parsley, 192
seafood
    freezing, 17
    frozen food lifespan for, 24
    Seafood Stuffies, 54
    See also individual seafoods
Shortbread, Miso-Caramel, 232
shrimp
    freezing, 17, 24
    Seafood Stuffies, 54
Slaw, Kale and Broccoli, with Pesto-Avocado Dressing, 144
smoothies
    Multitasker Smoothie, 238
    Strawberries for Morning, 251
soups
    Basic Butternut Squash Soup, 191–92
    Chicken and Kale Tortilla Soup, 203
    Chilled Tomato and Cucumber Soup, 197
    frozen food lifespan for, 25
    Italian Wedding Soup, 129
    Miso-Ginger Butternut Squash Soup, 192
    New Manhattan Chowder, 200–202
    Tomato and Greens Minestrone, 130
    Tomato-Dijon Bisque, 199
sous vide method, reheating with, 40, 253
speed thawing, 44

squash
    Basic Butternut Squash
        Soup, 191–92
    Charred Corn, Squash, and Onion
        Gratin, 215
    freezing, 24
    Miso-Ginger Butternut Squash
        Soup, 192
    Potato Pork Cakes with
        Marinated Peppers, Summer
        Squash, and Avocado, 90–93
    Seared Scallops with Butternut
        Squash, Apples, and Parsley, 192
    Zucchini–Poppy Seed Bread, 224
stocks
    Freezer Chicken Stock, 204
    freezing, 18
    Parm Stock, 128
strawberries
    Strawberries for Evening, 251
    Strawberries for Morning, 251
    Strawberry Puree, 251
sweet potatoes
    Beef and Coconut Stew with
        Root Vegetables, 106
    Chicken Piccata Farfalle with
        Sweet Potato, 99
    freezing, 24
Syrup, Jalapeño-Ginger, 248

T

Tacos, Carnitas, 85
Tahini–Brown Butter Chocolate
    Chip Cookies, 225
Tart, Provençal Onion (Pissaladière)
    with Tomato-Olive Relish, 150
tea
    Chai Concentrate, 246
    Spiced Chai Latte, 246
    Tea-Brined Pork Chop with
        Braised Greens and
        Tomatoes, 137–38
tequila
    Margarita Slush, 239
Tex-Mex Cheese Enchiladas, 211–12
thawing
    definition of, 41
    methods for, 41, 43–44
    reheating vs., 41
thermometers, 253
Toffee Cookies, Malted Coffee, 226

tomatoes
    Charred Corn, Squash, and
        Onion Gratin, 215
    Chicken Niçoise Salad, 96
    Chile Sauce, 175
    Chilled Tomato and Cucumber
        Soup, 197
    freezing, 24
    Guajillo Sauce, 211
    Harissa Lamb, Eggplant, and
        Potato Gratin, 155–56
    New Manhattan
        Chowder, 200–202
    Penne alla Vodka, 206–7
    The Quickest Risotto
        Parmigiano, 69
    Roasted Jalapeño Poppers with
        Sausage and Tomatoes, 183
    Tea-Brined Pork Chop with
        Braised Greens and
        Tomatoes, 137–38
    Tomato and Greens
        Minestrone, 130
    Tomato-Dijon Bisque, 199
    Tomato-Olive Relish, 150
    Turkey Chili with Goat Cheese
        and Chimichurri, 196
    Turkey Chili with Spiced Basmati
        Rice, Fried Shallots, and
        Yogurt, 196
    Turkey Chili with White
        Beans, 195–96
tools, 253
tortilla chips
    Chicken and Kale Tortilla
        Soup, 203
    Tortilla Breakfast Pie, 175–76
tortillas
    Carnitas Tacos, 85
    Egg, Potato, and Cheddar
        Breakfast Burritos, 168–69
    Tex-Mex Cheese
        Enchiladas, 211–12
turkey
    freezing, 17, 36
    Turkey Chili with Goat Cheese
        and Chimichurri, 196
    Turkey Chili with Spiced Basmati
        Rice, Fried Shallots, and
        Yogurt, 196
    Turkey Chili with White
        Beans, 195–96

turnips
    Beef and Coconut Stew with
        Root Vegetables, 106

V

vacuum sealing, 32, 34, 36, 253, 254
vegetables
    Beef and Coconut Stew with
        Root Vegetables, 106
    blanching, 12
    freezing, 12, 15, 36
    frozen food lifespan for, 24
    Italian Wedding Soup, 129
    See also individual vegetables
vermouth
    Boulevardier Slushie, 240
    Kait's Negroni, 242
    Vieux Carre, 242
The Vesper, 242
Vieux Carre, 242
vinaigrettes. *See* salad dressings and
    vinaigrettes
vodka
    Penne alla Vodka, 206–7
    The Vesper, 242
    Watermelon Collins, 245

W

Waffles, Cheesy Sausage and
    Sage, 170
watermelon
    Cornbread Panzanella with
        Watermelon, Cucumber, and
        Za'atar Vinaigrette, 53
    Watermelon Collins, 245
    Watermelon Juice, 245

Z

Za'atar Vinaigrette, 53
zucchini
    Charred Corn, Squash, and Onion
        Gratin, 215
    freezing, 24
    Zucchini–Poppy Seed Bread, 224

Published in the United States by Ten Speed Press, an imprint of Random House,
a division of Penguin Random House LLC, New York.
www.tenspeed.com

Ten Speed Press and the Ten Speed Press colophon are registered trademarks of
Penguin Random House LLC.

Library of Congress Cataloging-in-Publication Data

Names: Christensen, Ashley, author. | Goalen, Kaitlyn, author. | Allen,
  Lauren, photographer.
Title: It's always freezer season : how to freeze like a chef with 100
  make-ahead recipes / Ashley Christensen and Kaitlyn Goalen ;
  photography by Lauren Allen.
Description: First. | New York : Ten Speed Press, [2021] | Includes
  bibliographical references and index.
Identifiers: LCCN 2020035243 (print) | LCCN 2020035244 (ebook) |
  ISBN 9781607746898 (hardcover) | ISBN 9781607746904 (ebook)
Subjects: LCSH: Make-ahead cooking. | Frozen foods. | LCGFT: Cookbooks.
Classification: LCC TX828 .C47 2021 (print) | LCC TX828 (ebook) | DDC
  641.5/55—dc23
LC record available at https://lccn.loc.gov/2020035243
LC ebook record available at https://lccn.loc.gov/2020035244

Hardcover ISBN: 978-1-60774-689-8
eBook ISBN: 978-1-60774-690-4

Printed in China

Acquiring editor: Jenny Wapner | Editors: Kate Bolen and Kelly Snowden
Art director/designer: Betsy Stromberg | Production designers: Mari Gill
  and Mara Gendell
Production manager/prepress color manager: Jane Chinn
Food stylist/prop stylist: Lauren Vied Allen
Photo assistant/digitech: Bridgette Cyr
Copyeditor: Sharon Silva | Proofreader: Linda M. Bouchard |
  Indexer: Ken DellaPenta
Publicist: Jana Branson | Marketer: Monica Stanton

10 9 8 7 6 5 4 3 2 1

First Edition